PART ONE

Memoirs of My Missionary Life in Japan 1959–2010

PART TWO

A Glance at Contemporary Life in Japan Through Fiction

8/19/2014

Barbara

Thank you for your love
of Villanova and your
loyalty to the Augustinians

Thomas P. Dwyer OSA

THOMAS P. DWYER, OSA

Dedicated To

Fr. Daniel J.Menihane OSA
Long time friend and editor of this book. May he rest in peace.

Bishop Dominic Ryoji Miyahara
With special thanks for your kindness and understanding.

The Staff at Villanova Monastery
Thanks for your highly professional and loving care. I'm deeply indebted to you.

Fr. Anthony P. Burrascano OSA
Our most loyal supporter

Front Cover image: F. P. Fukuoka Complex, 1961

Back Cover image: New Church in Fukuoka

ISBN: 978-0-87723-114-1

Table of Contents

Preface

My book is divided into two parts. The first part is my memoirs of my ministry in Japan where I lived for fifty-two years. The second part is a collection of short stories to introduce our readers into contemporary Japan through fiction. I thought it was easier to portray modern Japan through stories rather than by essays. So in that sense, the two parts are really connected. That is, the first part is the journey of the Augustinians in Japan from nineteen fifty-two to the present and the second, a portrayal of modern Japanese society where we Augustinians worked.

The book of my memoirs is really an attempt to put into perspective the Augustinians journey from 1952 to 2010 when I returned to my beloved Villanova. I tried to put things in a chronological order from Nagasaki to Fukuoka to Nagoya and finally to Tokyo. Of course there are digressions along the way. For example, my language study did not finish after language school, but rather continued my whole life with private teachers. The encounters with graduates of our school in Nagasaki happened at various times in my travels throughout the country (I loved to travel and still do).

I tried to show our struggles from Nagasaki into other missions. We made some good decisions and some that lacked foresight that we regretted later. The good decisions are something to be proud of. In Nagasaki we setup the first parochial school in Japan. We built a prestigious kindergarten in Fukuoka which flourishes to this day. Fr. Joseph Masami Yamaguchi works full time in the maritime ministry and is very helpful to the many seamen who stop off in Nagoya. Our outreach to the poor and foreign workers in Nagoya and Tokyo are noted throughout the country. In the national newspaper our church in Tokyo was highly praised for its outreach to the homeless and foreign workers. It was called a model urban parish. The housing projects in Nagoya were so innovative that even the politicians took note. Although we had different opinions on some subjects, in the end, we all worked together in a brotherly Augustinian way.

Japan was a great experience for me. I lived a few years alone, sometimes when I rarely used English. I got to know many Japanese on every level of society. I came to love and respect the Japanese people and their ancient culture. Most of my work in later years was with non-Christians. This gave me precious insights into their ideas on religion and their attitudes toward Christianity. I had a happy, joy filled life.

In my short stories, I tried to portray contemporary Japan through fiction. They are a composite of the many Japanese I knew. There are dropouts, taxi drivers, sushi chefs, a police woman detective, the closeness of family ties, the strength of character of Japanese women, the compassion of Buddhist monks, survivors of the atomic bomb and other characters who show indirectly some modern social problems such as bullying, truancy, runaways, the class system and the difficulty to change from the family religion. While enjoying the stories I hope that our readers will recognize the insights I hope to give.

I could not finish this introduction without acknowledging my fellow Augustinians of this Province for their help both financial and spiritual. Our Provincials over the years, though often mystified, supported us right down the line. I salute the Augustinians in Japan and those who have gone to their reward or are retired here at Villanova. It was a good run and it's not over yet.

Thomas P. Dwyer, O.S.A
Autumn, 2013

Foreward

The directives of Jesus in those final lines of Matthew's Gospel, "Go, therefore…teach all nations…" recorded by the author, so perfectly and succinctly capture the life and work of Father Thomas Dwyer. His is a life of commitment, dedication, love of the Augustinian Family and the Gospel Message. "With the Augustinians in Japan" is the record of a journey that was begun by a newly ordained priest obediently dedicating his life to one of service and love.

One can only imagine Father's courage in accepting such a mission to Japan, a nation which was at war only a few years earlier and at that time in the late 1950s was in the process of rebuilding itself only to become one of the most important nations economically, politically and culturally. In reading the chapters that follow, one is drawn, through poetic precision and clarity, into a world that is contemporary Japan. At times, as one reads the descriptions of life among the Japanese in their effort at rebuilding their nation, one sees the rebuilding of spirit as well. In a style reminiscent at times of Endo Shusaku, the reader is easily taken back to the streets of Tokyo, Nagoya, Fukuoka and Nagasaki as Father and his fellow friars struggle to meet the needs and demands of parishioners and community life, whether in searching for property or building a new church or school.

The sharing of life and the formation of enduring relationships not only among the friars but the Japanese populace who were served, in the case of Fr. Dwyer, primarily through education and pastoral service, is an ongoing theme in this memoir. As a historian, I find this personal narrative especially interesting in the revelation of human striving and success at many levels—personal, religious, educational, pastoral and especially that of the Augustinian apostolic community.

The first Augustinians arrived in Japan in 1602. Through historical tragedies including persecution and war, Catholic missionary life was indeed brutally halted at times. However, the seed of the Gospel had been sown. The return of the Augustinians in the immediate post-world war two era, the missionary life and success of Father Dwyer's commitment to the Church in Japan, and the ongoing success of friars from many parts of the world including Japan, is testimony to the enduring commitment to truth and love as lived by the Augustinians and all whom they serve.

P. B. Reagan, Ph.D.
Department of History, Villanova University
Spring 2013

PART I

Memoirs Of My
Missionary Life in Japan

The Augustinian Martyrs of Japan

In any discussion of the Church as it exists in Japan one would be remiss if he did not devote a place of honor to the great sacrifices made for Christ by so many of the early Japanese Catholics. Many of those who gave their lives for the proclamation of the Gospel were missionaries, of our Order and other religious communities as well. We all expect that; it's almost a trademark among all missionaries in their generosity of spirit in the service of the Gospel.

However, in the annals of our Order regarding the response of our converts to Christianity, a place of honor must be accorded to the early martyrs of Japan. These were ordinary people who lived the Good News to an extraordinary degree. We honor them by placing the accounts of their sacrifice and martyrdom first in our memories of the Japanese missions.

The first Augustinians arrived in Japan in 1602 and quickly drew many people not only to the Catholic faith but also to the Augustinian way of life as religious, tertiaries and confraternity members.

In January of 1614, a governmental Decree of Extinction ordered the suppression of Christianity, however, and several years later, fierce persecution of the Christians began. Among those who suffered martyrdom were members of the Order from Spain, Portugal and Mexico as well as many native Japanese. Fr. Ferdinand of St. Joseph, the first Augustinian martyr of Japan, along with Andrew Yoshida, a catechist who worked with him, were beheaded in 1617. Fr. Peter Zuniga, a Spaniard from Seville, who grew up in Mexico but later joined the Order in his native country, was burned to death in 1622. Br. John Shozaburo, Oblates Michael Kiuchi Tayemon, Peter Kuhieye, Thomas Terai Kahioye, and tertiaries Mancio Scisayemon and Lawrence Hachizo were beheaded in 1630. Fr. Bartholomew Gutierrez, Fr. Vincent of Saint Anthony Simoens, Fr. Francis of Jesus Terrero, Fr. Martin of St. Nicholas Lumbreras and Fr. Melchior of Saint Augustine Sanchez were burned to death in 1632.

Fr. Thomas of St. Augustine, who was the first Japanese to be ordained a priest, was born around 1602. He was educated by the Jesuits in Nagasaki, becoming proficient in Latin and public speaking. He later moved to Macao to continue his studies, returning five years later to work as a catechist and preacher, often forced to flee from place to place to do his work. In 1622 he went to Manila to join the Order for the great admiration he had for the Augustinians and their work in Japan. He was professed at Intramuros in 1624 and was ordained in Cebu. After several attempts he was able to return to Nagasaki in 1631. Being Japanese, he was able to keep his priesthood secret and even obtained a position in the governorship of Nagasaki with the name Kintsuba. On All Saints Day, 1636, after being arrested for being a

Christian, he then revealed to his captors "I am Fr. Thomas of St. Augustine Jihioye, of the Order of Saint Augustine." He was tortured for several months with excruciating punishments but would not renounce the faith. On August 21, 1637, he was taken along with 12 others, men and women, some of whom were tertiaries, and members of the Confraternity of the Cincture, to be subjected to the torture of the pit in which they were suspended by their feet in a hole in the ground. Finally, on Thursday, Nov. 6th he was taken to the pit for the last time together with four others and died, as witnesses recalled, one of the greatest martyrdoms of the period. In November 1982 he was included in a list of 188 martyrs whom the Japanese bishops proposed for canonization.

The deaths of these Augustinians, religious and laity, men and women, natives of Japan and missionaries from foreign lands, bears witness to the universality and unity of the Order and the Church. The grace of Christ and the bonds of fraternity inspired and sustained the faith and fidelity of our brothers and sisters under horrendous circumstances. After enduring horrible tortures, their bodies were burned and their ashes scattered by order of the ruler Tokugawa Iemitsu. They were canonized by Bl. Pope John Paul II on October 18, 1987.

Another Augustinian martyr, St. Magdalene of Nagasaki, an Augustinian Tertiary of the Augustinian Recollect Order, was one of the many martyrs in Japan in the 17th century. Her parents had been martyred around 1620, while she was still a young girl. An enthusiastic Christian, she made contact with some Augustinians who arrived in Japan in 1623, and acted as their interpreter and later as a catechist. She was admitted into the Third Order of Saint Augustine at the age of fourteen by Blessed Francis of Jesus and Vincent of Saint Anthony, Augustinian Recollects. After their martyrdom in 1632, Magdalene hid in the hills and helped to sustain the faith of other Christians as well as baptizing converts.

To encourage those who were wavering in their faith, Magdalene publicly declared her Christian faith. Her brave act of faith resulted in her being tied by her feet, suspended over a deep hole dug in the earth until, after fourteen days, she suffocated to death. As she was only 23 at the time of her death in 1634, her Christian witness at so young an age made a great impression on all. She was beatified in 1981 and canonized in 1987 by Pope Bl. John Paul II.

With the death of St. Magdalene the tragic but glorious era of the Augustinian martyrs of Japan draws to a close.

American Missionaries Who Served in Japan

(Arranged Alphabetically)

Alfred Burke
Thomas P. Dwyer
Edward V. Griffin
Edward V. Hattrick
Michael Hilden
George M. Krupa
Maurice Mahoney
John McAtee
Patrick McStravog
Joseph X. O'Connor
Liam O'Dougherty
Thomas Purcell
Edward G. Robinson
Gerry Ryan
Michael Stanley
John J. Sheridan

From Rome To Nagasaki

As the sun rose over St. Peter's Square on that frosty New Year's Day, 1959, across the Square in St. Monica's, I wearily yawned my "Deo Gratias" to the caller's "Benedicamus Domino," little realizing what a tumultuous year this would be for me.

First, however, there would many serious items facing me in these last few months in Rome, after my Ordination on December 20, 1958. In the ordination ceremony itself there was a hint, maybe one could even say, a providential nod from the Lord as to what would lay before me in the decades ahead. As it happened, the ordaining bishop had spent his priesthood serving in the missions in China. He had recently been expelled from the country by the Communists who had defeated the Chinese Nationalists in 1949. None of that, of course, was on my mind that morning as my classmates and I entered the church on the Piazza Navona to receive the sacrament that would unite us to Christ by a very special bond.

After a brief flight home to celebrate my First Mass with my family, relatives and friends, I returned to Rome to finish up my studies at St. Monica's. Those months passed quickly and then it was time for last goodbyes to the many Augustinians from Italy, Spain, Ireland and other European countries with whom I had lived and grown close to in my four years at St. Monica's. Then it was off again over the Atlantic to return finally to the United States to begin my work as a priest in one of our high schools or parishes along the east coast as a member of our Province of St. Thomas of Villanova.

By the time I reached Villanova many of my classmates had received their Letters of Obedience and had reported to their new assignments, many went to Msgr. Bonner H.S. in Drexel Hill, some others had gone down to Washington to teach at Archbishop Carroll High School and one or two had been sent to work in parishes.

A very small number of us remained and were puzzled when we were called into the Provincial's office. Puzzlement turned to disbelief when the Provincial said that he wanted to send one additional priest to serve in the missions in Japan. Would any of us consider taking that appointment? After a momentary pause while we considered the full meaning of what he had just said, I spoke up and replied "I'll go." It was as simple as that—my whole future wrapped up in a response of but 2 or 3 words!

Right away things began to happen. A passport I already had from my trip to Rome, but airline tickets, health checks with the doctor, and a myriad of other smaller details needed to be attended to before my departure.

My plane touched down at Tokyo's Haneda International Airport where I was greeted warmly by Fr. Joe O'Connor. After clearing Customs and exiting the airport terminal we hastened across the city to the railroad station where we were fortunate to secure seats on an overnight train to Nagasaki. That's when I got to learn my first lesson about the geography of Japan, that as small as the country may look on an international map, it is in reality quite sizeable, especially when you have just completed a very long airplane trip and are anxious to meet and relax with all the members of the new Community, fellow American Augustinians who would be both my companions and my mentors in the days and years ahead.

There was indeed a lot to discover and learn about this land that was to be my home for so long a period in my life. Learning the language alone would be quite a challenge. More about that later when I describe my days in language school. First, it was important to learn some basic facts about the country about which I had only a textbook knowledge, as is true of most westerners journeying to the Orient for the first time. Japan, however, had established itself very prominently on the world scene in the twentieth century, and would become a world leader in the electronic and automotive fields in the latter years of the century. It would be important for me, as it would be for all missionaries, to recognize these achievements and to become well acquainted with the language, customs, history and geography of Japan.

In geographical terminology, Japan is classified as an archipelago, that is, a group of an astounding number 6852 islands, the largest part of which, quite obviously, are extremely small and uninhabited. There are, however, four main islands which constitute the nation of Japan as the world knows it. From north to south, the distance is quite extensive, over a thousand miles, a distance which gives rise to many cultural, linguistic (dialects), and other differences, owing to ancient difficulties in traveling, local agriculture, and other regional differences. Let us now, however briefly, examine each of the four main islands which make up the nation of Japan.

Hokkaido, the northernmost large island, has a climate that reflects its proximity to the North Pacific. Indeed, it received prominence in the 1970's when it was the sight of the Winter Olympic Games which were centered on the snow and cold weather conditions found on the island.

Honshu is the largest and most highly developed of the main group of islands. This is the largest of the four main islands, and indeed is so prominent on maps that for many it is thought to represent the whole nation. On it is found the beautiful, perfectly cone- shaped Mount Fuji whose majestic beauty is world-renowned. Tokyo, the nation's capital, and such major cities as Yokohama, Nagoya, Kyoto, and Osaka are all located on Honshu which is the heartland of the country and the site of its electronic, automotive and industrial activity. Nagoya, along with Tokyo, would become a center of our Augustinian missionary activity once we began to expand beyond Nagasaki is located on the island of Honshu. Later, the members of our Midwestern Province would select Yokohama, a principal port city on Honshu, as the site of their expanded mission after having served for some years with our Villanova mission in the Nagasaki area.

Shikoku, perhaps the least well known of the main islands, extends just to the southeast of Honshu. It is mainly agricultural, contains no major cities, and is not connected with our apostolate in Japan.

Kyushu, southernmost of the four major islands, is the focal point of our missionary work in Japan. In time we would establish parishes in Nagasaki and Fukuoka, the two most prominent cities on Kyushu. Surprisingly, for a nation with only a very small number of Catholics in relation to the total population, Kyushu has had a long and spiritually fruitful connection with the Church, dating all the way back to the time of the great missionary St. Francis Xavier who set foot on this very island in 1549. Other Jesuits followed him as did some Franciscans a short time later. We Augustinians arrived in 1602. But those were unsettling times, and fear among the native rulers about the intentions of these new Westerners led to outright persecution of Christians in the late 16th and early 17th centuries. A description of those difficult years is given earlier in these pages, in the "Tribute to the Japanese Martyrs" section of this booklet.

A unique and fascinating period developed after the years of persecution ended around the year 1650. All missionaries, and indeed all westerners, were banned from the country. Japan would remain isolated from the world until the Meiji Restoration Period of the mid 19th century. During that period of nearly 300 years, the Japanese Catholics continued to observe the basic rudiments of their faith as best they could.

They retained abbreviated forms of prayers and liturgical practices; Christian statues were disguised in forms that closely resembled Buddhist statues, and so on. A real tribute must be given to the "Kakure Kirishitan" (Hidden Christians) who remained faithful to their religion and who later would emerge in the 19th century to become full members of the current Japanese Church.

Nagasaki: Beginnings

We begin with a word about our community. We Augustinians are a community of men who have come together and pledged to follow a way of life exemplified and outlined by our Holy Father Augustine for his companions centuries ago, approximately 395 A.D., shortly after his own conversion to Christianity. A hallmark of Augustine's Rule is the call to live a "community life" which we look upon as our charisma, an identifying feature which distinguishes us in the way we are responding to the call to follow Christ.

There was a real spirit of welcome and camaraderie in the air that evening as Fr. O'Connor and I arrived at our parish, Shiroyama, and I was shown my room. In spirit of the biblical passage, we "killed the fatten calf" and enjoyed one another's company in conversation around the table. I had news from home and from Villanova. They in turn assured me that they would be with me to assist in mastering the basic rudiments of the Japanese language and customs.

Who were these men? What turn of events brought us Americans, members of the Province of St. Thomas of Villanova to this particular corner of Japan, an area I was to learn that was connected in a rather interesting way to our Augustinian Order and way of life?

Father Tom Purcell was the founding father, the "soritsusha" of this mission to Japan. He, along with Fr. George Krupa and Fr. Ed "Rusty" Robinson were the three pathfinders who had arrived here in 1952. Two years later Fr. Ed Griffin and Fr. Gerry Ryan joined them. Fr. Robinson and Fr. Ryan were members of the Midwestern Province of the Order, with its headquarters located in Chicago. A third group of men arrived in 1958, Fr. Ed Hattrick, Fr. Joe O'Connor and Br. John Sheridan. Then came I, the least of the flock, fresh from the seminary and eager to begin.

There is an interesting history leading up to our coming to Japan at this midpoint of the 20th century. Its origin can be traced back three centuries to the very earliest days of 1602. Those were tumultuous and dangerous times which ultimately led to the martyrdom not only of foreign missionaries of various religious communities, but of many native Japanese priests, religious and lay people as well. There is a saying in Christian history, dating back centuries to earliest Church in the Roman Empire, the "the blood of martyrs is the seed of Christians." Our Augustinian missions today, with their growth and success, are a testimony to the truth of that saying.

In the early 1950's, Bishop Paul Yamaguchi, the saintly and revered bishop of the Diocese of Nagasaki, and himself a survivor of the atomic blast on Aug. 9, 1945, decided to invite back to Japan members of the several religious orders who had labored and suffered in Nagasaki in the seventeenth century. Invitations were sent to the Jesuits, Franciscans, Dominicans and Augustinians with mixed results. The first two communities accepted and sent some priests in response to the plea of the bishop. The Dominicans were hard pressed with the availability of personnel at the time and were unable to offer any assistance.

Perhaps by coincidence, but ultimately through Divine Providence, Fr. Thomas Hunt, Provincial Superior of the Augustinians in Australia, happened to be on his way to an International General Chapter in Rome and just stopped over in Nagasaki to view the devastation caused by the atomic bomb just a few years earlier. Fr. Hunt met with the bishop as a matter of courtesy and the two men discussed among other things the return of the Augustinians to Nagasaki.

Later, during the course of the Chapter meeting, Fr. Hunt spoke openly of Bishop Yamaguchi's request and the matter was taken under discussion. Fr. Joseph M. Dougherty of the Villanova Province, and Fr. Clement McHale, Provincial of the Midwestern Province of Our Mother of Good Counsel, were open to the idea and elected to join in what was initially a joint inter-Province venture. The Villanova Province, being larger at the time would send two men while the Midwest Province would send one man in the beginning. Fr. Tom Purcell and Fr. George Krupa came from Villanova and Fr. Ed "Rusty" Robinson was chosen from the Chicago Province. The new missionaries were formally commissioned in departure ceremonies in their respective Provinces in the spring of 1952 and left for Japan shortly thereafter.

Two years later, once the community had been established in Nagasaki, two additional missionaries were sent in the persons of Fr. Ed Griffin from Villanova and Fr. Gerry Ryan from Chicago. Fr. Tom Purcell was named Superior of the Community and of the Augustinian Missions in Japan. Nineteen fifty-eight saw the arrival of Fr. Ed Hattrick, Fr. Joe O'Connor, Fr. John Sheridan (Brother Patrick at that time). I came a year later, in September 1959.

Meanwhile a great deal of foundational work had been done in order to establish the Order on a firm legal and canonical foundation in this new field of endeavor. Bishop Yamaguchi offered the Augustinians a section of the Urakami Catholic Church which had been at the very epicenter of the atomic blast. Indeed many of the parishioners were survivors of the atomic bomb attack. The presence of these new priests, and Americans at that, caused some uneasiness at first. A lot would depend on wise decisions that would have to be made by the Americans in their need to understand and to adapt to the oriental mind and customs of their Japanese hosts. The Urakami church itself had been built by the Christians themselves under the direction of a French priest as architect and suffered complete destruction in the attack of Aug. 9, 1945. At the time of our arrival and the transfer of the parish to our care, Fr. Manri Nakashima was pastor. He very graciously handed over to Fr. Purcell all the names and files of his parishioners and became a very loyal supporter of our new parish, cooperating in every way, and serving as well to facilitate the smooth transition which needed to take place as the administration of the parish changed hands. The parish contained many veterans of the Japanese army who had lost family members in the atomic bomb and were re-establishing themselves and building new lives in the war's aftermath. Additionally there were a number of families from the Goto Islands who had migrated to the area seeking employment in the new ship building industry that was developing.

Shiroyama Parish and St. Mary's School Develop

Having finished with the formal meetings with Bishop Yamaguchi and the outgoing diocesan pastor, Fr. Nakashima, the time to begin our apostolate in Japan arrived. There were a number of challenges confronting Fr. Purcell and his two fellow Americans. They were Westerners in the Orient for the first time, arriving only seven years after the war, facing some very daunting adjustments that had to be made, among them learning to speak and read the Japanese language so very different from their own English language, and as well, accepting and respecting the time honored customs and traditions of the people native to that area. However, they had come with the grace of God, the blessing of their Christian faith and with hearts open with love for the people with whom they would share their Catholic faith and values. Spurred on by these thoughts and motives, in time their work would bear much fruit.

One story illustrates how necessary it was to be patient in starting the new mission, to be able to communicate clearly from one language to the other, and to honor and respect the customs and needs of the local people.

Obviously it was necessary to build a church for worship and a friary to house the priests and to serve as a small center for parish needs. As the meetings progressed and other needs were brought forth, the people urgently requested a "yochien," (a kindergarten). After he had looked up the word in his pocket dictionary, the puzzled look on Fr. Purcell's face indicated his lack of understanding why the people wanted something so basic, even before a grade school, at a time when funds for building would be hard to come by. Later, in discussing his plans with the Vicar of the diocese, Fr. Satowaki explained to him that in Japan the government would advance loans for building a school and afterwards give direct aid to the institution, even if it were sectarian. Armed with that information and encouragement, Fr. Purcell decided to proceed with the construction of the kindergarten, to the great delight of the parishioners and the local community. And so the parish of Shiroyama took shape, a church, a friary and—a kindergarten!

Now that the first step had been taken in providing for the needs of the little children, it soon became apparent that further development in educating the oncoming generations would be necessary. The full extent of what Fr. Purcell was envisioning would be a parochial facility constructed along the lines of what was common in the United States, a parish church, a friary for the Augustinians, a grade school and the aforementioned kindergarten. However, certain significant changes would have to be made in order to adapt to Japanese laws and property restrictions.

First, in a country with such a large population and a very limited amount of land, the purchase price for a piece of land would be quite expensive. The Augustinians had already purchased a sizable piece of land with the intention of fully developing the Nagasaki mission according to a prearranged plan. One of the larger areas of this land would be used to erect the grade school. It was at this point that the Order came face to face with a requirement of Japanese law that was substantially different than anything it had experienced back in the United States.

The issue revolved around construction of a school which would be subsidized in some way by the government. Aided by advice from the Vicar General of the Diocese, Fr. Purcell discovered that, if he were to construct a school building, he would have to cede permanently to the government the land on which that building was to be erected. Here he was faced with a dilemma. The Order had already purchased a large plot of land with the intention of it being used by the Augustinians to develop their foundation of a permanent mission in Nagasaki. Part of that foundation would be a grade school. But would such a school succeed in a land with such a small population of Catholics from which to draw its students? Would it not be more advisable, for instance, to build instead a sizable community center for diverse activities of the parish?

On the other hand, Fr. Purcell was an American who grew up in Shamokin, PA, and had seen first hand the beneficial experience of a Catholic grade school and the impact a well run religious school taught by devout Sisters had in forming in young people a strong and vibrant faith. This would be a new experience for the largely non-Catholic children and their families, but the importance of providing them this opportunity overrode all other considerations. Permission for the transfer of property was granted by the Provincial back at Villanova, and so a large portion of the property was given to the government for the construction of a parish school with grades from first to sixth.

The Order retained the small section of the remaining property on which the church and the friary would be built. From a legal standpoint, two corporations were created, one the religious corporation for the Augustinians and the other a school corporation owned by and under the direct control of the government.

Next came the need for selecting a staff to operate the new school. Back in the United States, especially back in the 1950's, it was still possible to seek out and obtain Sisters from one of the local Congregations to fulfill this task. It might be an entirely different matter in a country like Japan with an extremely small number of Catholics, both lay and Religious, to find such assistance. We were blessed when the Sisters of the Infant Child Jesus, a well-respected congregation of native Japanese women agreed to assist us at St. Mary's school. A convent was set up for them on the second floor above the classrooms of the primary school. They were of great assistance to Fr. Purcell when it came time to interview lay teachers and other staff personnel for the school. Although the Sisters had taught elsewhere in some rather prestigious schools (mostly for non-Christian students), the parochial school arrangement at St. Mary's would be quite different for them since this was to be the first "parochial" school in the country.

As the life of the school continued with continuing success being achieved by its students, plans were being made to expand the program to the next level. A new middle school would be erected. Much of what is recounted here regarding our parish educational program might seem quite basic and ordinary to American readers of these events. However one must put them in the context of the Catholic faith as lived in Japan where the number of Catholics and church sponsored institutions is minuscule in comparison to what Americans are accustomed. Also one must take into account that this was all being done in the 1950's and 1960's at a time when the whole Japanese nation, and the devastated city of Nagasaki especially was struggling to recover from the ravages and devastation of war. The continued support by the Augustinians and those they served back in the United States was deeply appreciated by all of us working in the missions in Japan. On a personal note and as an example, I remember hearing of the "Shamokinaki" dances put on by the students at Villanova to raise money for the new Augustinian mission in Japan. (For all of you, of either nation, "Shamokinaki" is not a word found in either language. Fr. Purcell was from Shamokin, PA and the Villanova students used that name with the Japanese-sounding ending to draw attention to the dances that were being held to support the mission.)

Before going on to another topic in these Memories, I would like to relate some of the achievements attained by our students after they left St. Mary's to compete and to find their place in the local and national scenes.

First, in sports our students competed in basketball, tennis, volleyball and table tennis. Both boys and girls teams did rather well locally and in regional competition. They placed well in the standings in table tennis, a sport especially popular in the Orient as a result of the Chinese - American contests in the 1960's. In tennis, two of our students won the Prefecture finals. Our most notable achievement occurred during the Melbourne Olympics when one of our girls placed third in the backstroke competition in swimming. She became famous throughout the country with Japanese television showing the contest on a nationwide broadcast with inserts of our students cheering on their "neechan" (elder sister).

It wasn't in sports alone that we had, for a small school, a few graduates who went on in careers to achieve national, and even international, prominence. In the field of medicine Kenji Nakashima went on to become an expert in the treatment of thyroid gland disease, and worked for some time in the Chernobyl area disaster treating the effects of the radioactive material that was emitted at the time of the explosion. Later, back in Japan, Dr. Nakashima became the youngest full professor in the history of the Nagasaki Medical School. After that he went on to continue his practice working for the World Health Organization in Geneva, Switzerland.

We also felt honored when one of our girl graduates, Minako Motomura, was accepted at a prestigious Protestant University in Kyoto. After graduation she went on to become a television newscaster and became a very well known face on TV in the Nagasaki area and throughout the region of Kyushu.

It is a fact of life that change happens. And when it does happen, it often hurts those involved to see something cherished diminish in size, in its perceived value, or even to disappear altogether. Such would be my experience with regard to our cherished St. Mary's kindergarten, primary and middle school combination which was so distinctive a part of our parish structure and which distinguished our parish from others around us. During its early years, as it was first envisioned and then developed by Fr. Purcell and later by Fr. Hattrick, it was something new, different and unique in Catholic Japan. This was also at a time when the nation was re-establishing itself after the trauma of World War II when the Christian faith was beginning to grow stronger and become a force of greater importance in Japanese society. All these factors, plus the presence of the Sisters and the other factors everywhere associated with a Catholic school came together to support the decision of the parents to entrust their children to our care. We were different and we were good.

However, in Japan as in the United States, alongside the Catholic schools, known for their faith filled atmosphere as well as their academic excellence, were the public schools under the direction of the government. As the years went by and the nation continued to make enormous strides in its redevelopment, the support it provided for the public school system grew stronger and it became more competitive with our school. In addition, during the 1970's and 1980's when Japan developed into a commercial and industrial colossus, the importance of getting into prestigious schools as stepping-stones to successful careers put added pressure on students and families to make every effort not to miss every opportunity that would lead to that success. All these factors impacted us at St. Mary's when a number of parents transferred their children to the public schools and it became increasingly more difficult for us to maintain the facilities and provide the diverse educational offerings of the public schools.

So change came to St. Mary's. And as I said above, change brings with it disappointment and challenges. It also offers the opportunity to take those changes and make them work for us rather than just wring our hands at the fact that things were not going to be the same as always.

At the time that those difficult days were happening I was pastor of Shiroyama Church. As the number children not returning to our school grew, it became apparent that we would have to go in a different direction. I decided that we would utilize our available classrooms to provide instruction, limited though it may be, to those same children who no longer were receiving religious instruction. We would open a Sunday school. This would enable the Catholic children to prepare for the sacraments and to obtain additional knowledge about their faith. Our school would be open likewise to non-Christian children to open their minds and hearts to the Christian faith, and perhaps lead to future conversions on their part or their parents' part. Many years later, as I prepared to depart from Japan, our school had more non-Christian students enrolled than Catholic children and our Sunday school is filled. Clearly the educational work of the Church in Nagasaki continues and, with God's blessing, will continue to bear fruit. A new primary school was dedicated in April, 2013.

Tokyo...and Language School

One of the most daunting challenges facing all missionaries to Japan is the need to learn the language of the country, and even to master it as much as one can. After all, we came to Japan to serve its people, and even though some of them spoke our own native American English, it was imperative that we learn to communicate in their tongue. Looking back on my own situation, I have to smile because here I was, having spent the previous four years learning the Italian language while studying at St. Monica's in Rome, and now I was starting all over again, this time facing the far more complex and challenging language of Japan.

And so it happened that shortly after I had settled down in the new parish of Shiroyama I took to the road once again, this time heading for Tokyo and the Franciscan Language School. Fathers Ed Hattrick and Joe O'Connor, and Brother Patrick Sheridan who were returning for their second year term at the school accompanied me on the long train ride north.

The school was run by European Franciscans and was located in a district of Tokyo called Roppongi, about which I will have more to say later. The school offered a two-year course in basic conversational Japanese with an emphasis on speaking, reading and learning to write in the appropriate characters that make up the language of Japan. Quite a number of us were from English speaking countries or were well acquainted with English which allowed us to converse rather easily and comfortably around the dinner table and at recreation.

It was a different matter in the classroom. All language teachers will tell you that it is most important, and indeed necessary, to conduct language classes in the language that is being studied. So it would be for us. Our English tongue is rooted in an alphabet consisting of 26 letters, comprised of 5 vowels and 21 consonants. That is really easy and straightforward. The Wikipedia Encyclopedia, on the other hand, describes the Japanese language as having 99 sounds formed with 5 vowels and 14 consonants, all written in Japanese kanji characters. Right away one can see the emerging challenges. We, however, were highly motivated; our whole missionary endeavor was intended to mingle with, speak and communicate with the people with whom we had come to share the Good News of the Gospel. God's love radiates from people who are caught up in the love Jesus has for us, a love that was shown without reservation throughout His passion and death. The Holy Spirit also would see to it that the message of the Gospel would be communicated to our new Japanese friends by the way we Augustinians interacted among ourselves and with them. Love transcends all barriers!

The most striking difference between our two languages became immediately apparent every time we picked up a Japanese newspaper or book. Our American manner of reading is to read the print horizontally, from left to right. It's quite different in Japanese in which the message is read from right to left and from the top of a column of kanji characters downward.

To succeed in mastering such a different tongue, it was quite necessary for us to do some intensive studying. And that we did, each evening in our rooms! We were aided by reading simple children's books, comic books, and by watching and listening attentively to TV news broadcasts, etc. Joking around with the Japanese children, or playing soccer with them, was especially helpful. Little children are so patient; they never tire of repeating words or expressions, and take great delight in laughing at our fumbling pronunciation of words that come so easily to them.

Let's take a closer look at what we did in the classroom to better understand the methods that were then in use in the 1950's compared to the method of teaching the Japanese language today. In our day we used the Naganuma readers which guide the student from the Japanese symbols to the Chinese characters. We did this only after having studied for a few months using our familiar English letters to spell out the Japanese words. One can get very comfortable doing that, but it gives a student a false sense of accomplishment, something which is really looked down upon today. We started by working with the two kinds of Japanese writing (the Hiragana and Katakana alphabets) and only then did we advance to Kanji (Chinese symbols or characters.) We first read traditional Japanese fairy tales, after which we progressed to stories for primary school children. In our second year we advanced to short stories, newspaper articles, and, to pay homage to the ancient customs of Japan, we examined the ways of Haiku, flower arrangement and the making of pottery. In our readings in class we learned Chinese characters as they came along in the text, just as the Japanese children did. As an added motivation to do well in our studies, there were tests for writing (called "kakitori") every day, once a week, and once a month. Finally a complete comprehensive test was given of all the characters we had learned during that semester. I remember getting B's for perseverance for my homework and attention during class. Getting those B's was no small accomplishment, and I felt very satisfied at what I had achieved. The grades we had attained were in turn sent by the Franciscan Principal of the school to a central office at the request of the Regional Superiors of almost all the Congregations which had students enrolled in the language school. The modern Jordan scientific method of reading and writing Japanese which is in use today did not appear until a few years after I had left the language school.

As I said in an earlier paragraph, the language school was small in size and our daily class routines enabled us to bond closely to one another and to form relationships which continued to strengthen both in class and for many years after we had left the school behind us and began in earnest our missionary endeavors. At times in class we were asked to make up little sentences in order to help ourselves become familiar in expressing ourselves in Japanese. We often used these opportunities to make up humorous sentences to lighten up the class and to kid one another. I remember one such incident in which I was involved. We had in our class a German Franciscan, Fr. Rupert, who was probably a little older than I, who was always very serious—and who was quite bald. When the teacher called on me to make up a sentence using the word "ue" (which means "on or above"), I said in Japanese "There are no pine trees on a mountain called Rupert." He smiled a little, but his body language told me that he was not amused. But we all laughed it off and continued on kidding one another whenever the opportunity presented itself. After all, we really didn't take ourselves seriously and we knew that humor is so often the direct road to a lasting friendship.

I can't move on from describing my early days in this school without mentioning one piece of advice given us which proved to be invaluable as a means of assisting me in learning Japanese, in what I consider the best way possible: being tutored directly by a native Japanese, gifted as a teacher and loyal and gracious as a friend. I thought it was excellent advice, and I made it part of my life for the entire fifty-two years I was to remain in Japan. Over those many years I must have had five or six such mentors all of whom guided and directed me to an ever-deeper understanding and love of their native language and customs. Mrs. Naomi Shiraishi, my last teacher, was very patient and understanding. We concentrated on reading novels, biographies and editorials from the national newspapers. Naomi also helped me with important sermons, talks and retreats I had to give. Over time I became fast friends with Naomi and her husband Hiroyuki.

One way of expressing my appreciation for all that Naomi did in assisting me in the course of each year was to invite her and her husband to share a "bonenkai" (end of the year party) which I personally cooked and served as host. I also invited Mrs. Mitsuyo Uchiyama and her family to the "bonenkai" as well. I had known Mitsuyo from her days at the local university at which time I had hired her to assist me in running a small school I had opened. In this school our goal was to teach English as a second language to young primary school children. The parents of the children were enthusiastic supporters of the school because it offered a well organized, structured six year program taught by a professional Japanese teacher, Mitsuyo, and a native American, myself. A highlight for the children took place each year before the Christmas break when we celebrated with a public presentation by the children of their ability in speaking English, followed by a party of cake and tea to close out the celebration. Mitsuyo and I worked together in this venture for a total of some twenty years in all. Happy memories all the way!!

I relied on Mitsuyo in other ways as well. She had an intricate knowledge of the mysteries of the computer which counter-balanced my awkward attempts to learn and deal with its many challenges. In her frequent frustrations with the many small problems I presented her with, she often used the word "Mohhh"–an expression Japanese women often use when they are irritated. It is really untranslatable. I heard her having to use the expression so often in her work that in jest I gave her the nickname "Moh-chan" or (Little Miss Moh.) She always contended that I was very forgetful. (Boy, was she ever correct on that point!!) She often repeats the story when once she asked me to get my personal seal to put on a document. I picked up the seal okay, but on my way back to the office I started talking to a visitor, and kept at it for over half an hour. When I finally got back to the office Mitsuyo was whispering to herself "Mohhhh." She asked, "where is your seal?" I answered "what seal?" There was another "Mohhhh." I knew I had put it into my pocket, but could not find it. Finally she had me turn my pockets inside out until at last out of one of them the seal fell out onto the floor. She just looked at me and uttered still another "Mohhhh." Later Mo-chan was married in our church even though both she and her fiancé were non-Christians. Her daughter, Miyu, can imitate me perfectly and is so cute. No doubt she will turn out to be as generous and open minded as her mother. Naomi and Mitsuyo were so very kind and helpful to me!! Our "bonenkai" parties at the end of each year bring back so many good memories. The Japanese are such delightful, gentle and humorous people! All those good times and happy memories grew out of that one bit of advice given by our instructor in language school: be sure to get a good mentor who will work along side you to assist in getting a deeper understanding of the language and the people. How right she was!!

Before concluding this section dealing with my remembrances from language school, I want to include a few thoughts on how important and valuable an experience it was to have been introduced to the Japanese literary and cultural traditions. I am referring to Japanese Haiku poetry with its specialized format and imagery. As we read more deeply into the Japanese literary tradition, I began to see how the Chinese Confusion ethic had greatly influenced Japanese writing.

Something else that became very interesting was the rise to great prominence of Japanese women as writers. On the other hand, I read translations of such famous male writers as Mishima in his work "Sound of Waves" and Kawabata with his equally noteworthy "Snow Country." I also read works by Catholic authors such as Shusaku Endo and Ayako Sono. This last named author, a lady, we invited to give a lecture to the parishioners of our Nagasaki church on the occasion of its twenty fifth anniversary as a parish. Ms. Sono is a very lovely person, quite cultured, yet one who mingled very well with our parishioners. We were quite happy and pleased to see that the novel she was writing at the time of her visit went on to become a national best seller.

With those tributes, I bring to a close my time at the language school in Tokyo together with the many significant experiences and friendships that grew out of my days at the school. Now with the close of the school year at the language school behind me, I headed over to the Tokyo railroad station to once again board the southbound train to take me back to Nagasaki. But this time it would be different; I would no longer be returning to the school but instead I would be starting my life's work as a missionary bringing the message of the Gospel, the centuries old story of God's personal love, to these lovely people most of whom had never before heard the beautiful story of redemption.

The plan was for me to join Frs. Purcell and Ed Hattrick as an associate in the parish at Shiroyama. Fr. John Sheridan, (at that time still known as Bro. Patrick,) was working full time with the children in the school. Fr. Joe O'Connor had joined Frs. George Krupa and Ed Griffin in the mission in Fukuoka.

At that very time, however, the community was saddened to learn that Fr. Krupa had recently been diagnosed with a form of cancer, the treatment for which required that he return to the United States. Fr. Joe O'Connor was selected to accompany Fr. George on the long flight home, which meant that Fr. Ed was left by himself in Fukuoka running not just the parish itself, but also caught up in the midst of a construction program for a new church, friary and primary school. Needless to say, his situation called for someone to assist him in the parish. I would become that someone, at least until it would be possible for Fr. Joe to return from his trip to the United States. Working and living with Fr. Ed. proved to be very enjoyable and his guidance very valuable.

My Teaching Career in Nagasaki

After my stay in Fukuoka, I returned to Nagasaki and the parish of Shiroyama where Fr. Purcell had an immediate assignment waiting for me. I was to go over to the school, and pitch right in even though the children were fast approaching the end of the first semester. Perhaps his thinking in part was that by starting in right away in a classroom situation I would have no choice but to put into practice the basic skills I had learned in language school. And he was right. As intimidating as it might at first appear, being in front of a class of teenage students as their teacher, "Sensei", I struggled initially but gained more confidence as time passed. The students were absolutely wonderful. They were so forgiving of my mistakes, giggling as they sought to correct me and enjoying every minute with their new *Sensei*.

In Japan the school year begins with the first semester in April and ends in July. The second semester begins in September and concludes in March. I walked into the classroom in January of 1962. Those first few months are only a blur in my memory now for a number of reasons: we were well into the semester and I had no idea of what had been accomplished thus far; I had little knowledge of the standard implements all teachers looked for in situations like this, such as lesson plans, textbooks, outlines, notes, to say the least. Moreover there was the ever present realization that this was going to differ remarkably from the classroom experiences I remembered from St. Denis's in Ardmore, PA or in the seminary classes at St. Mary's Hall at Villanova. In a word, I was on my own! But with a little reflection I realized that such was not the case. I had my Faith, that gift from God that had so formed, motivated and brought inner happiness and peace to my life. This precious gift I was now going to share with those Catholic teenagers.

I used those days from January to March in part to plan for the start of the next semester, which as I said above would begin in April. Fr. Purcell's plan for the school was for Fr. Eddie Hattrick to teach the third year students while I would do the same for the second year students. A Japanese Sister taught the first year students and also prepared them for Confirmation.

Before I write about our school in Nagasaki, I'd like to mention a small personal story, one that still remains in my memory and depicts the age-old reality of the lasting impact a teacher can have on his students, even if as in this case it is a story that goes beyond the two very different cultures and languages that existed when the events began.

In those initial two months of 1962 when I first entered the classroom and introduced myself to the students, we knew little about one another and the questions came in a very cautious and uncertain way. Many years later I was told that, like teen age girls everywhere, they thought that I was "kawaii" (cute). But there was a serious part to their lives too as they advanced through adolescence into the far more demanding challenges of trying to succeed in the "real" world awaiting them. Even after all these years I can still picture them in my memory: young teenage boys and girls, only sixteen from our first graduating class, gathered with their parents at the railroad station, the parents weeping, the boys and girls trying to remain stoic and brave. As the whistle blew and the train departed, they would be leaving behind their childhood and heading for life in the factories of Nagoya or to a nursing school in Tokyo. This was a special train provided by the companies for students who would continue their high school education at night but work during the day. The one personal bright spot in this little story occurred many years later. One day while I was making sick calls in a big hospital in Tokyo, I discovered that the head nurse on one floor was a graduate of our school. She had left Nagasaki on that company train when she was just turning sixteen, and here she was now in Japan's capital city, in a position of authority in one of its largest hospitals. When she saw me at the end of the corridor she called out "Shimpusama." (Father!!) She wept profusely as we remembered old times, people from long ago in her life, and so many other reminiscences. She walked along with me, talking all the while as we headed for the elevator where I left her.

But getting back to my days in the classroom in Nagasaki, I had to make some basic decisions and plan my approach to my young charges. First, I needed a text that met both their needs and my own as well. A catechism with the rather unusual name of The Junior German Catechism seemed best suited for us. This was, of course, written in Japanese, although not in a complicated Japanese. Nonetheless, because I was just starting out, there were a number of words I did not know. This necessitated my spending hours each evening looking up vocabulary words for the next day so I could keep ahead of the class and be in command of the material we were studying.

Since I had looked up beforehand the necessary words in the catechism, I came across to the students as being really good in Japanese. When I had them read from the text, some of them would stumble over difficult Japanese symbols; I would stare at them and say, "Don't you know those easy Japanese characters?" Little did they know how false my "stare" really was!! (I used to practice my "stare" looking into a mirror each day just to be sure I looked serious enough!!) Then I would ask the whole class and they would all shout out the correct pronunciation and reading. At that point I would call on a girl named Hisako to write the Japanese characters on the board and we would practice saying them over and over again just to be sure that we all knew them. As my American readers might well remember from their own school experiences, this method of class repetition works well with children as a means of helping them learn some basic material. My little scribe Hisako continued to be reliable up at the blackboard, her letters sure and her characters very legible and easy for the others to copy.

It was a joy for someone like myself who had known nothing but the experience of a Catholic school atmosphere, with almost every grade being taught by Religious Sisters, and living in the shadow of the parish church and rectory, to see and be part of re-creating a similar scene half a world away in Japan. The positive support coming from such a profoundly Catholic setting did so much to strengthen my faith and serve as motivation to continue the whole process as our generation married, had families and passed on the same traditions and faith practices to oncoming generations.

Such an ideal vision fired the imaginations of all of us working with these Japanese children sitting before us in the classrooms at Nagasaki. But there were differences, one major difference in particular. Philadelphia, and indeed the entire northeast section of the United States, has one of the highest concentrations of Roman Catholics in the entire country. It is not uncommon, for instance, for a person, when asked in what particular section of a city he lives in, to reply that he lives in St. Denis' or BVM or Most Blessed Sacrament rather than his territorial area of Ardmore, Darby or West Philadelphia. This "Catholic spirit" that is so much part of life in the northeastern United States does much to support and strengthen a person's faith, even if it is only in a very indirect and non-intentional way.

Life in Japan is quite the opposite. The Catholic population is very small in comparison with other religions in the country. The Buddhist, Confucian and Shinto cultures predominate, both in the general atmosphere of a community, and quite often within most extended families. Often this leads to a very personal problem when a young person steps out into adult life and approaches marriage and the starting of his or her own family. We experienced this many times when many of our students later fell away from the Church with almost all of them choosing non-Christian spouses as their mates. It was always sad for us to see this happening, but quite understandable at the same time. From that point on our concern, our work so to speak, was to pray for them and to rely that God's grace, which was so much part of their lives while they were under our care, would remain always with them as a source of strength helping them to preserve the values of their Christian faith and Catholic traditions.

There was a practice, something quite beyond the experience of Americans, which indirectly interfered with and put pressure on the young students as they entered the job market and began their careers. In Japan the work ethic is so demanding and the pressure from the large companies and corporations is so powerful that the average worker feels obliged to fall in line and do whatever is required of them in order to succeed. It is not uncommon for a company to demand that work be done on

Sundays, or that one must participate in some form of company recreation. Women workers were especially the victims of discrimination. Not only were their wages low, but they were required also to arrive early in order to set up the office, after which they had to prepare and serve tea to the staff, and of course clean up afterwards.

Our Nagasaki Graduates In Later Years

One of the joys of being a parent is that of seeing one's child develop from young childhood into the full bloom of youth, filled with energy, enthusiasm and a desire to go out into society and make a significant contribution, a contribution whether large or small that will be of benefit to others improving their lives and bringing honor to one's own family.

Such feelings of satisfaction and fulfillment are not limited just to parents but can be a source of much personal happiness and joy to teachers as well—and to missionaries also. We leave home and homeland to spread the Good News of God's personal love for all people, sealed forever in the passion, death and resurrection of Jesus, to people who until they hear this message of hope and joy, have personal horizons that do not rise above what they can see around them. The Christian message of the Gospel pulls aside the veil of this material world and reveals a life and a destiny unmatched by any other faith, a vision and a promise of a new life reaching out into eternal life with God.

I mentioned elsewhere that for our young Catholic graduates of St. Mary's, stepping out into the complex business and material world of modern day Japan held its own challenges. Those challenges became more personal when they focused in on marriage and the establishment of a family. Catholics make up a very small portion of the total Japanese society, the remaining majority being comprised of the traditional faiths of Buddhism, Confucianism and Shintoism. There arose, as a result, the ongoing problem of slipping away from one's baptismal beliefs into the prevailing culture and faith of so many of one's peers.

It was always a comforting and heartening experience to hear from one or more of our graduates who remembered in a positive way the life and times at St. Mary's. The following two vignettes, excerpts from the lives of Junko and Kazuko, and also the account of a brief visit with some graduates of St. Mary's serve to illustrate the joy that comes from learning that our missionary lives and the Christian ideals we fostered really did leave lasting impressions in the lives of many of our students and parishioners.

The first story has its origins not in Nagasaki but in Nagoya, the site of our third mission after coming to Japan. Some parishioners and I used to frequent a local Chinese restaurant which was run by a family from Nagasaki. As is so often the case in family run businesses, Junko, the daughter of the owners, was a waitress in the restaurant. I remembered Junko from her days in our school and we both enjoyed recalling memories of the days long past as we chatted away in the Nagasaki dialect, making the past come alive in an even more personal way. Shortly before I was to return home for the final time in May of 2010, I was visiting the Friars in Nagoya and decided to visit the restaurant and say good-bye to Junko. Since she didn't know I was coming, and in a surprised voice she said, "Shimpusama" (Father). I answered "Junko-chan," the name I had called her since she was a little girl. (Chan is attached to a little girl's first name.) All eyes turned toward this elderly foreigner. She was very busy and we didn't have much time to talk together. When she brought me some very spicy food, she said, "There ya go, Father" in a loud voice. Since I knew I would never get a chance to speak with Junko again, with a ball point pen, I wrote on a napkin in Nagasaki dialect a phrase I had used when teaching many years before, "shinkou senba" (keep the Faith.) I could see tears well up in her eyes. After a while, when I had finished eating, Junko picked up my check and walked me to the door of the restaurant. She took my two hands, looked at me for a long time and said, also in Nagasaki dialect, "Shimpai sen de ne, Shimpusama" (I'm okay, Father, don't worry about me.) She came out on the sidewalk outside her restaurant and continued to wave as I walked to the subway.

My visit with Kazuko began with a simple and unexpected phone call. Kazuko, who was working as a secretary in a Catholic school in Tokyo, had heard through the grapevine that I was visiting in Nagoya. She called and asked if I could meet with her in the railroad station. When she exited the turnstile from the bullet train and spotted me there waiting for her, she took made a few bows and, with tears in her eyes, said "Shimpu-sama" (Father). I answered, "Kazukochan, sashiburi" (Kazuko, it's been a long time).

Since Kazuko intended to return to Tokyo that same evening, she suggested that we find a Japanese style restaurant located on the top floor of the train station. She took my arm as we walked through the station, used the elevator, and chose a place she liked for dinner. In deference to my age, we asked for a table with chairs (I found it very difficult to sit on the floor, Japanese style, in my latter years). When we were seated, Kazuko ordered a dinner consisting of several courses. I could see that this meeting meant a lot to her and that she wanted to talk about many things.

She began by presenting me with a special gift for the occasion, a beautifully wrapped box containing the newest I-pod available at the time. I was deeply touched by her thoughtfulness. Caught so much by surprise, I responded by giving her my Phillies cap as a remembrance. She laughed and put it on right there. As the meal came and we went from one course to the next, she began to tell me how deeply I had influenced her life. She said that amid the several difficulties that she had faced in life, she always found courage in my words, "Shinkou senba" (Keep the faith). We talked at length about the old days in Nagasaki. She didn't tell me in detail about the difficulties she had endured at times in her life, but as she continued on in her indirect Japanese way, I sensed that she had indeed suffered through some sad experiences, which are all part of the human condition. We went on to reminisce about her classmates, how some had died, and how others had turned out in life. She recalled Hisako writing on the blackboard and of my "cold stare" in class. Of course, she said that I was "yasashii" (nice). Kasuko went on to relate in detail of her Catholic devotions and of how much the faith meant in her life over the years. She commented, as Catholics do all over the world, on the homilies priests gave which showed poor or hurried preparation, something which annoyed her because it wasn't fair to so many parishioners who were looking for direction and guidance in applying their faith to the many challenges they were facing in their daily lives. The different courses of the meal, each small in keeping with Japanese style, kept coming as we talked.

When we finished the meal, Kazuko suggested that we go for coffee to a small parlor in that part of the station that overlooked the city. We recalled with great nostalgia many of the days and events that had occurred at St. Mary's school in years gone by. She repeated again how much I had influenced her life and how much she valued all that she had experienced at St. Mary's. As the time approached for her to leave and head back to Tokyo, she took my arm as we walked through the station. With her Phillies cap on her head, she went through the turnstile and headed for the train. I waved to her and said, "shinkou senba" (keep the Faith). As she got on the escalator she returned my wave and called back, "shimpusama mo" (you too, Father). Then she was gone.

My attention now turned to Nagasaki for another, and perhaps final, visit with some of my former students at St. Mary's. Fumitoshi Iwamoto, a member of the first class to have graduated from St. Mary's, had finished his education and returned to teach at the school. At the time of my visit he had risen to the rank of head teacher. Michie Shirozaki, from the third graduating class, also had returned to the school and was a homeroom teacher in our Junior High school and taught Social Studies. I met several other former students, among whom were Akemi, Yoshiko, and Sayoko. Nabuko came all the way down to Fukuoka from Nagoya just before I was to depart for the United States and took me out to lunch.

Many of those of whom had the opportunity to visit with before leaving Japan were now parents who I remembered as shy boys and girls when we first met years ago. Back then it was hard to get them to speak at all. Now as parents and grandparents they were so much like their counterparts everywhere. I just had to shake my head and smile as I heard them voice the universal complaint of parents everywhere: "The kids nowadays never study, won't listen to their parents, and are always on the phone." Ah life, we're all so very different, yet so very much alike!!

Shiroyama Parish Grows and also Struggles

After I was transferred from Nagasaki in 1981 where I had been pastor for about eight years, Fr. Jack McAtee replaced me. Fr. Jack and I had worked together for a few years and were good friends. He had spent many hours in the classroom after he arrived in Japan teaching English and Religion, and in addition had considerable experience in parish ministry.

What is perhaps most interesting about Fr. McAtee, however, was the rich diversity of his talents in a variety of scenes. Fr. Jack had a superb command of the Japanese language and on one occasion was featured on television discussing Japanese culture with a noted television reporter. He wrote out his sermons in Japanese characters, not at an easy thing to do for an American relatively new in the country, and had an excellent and smooth delivery in transmitting those thoughts in his homilies. He also jogged through the streets of Nagasaki, and even competed respectably in 10 k marathons. He was also an authority on Japanese food, especially sushi, and could banter humorously with chefs and their clientele. The new pastor was indeed a man of diverse talents and was well received by his parishioners. Amidst all of this he had to face the death of his beloved parents, one shortly after the other.

When Fr. McAtee assumed his office as pastor of the church at Shiroyama, he was faced with some serious challenges regarding the physical facilities of the parish. Confronting him as he began his work in the parish were three major projects, each in dire need of attention. A new and enlarged Monastery had to be constructed, the parish was in need of a hall to serve a variety of needs, and the kindergarten had to be rebuilt.

It was decided to focus attention first on the Monastery because its structural weakness was of grave concern. That situation, plus the fact that it was in constant use by two different groups, the Augustinians and the parishioners, each vying for space in an overcrowded condition, called for immediate attention. For example, besides two offices there were only two rooms, the monastery dining room and kitchen, available for use. With all the activities going on in the parish, both rooms were needed, sometimes simultaneously, for adult catechism class, pre-Cana talks, Legion of Mary meetings and for planning sessions for the St. Vincent de Paul Society.

In addition to the above, there was the question of reasonable privacy for members of the community. The one shower was located on the first floor which meant that the Friars had to descend the stairs in our bathrobes in the midst of one or another meeting to use the shower. Not a good situation! All these conflicting problems would quickly be resolved, however, when the issues were addressed by the Provincial, Fr. Joseph Duffy and his Council. The Provincial Council authorized a grant of $600,000 (In today's currency, a million dollars) which would enable the construction to go forward.

Back in Japan, the parishioners were ecstatic and in short order they assumed responsibility for the new hall, and energetically entered into planning the details of the construction. They requested a room for wakes, and also asked for a mat floor room with large closets so that the grieving family could stay right there overnight after the wake itself had ended. This service was made available to the parishioners at a minimal cost so that even the poor people would be able to afford it. This foresight and planning, taking into account the needs of the poor, in the long run paid rich dividends in good will among the people and provided a financial benefit to the parish as well. It proved to be a win-win situation all the way!!

As the planning for the hall went forward it was decided that the new hall would have separate offices for the priests and rooms as well for the people to have their own meetings. In addition, there would even be a spacious room for large parish meetings and parties. Fr. Jack also made provision for a receptionist room that was easily accessible. He later hired two expert secretaries to offer good and efficient service for the people. This was a level of service far beyond what had been available earlier and was greatly appreciated by the parishioners who came seeking documents or to request Masses for the dead.

Turning next to the much needed plans for improving the living conditions for the Friars, Fr. Jack went all the way to Tokyo to obtain the services of a well known architect to seek advice and to develop a basic plan that would meet the needs of the Friars. As they discussed the plans for the Friary, Fr. Jack expressed his desire for the architect to provide two rooms for retired Friars with walk-in showers together with safety bars to help avoid accidents. The Friars asked for two additional features, a common room close to the entrance, and a chapel on the first floor. Altogether seven bedrooms were requested, including the two rooms for the elderly retired Friars. Later at one of our regional meetings, the architect himself came down from Tokyo and graciously accepted the suggestions of the Friars. The people of the parish chose their own architect for the hall with Fr. Jack's permission and supervision. In the end, after everything was completed, both the Friars and the parishioners were satisfied that the new structure filled everyone's needs and was in harmony with the native customs and traditions.

Years earlier, when I was Pastor of the parish, I foresaw the need of rebuilding the kindergarten. However, financial and other considerations at the time were such that any construction had to put off to a later date. By the time Fr. McAtee arrived the needs were greater and construction could not be delayed. This time Fr. Jack sought out a local architect, a person who had designed and built several schools and churches in the Nagasaki area and hired him to take on the project of rebuilding the kindergarten. The new building would be somewhat larger than its predecessor, but at the same time the architect was able to allow enough free space for the children to use for their recreation periods. In the end he designed an outstanding kindergarten which is still in use to this day.

Looking back on everything, I can surely say that Fr. McAtee did indeed maintain the vision of Fr. Tom Purcell. The grade school continued to function and the kindergarten maintained its original purpose of providing training for the young neighborhood children. All the while, throughout his pastorate at Shiroyama, Fr. McAtee continued to do excellent work in the parish as well as in the school.

Fr. Jack's life as a missionary continues, although in an entirely new setting. He is now engaged in a mission in South Africa, not far from the home of the well known author Alan Paton who wrote the great novel "Cry the Beloved Country". Fr. Jack's missionary zeal and activity is now focused on members of the Zulu Tribe and is both interesting and dangerous due to the local political situation in that country. But that is a whole other story beyond our present work.

As the closing years of the twentieth century approached, the parish and schools at Shiroyama were beginning to show signs, both good and bad, that years of constant use and burgeoning growth had to be addressed. A first step in trying to fix these problems coincided with the routine personnel changes that occurred in 1990, at which time Fr. Ed Hattrick was brought back to Nagasaki. He had worked in the parish earlier and knew the area and the people very well. Additionally his work in the schools during his first stay in Nagasaki gave him an insight into the background which gave rise to the problems facing the schools at that time.

The grade school at St. Mary's was beginning to decline in enrollment and was facing serious financial problems. Long discussions were held with the parishioners about the possibility of raising the tuition, or of developing ways to generate additional operating funds from within or outside the parish. Fr. Hattrick began by trying to put the school on a firm financial footing. He tried in many ways to raise money and sought procedures to bring down the annual budget. One factor which helped in this regard was the fact that in Japan the school received direct financial aid from the local government. That meant that the teachers' salaries were almost on the same par as those of the teachers in the local public schools. After lengthy discussions, our teachers agreed to take lower salaries which helped considerably. The raising of tuition, on the other hand, was met with opposition and disapproval by the parents. The great respect which the parishioners had for Fr. Ed did assist him in gaining some support among the people and enabled the schools to continue on for another five or six years but with only limited success. In the end, very reluctantly, Fr. Ed came to the conclusion that the schools must close. This, however, was out of the question for various reasons, the principal one being that the property was under the Government's supervision, a legal reality unique to Japan. At his point, being extremely disappointed and seeing no option open to him, Fr. Ed asked to be changed.

Fr. Michael Hilden took over the parish as pastor and in keeping with that role, became President of the Corporation and of Board of Trustees. As is so often the case in both business and even in sports, he brought a fresh perspective to the problem, which aided him in working out a solution to the matter. It was not easy, but after many negotiations, concessions and other adjustments, a workable agreement was ironed out. Under Fr. Mike's direction a way was found to maintain the schools by raising the tuition and by working out a system with the Prefecture Government that would ensure more income for the school. At this writing there is a new school, both beautiful and functional, still with many non-Christian students enrolled along with the children of the parish. In 2013, a new primary school was built and the Junior High School was closed.

A very significant date in the history of the parish became the next major item to be addressed. Soon, the church at Shiroyama would celebrate its fiftieth anniversary and plans were already afoot to celebrate that event in a very significant way. There was good reason to plan a celebration. Fifty years had gone by since the parish began and God had blessed the efforts of the Augustinians in many ways. A parish community had been generated, children had been educated, a significant number of converts to the Christian faith and the Catholic Church had been made, a regular sacramental life had been introduced to the parishioners, and some vocations to the Augustinian community had been realized. Yes, God had indeed blessed the parish and it would be highly significant and vitally important for the parish to respond in an appropriate manner.

Fr. Hilden suggested that a new church be built. The original structure that had been built when the parish was just getting underway was now too small and had neither heating nor air conditioning units. Surely it would be appropriate to construct a building that reflected and served the thriving parish that the Shiroyama parish had become! The people of the parish were in accord with this proposal and committees were formed to assist in the planning. In a democratic style, four architects were asked to offer designs. The winner, a Catholic from Tokyo, was chosen by the people and approved by the Augustinian Order. The architect was president of a prestigious firm which had an extensive portfolio of creative work which had earned it a high reputation in the Catholic community for designing schools and places of worship throughout the country. The design which the president offered to the parishioners was quite artistic and was in line with modern Catholic liturgical practice. The accompanying budget was in line also with comparable construction going on in the Nagasaki area, and very importantly, was in keeping with the basic financial abilities of our parishioners. Approval from the people quickly followed, and substantial aid was promised from the Augustinian Order. Fr. Hilden tells the story that when it was announced how much each family would be assessed for the building of the new church, the next day there was a long line of Christians waiting to give their contributions—in one lump sum! Certainly this speaks highly of the Catholics of Nagasaki who had endured two hundred years of persecution for their faith, and on top of that suffered the devastation of the atomic bomb. Personally, after seeing the new church, I think the it is a credit to the architect, to Fr. Mike Hilden who forged ahead with this idea of a grand tribute to the parish, and especially to the great people of Shiroyama who had sacrificed and given so much over the years as a testimony to their great faith as a Christian community.

Fukuoka: Our Second Mission

It wasn't too long before we began talking about the possibility of expanding our apostolate. We had succeeded, at least partially, in establishing and running a Japanese parish along the lines of an American parish as we understood one to be. We had a rudimentary knowledge of the Japanese language and a growing appreciation of the culture of the Japanese people. Our approach, both professional and personal had captivated the interest of the non-Christian people of Nagasaki, as well as building support in the ranks of the Catholic population in this city, arguably the most Catholic city in all Japan. Finally, and perhaps most important of all, there were people out there to whom the Gospel had not yet been preached. Everything within us as missionaries called out for us to search out a suitable locale to which we could direct our efforts for Christ and for the Church.

Fortunately we didn't have to look far at all. Fukuoka, the largest and most important city on the island of Kyushu, was reasonably close by and fulfilled our every need. Historically and geographically it presented several advantages that were attractive to us in our planning. Reputed to be the oldest city in Japan, Fukuoka was originally known as Hakata. It is the capital city of the island of Kyushu and is the center of the island's cultural and intellectual activity with many universities and an active social and cultural agenda. In addition, the distance between Nagasaki and Fukuoka is a reasonable 90 to 100 miles, short enough to enable us to maintain a close relationship between our two locations.

Geographically, Fukuoka is located along the coast in the northeastern shore of Kyushu directly opposite Korea and relatively close to China. This proximity to the mainland of Asia became the focal point in the early history of Japan during the reign of the Mongol emperor Kublai Khan. Twice he sent his forces across the sea bent on invading Japan at Hakata, and twice they were repulsed. The second attempt at invasion in the late thirteenth century is remembered in special regard by the Japanese by the way it ended. As the invasion got underway the Mongol forces were devastated, their plans and their fleet totally wrecked by a savage typhoon. The Japanese looked upon this saving force as the work of the gods and gave it the name "kamikaze" or "divine wind," a name that would reoccur in the closing days of World War II to describe the suicidal action of sending young Japanese pilots to crash their bomb-laden planes into American ships during the battle for Okinawa.

Fukuoka also emerges in other ways in connection with the war, quite a few of which are quite unsavory and atrocious. Kyushu Medical School, for instance, is very famous and quite noteworthy for its achievements in medicine during the Taisho era, a reputation that was sullied and damaged by the medical experiments performed there on captured American pilots. Shusaku Endo, the famous Catholic novelist, wrote a very moving account on these atrocious acts. I might also add that on the last day of the war some American airmen were shot on a hill right near the church where I ministered. The city itself did not escape the ravages of war, having been burned to the ground by incendiary bombs with a great loss of civilian lives in 1945.

The city as well as the country in general was to witness a massive and even astounding recovery from the ravages of the war in the decades after the cessation of hostilities. It is well known that Japan was not a recipient of the famous Marshall Plan which so transformed the European continent. The American General, Douglas MacArthur, however, was empowered to rebuild Japan and was largely responsible for its amazing rise to respectability and economic prosperity on the world scene. In addition to the rule of General MacArthur, down on the local level where the ordinary people lived, the transformation of the public attitude was aided tremendously by the way the American GI's interacted with the Japanese people during those early days of occupation. The kindness and generosity of the American soldiers greatly impressed the Japanese who in turn earned the respect of the Americans by their zeal and determination to rebuild their country, their society and their national image. My own brother Bill, a highly decorated marine, was on the first wave to enter the port city of Sasebo. He often said that they were prepared for terrorist attacks and other forms of opposition, but the Japanese military and ordinary citizens came forward and laid down their rifles, swords and revolvers at the feet of the American troops. MacArthur had made it known to those forces under his command that he would punish severely, even to the point of hanging, any member of the military who was convicted of committing serious crimes against the Japanese civilians. This was a far cry from what was reported of Russian soldiers wreaking revenge on the German women who they savagely attacked in great numbers. That the American GI's are remembered so well for their generosity, restraint and good humor says a lot about both MacArthur and all those who were part of "the greatest generation."

After hostilities had ended in 1945, Fukuoka city was rebuilt. However, the American reconstruction engineers and their bulldozers failed to make streets wide enough for the post war era. Also, there seems not to have been adequate planning for the city in general. As a result, the roads are too narrow to hold the great number of cars today. Gradually, however, the city did manage to develop into the great metropolis it is today.

Fukuoka has developed into a city with a wide variety of offerings which, combined, have made it the largest city on the island of Kyushu and a cultural and educational center as well. In the field of education, it is the home not only of the famous Kyushu Medical School, but also of the outstanding Protestant universities of Seinan and Jogakuin from which have come many famous Christian converts.

The city itself is partly inaka (country-like) and partly tokai (city-like). Thus it is a perfect spot for families and to raise children. The sea is close by and is favorable almost all year long for sailing. Student clubs from the local schools and the universities are often on the water practicing for competitions or just enjoying the good weather and favorable sailing conditions. The water remains very clean and is good for swimming in the all-too-short season from mid-July to mid-August. For those whose interests lie inland, the nearby mountains beckon and are accessible and good for hiking. Fr. Joe O'Connor and I used to hike there frequently with our parish youth club made up of Christians and non-Christians alike. Fr. Joe enjoyed this interaction with the young people and attracted many of them to the church. Our parish is located in an area that was originally made up of rice fields. However, on the advice of the city office we bought property in an area that developed very favorably and became a very comfortable place in which to live.

Culturally Fukuoka developed as well. Because the city prospered and grew into a large and prominent business center, its importance was emphasized when it became the last stop on the famous bullet train from Tokyo. This enticed many Japanese and foreign musicians to come to Fukuoka on tours. The city's symphony halls, while not as magnificent as the Suntory Hall in Tokyo, are nonetheless spectacular in their own ways. The halls were built strategically on bus and subway lines which made them very accessible for the people and had the added advantage of eliminating the need to find and pay high prices for parking facilities. I frequently received tickets to concerts from my many friends. Imagine receiving free tickets to hear Yo Yo Ma, Midori Goto, Russian choirs and European orchestras! The Japanese love western classical music and my friends and I not only enjoyed the concerts but also had many interesting and spirited conversations during the intermissions as well. I must say a word about the Fukuoka Philharmonic Orchestra which is truly superb. I was fortunate to have been at the last concert of the wonderful director Hiroshi Ishimaru who died just a week after his last performance. I'll never forget the moving events of that final concert by this great man. At the end of the concert there were tears and warm applause, more tears and more applause. It was a truly unforgettable moment! His final symphony was the one he loved best, Brahms No. 4 in E Minor. Again, an unforgettable moment!

The decision to expand beyond Nagasaki and to establish a church and Augustinian community in Fukuoka proved to be fortuitous indeed. The city as I have described it was ideal in so many different ways. Even the particular area within the city that we, on the advice of the local authorities, chose turned out to be blessed as it developed from being just some rice paddies into a delightful residential locale.

We were fortunate too in having available just the right personnel to guide and develop the fledgling parish. Fr. Ed Griffin, a wise, kind and seasoned priest with a diverse background from being chaplain in a federal prison to having spent many years in various parish communities proved to be an ideal choice to head this new endeavor. He worked well with Fr. Joe O'Connor who joined him in Fukuoka shortly before I arrived on the scene.

Under Fr. Griffin's supervision our kindergarten and church complex were completed and dedicated in 1961. In our plans for the future development of the parish we focused on a multi building complex which would even include a house for future Augustinians training for the priesthood. With that idea in mind we chose a location near the Major Seminary which was run by the Sulpicians. That part of the plan never really worked out, but as they say, that's another story. The kindergarten, however, was very much welcomed by the local community and has flourished ever since. Slowly the parish began to develop and increase in size from a lowly beginning of but ten Catholics to a sizable parish of some eight hundred parishioners today.

I would like to emphasize my remarks on the kindergarten because in my opinion it is an important feature in the development of the Augustinian Vicariate in Japan. Fr. Ed Griffin, the builder and first Principal of the kindergarten, with great foresight laid out a plan for the education of small children, catechism for their parents, and at the same time a program so constructed that it would be on a firm financial footing to enable it to continue long into the future.

Fr. Griffin enlisted a Congregation of Sisters called the Knights of Our Lady. The Provincial of the Congregation assigned one of her best teachers to be the head teacher and two young Sisters who were wonderful in the work they did and the relationship they had with the young children and their families as well. As is true just about everywhere in the world, Catholic Sisters are well respected, indeed beloved, in every country and by people everywhere. This trust and complete acceptance of the Sisters would help assure the continued success of the kindergarten even as stiff competition developed in later years.

At this point I feel it is important to offer a few recollections on matters financial, if for no other reason than that otherwise they would be neglected and go unnoticed. Anyone who has ever been in an office of administration can clearly appreciate this matter. In regard to financial administration special mention and praise must be given to Fr. Griffin for the expertise he showed in establishing a financially secure basis for the parish and the Order in Fukuoka.

Fr. Griffin repaid the initial investment for the kindergarten in a short time. Very shortly thereafter he started a new fund under the Religious Corporation body which had as its purpose to provide continuing income for the support of the kindergarten.

According to Japanese law, such a fund could be used for other purposes within the Corporation itself. This was an unexpected but very helpful benefit to the Vicariate to help it to become self sufficient thereby reducing it's financial dependency on the mother Province of St. Thomas of Villanova. There is a history of loans and direct gifts to other Augustinian projects throughout the country which are too numerous to mention here. For example, in 2002, many years after Fr. Griffin had returned to the United States, when we found it necessary to construct a new kindergarten the Private School Association graciously gave us a loan of $800,000, to be repaid over twenty years at two percent interest. With the two million dollars we had set up, we repaid the loan easily and in a short time.

Although Fr. Griffin's vision will never show up in our archives at Villanova, I have the highest admiration for him. I might add that he was extremely kind and supportive of me in my first year of ministry after finishing language school.

Along the same lines of a person being kind and supportive of me as I began my ministry in Japan, there is the person of Fr. Joe O'Connor. We got along very well together, and even as I began preparing to return to the States in 2010, Fr. Joe is still remembered as Principal of the kindergarten for his kindness, good humor and friendship with the parents of our children.

After Fr. Joe's return to America, I was put in charge as Administrator of the kindergarten complex although I was not yet appointed officially as Principal. In my beginning years as Principal I was extremely fortunate to have Sister Paul Miki from another Congregation who became our head teacher. Besides being quite cultured herself, (her command of Japanese polite language was kind of mind boggling), she was wonderful with both the young children and the other teachers. We were able to have almost perfect Japanese harmony in our school, something very highly prized in Japan. Sister, who came from a high class family, proved also to be highly skilled in the manner in which she invested our portfolio. Through her skills in management she increased our funds two or three times over. However, in spite of her skill and attentiveness to detail, we were dismayed when the market took a downturn and the interest rates dropped from 8 percent to 6 percent. But such is life in the investment field, whether it is Wall St. or downtown Tokyo!

In 2002 we decided to change our corporation into one that was directly under the government (called "gakkou houjin" in Japanese). Even though we gave up control of our portfolio, we were funded by the government and were allowed to receive the going salaries appropriate for the work we were doing. Along with this aid we were able to give our teachers decent salaries, bonuses and upscale benefits. The very idea of financial aid being given by the government to sectarian schools is unheard of in the United States where there is a strict separation of church and state. The situation is rather different in Japan. The Japanese government not only allows but also helps schools with financial aid. The Board of Education, highly centralized in Japan, even urges sectarian schools to instill moral values in the children.

I emphasize this financial area of our kindergarten program not because it is more important than the education of the children, but because it gives an insight into the development of the Order in Japan. This financial aspect of the Fukuoka project is helpful in understanding how a small group of Friars could become virtually self supporting. We in Japan have not been a financial burden on our Province at Villanova for many years. All this is thanks to Fr. Eddie Griffin who is now living in retirement at Villanova.

Although I cannot recall precisely when Fr. Ed Hattrick and Fr. Jack McAtee ministered in Fukuoka, they both made extraordinary contributions both to parish life and leadership in the kindergarten program.

Fukuoka: The Parish and its Important Kindergarten Program

My priestly life in Japan was a mixture of education and priestly ministry. Never once was it either/or but always both/and. Right now as I reflect back on the time I spent in Fukuoka my thoughts are drawn mostly to my work on the kindergarten level, especially over the past 26 years when I was the principal. The caring teachers with whom I worked and the precious children under our care together were a joy that is difficult to put into words.

My aim was to make a family life atmosphere not only for the children but also for the teachers who stood in place of the parents for a few hours every day. We also endeavored to bring the young parents into the circle. This approach would not only be a plus in its own right, but also would serve as a means of assisting the women to form friendships with one another. Even with today's cell phones, computers and satellite stations, many people, especially women, are often very lonely. We found that families which had close ties from the days when their children were in kindergarten together, would often continue their close relationships over the years.

Asian people by nature are community minded in sharp contrast to our American and western sense of individualism. In my long experience I've found that Japanese children seem to have an almost innate sense of community. Although the younger ones cried at the beginning of the school year, when later they began to see that their home room teacher was caring and warm hearted, the children then made friends quickly and seemed to form, without anyone telling them, a kind of family. They called each other "tomodachi" (friend) or "nii-chan" and "nee-chan" (older brother and older sister). The older children tried to look out for their younger friends. When I addressed the children, I would start by saying "chiisai tomodachi" (my little friends).

From 1961 on, our kindergarten progressed along with other private kindergartens, comprised mostly of Buddhist families. Even though there was always fierce competition, our kindergarten continued to expand. As administrators, Fr. Griffin and Fr. O'Connor built extra classrooms to admit the large number of applicants.

The reputation of our school continued on into my time as principal, but at that point we began to be outpaced by some of the other kindergartens by their purchase of new and costly equipment, additional furnishings, and even by superb new constructions, some with the latest in solar energy and others with new architectural designs. We began to worry that our facility might go under financially if we failed to take some necessary steps to survive. So the Augustinians at our Regional meeting decided, at my suggestion, to build a new kindergarten and place part of our Religious Corporation directly under the government so that we would be able to obtain government aid. Both suggestions were adopted and in time were carried out successfully. The results were impressive. For the construction of our new building we chose to use timber imported from the western coast of the United States because such lumber promised greater longevity, was more sturdy and had an attractiveness that local lumber could not match. The new facility pleased just about everyone and the number of our students grew to over two hundred children. Also the heavy financial aid we were now receiving from the government enabled us to purchase supplies and materials that we could never have afforded under our former Religious Corporation. The direct grants we received came from two sources: the Prefecture Office and the City Office. Even though such an arrangement is foreign to the relationship between the church and the state in America, in Japan such a situation was completely legal and worked to our advantage in serving the people and especially the little children of Fukuoka.

Now, a few words about the children of Fukuoka and highlights from our program for them for them. Since almost all of the children were non- Christian, we tried first of all to respect the spirit of prayer and thanksgiving in both Buddhism and Shintoism. In a process of inculturation, we endeavored to incorporate into our programs the festivals of the Japanese that had come down from olden times. For instance, we celebrated "shichi-go-san" (ages seven, five and three), an old Shinto ceremony where the parents give thanks at the Shrine for their children who survived those three stages in life. We had a ceremony in our church in which we blessed and gave out Miraculous Medals on beautiful ribbons which were placed on the shoulders of the children. They also received a kind of candy that is given out at the Shrines. Of course, even though the children went to the Shrines again with their families, our ceremony was filled to overflowing with parents and grandparents. On this special occasion I always made it a tradition to speak about the meaning of this ancient festival and how it related to the Family. First I would tell stories to the children so that they could understand their native customs. Then I was able to give a rather long talk to the parents about God and family life.

We also celebrated the summer solstice with an evening of drum playing, dances and other festivities. The parents sold food and drinks during the evening, the proceeds from which they used to fund activities for the children. The two biggest celebrations of the year were the Fall Field Day and our own Catholic Christmas. Over a thousand people came to these activities. All clapped for the children in the races and applauded for the Nativity play. Over the years I would meet on occasion various graduates from our school, and without fail they remembered the different parts they had played in the Nativity Drama. In Japan, the Bishops allow weddings for non-Christians to take place in our churches, and sometimes our graduates would return to be married in this setting which meant so much to them. In the course of the festivities connected with their wedding celebration the bride or groom would recall with nostalgia the parts they had played in the Christmas play. On an overhead screen at the reception, the families often showed pictures when the newlyweds were serious actors or actresses in the Christmas pageant when they were still young children.

Shortly after the second semester was finished in early December, on a volunteer basis candle services were held twice in one day to accommodate all the families. The children along with their parents placed candles around the manger and placed a gift of money into a box which we used to send to the missions in Africa. At the same time I gave a long talk on the meaning of Christmas by holding up each of the statues from the Nativity scene and by explaining its significance. The children and their parents were delighted to see the various animals, the shepherds, the three kings and the Holy Family. I always spoke on the true meaning of Christmas to the parents after the children left to eat cake and tea in their homerooms. I invited the parents and their children to the six o'clock Christmas Eve Mass which was celebrated in a way which had special appeal for the children. Both the Christian and non-Christian parents celebrated the Lord's birth and were accompanied by violins, bass fiddles and chimes as they sang traditional Catholic hymns. The Catholic parents were outstanding leaders as they coordinated all parts of the celebration. Christmas was a perfect time for evangelization!

We were therefore able to create a catholic atmosphere even when we incorporated into our programs the ancient customs of Japan and our own Catholic feasts. In all these endeavors our aim was to build a bridge between the Church and the neighborhood community by using the kindergarten as a base.

We also taught the children Catholic prayers. The two and three year olds memorized our traditional prayers in a few days even though they didn't have the faintest idea what they meant. During the school year at the morning assembly the teachers took turns explaining the meaning of the prayers by using paper slide picture shows and puppets. These traditions of teaching children go back long into Japanese history when itinerant groups would tour from village to village to the delight of the little ones and their families.

I once interviewed a family which was intent in putting their child into our kindergarten. I learned with interest that the mother was a graduate. I asked her what she remembered of the days when she was a student. She responded without losing a step "Ten ni mashimasu" (Our Father who art in Heaven). She then recited the Hail Mary also in Japanese. I asked her what else she remembered. She smiled and said, "Well, there was this principal whose stomach stuck out and he used to tell us that he had swallowed a watermelon." I said, "I wonder who could that be?" "Well," she answered, "I hear that that principal says those same jokes to the present children that he told us." Most graduates of Catholic kindergartens, even though they were never baptized, continue to recite these basic prayers even into old age. So I don't think that one can judge mission activity by actual statistics of adult Baptisms. On the other hand, many converts to the Catholic faith in Japan are overwhelmingly graduates of our kindergartens and schools. Missionary work must be viewed with a long term vision.

Besides these Catholic customs directed toward the children, I also provided classes for the mothers to teach them about the meaning of the prayers their children were reciting. I also held Bible study classes and concentrated on the first few chapters of the Book of Genesis and St. Luke's Gospel. Somehow Japanese non-Christians think that we Catholics believe that the Genesis account of creation is taken literally as a scientific fact. They are very pleased to see that the beautiful poetry of Genesis can be a key to the meaning of life. The gentle St. Luke is very well received by these non-Christian mothers. I don't think there is a better account of the meaning of prayer, God's infinite mercy, and the Breaking of Bread than what is contained in St. Luke's Gospel. In fact, I think it is the door to the Japanese heart! I enjoyed very much meeting graduates and parents from years ago. Some of the parents of the children a few years back are now grandparents. I met them all over, in restaurants, bookstores, on the subway, on the bus, in department stores, in the supermarkets, outdoor markets, and well, almost everywhere. They would wave and call out, "Shimpu-samaaaaaaaaaaaaaaa" (Fatherrrrrrrr). Some also called me "Enchou Sensiiiiiiiii" (Mr. Principallllllllll). They all have stories of my antics when they were kids. I loved to take walks through our neighborhood. People always stop and talk. Even people I didn't know, knew me. In Japan the principal of a kinder-garten is very much respected by all. I call your attention to the Japanese word "sama" joined to the word for Father. You must understand that this is the highest honorific title in the Japanese language. People in department stores, for instance, really look around when they hear the sound "sama", It might be the Emperor or God Himself. No, it's only me. I had so much fun meeting old friends and making new ones on the frequent walks I would take. I wish I had some hardship stories that missionaries usually tell. It would make this journal more interesting perhaps. But all I have to share with you are these fun stories.

In the kindergarten itself, every day was happier than the next. You can tell the same stories to children and repeat them every day. That is, if you don't change anything!! If you do change one little thing, you have a problem. "Iyaaaaaaaaaaaaa" (Noooooooooooooo). So I used to change the stories frequently just to get the word "No" out on the table. The children knew it was a joke, but they waited for my stories. In the winter when I ran around the track with the three year olds, we would come back to the classroom and I would ask, "How many laps did we make?" They would answer in unison "hashu, hashu" (eight, eight) and I would hold up seven fingers. They would all give a big huff, come over, pull up another of my fingers and say, "Mr. Principal, why do you make the same mistake every day?" They then would laugh so hard they had to sit down. It's kind of embarrassing when I met graduates in the supermarket who hold up seven fingers and shout "hashu, hashu"!!

One of the most touching ceremonies we had was created by our teachers. At the end of the school year, the five year olds who were about to graduate would receive little gifts from the younger children and give another gift back. The head teacher would say, "This is not only a change of gifts, but an exchange of hearts." The five year olds stood still while the younger children went around and shook hands with each of their older brothers and sisters. There was a lot of weeping because the children considered each other as family. I always got choked up myself as did the teachers who would wind up red eyed all day long.

I used to have lunch with a class once a week. It took me six weeks to get around to all the classes. Four children would come into the teachers' room, bow and say "Please come." They would then lead me to their classroom and the other children would all applaud when I entered the room. In this way I got to know the children very well. I used to pretend I was going to steal their jello with my white plastic spoon. The ones near to me would cover their jello and say, "Iyaaaaaaaaaaaaa" (Noooooooooo)!! It worked every time. At the end of the lunch, the homeroom teacher would have them ask me questions which were almost the same every week. When I would answer that my favorite food was noodles, they would all give a big huff and say "Last week it was curry rice." When I said my favorite color was red, they would huff again and say that last week it was green. At the final end of the lunch period, the same four would lead me back to the teachers' room. Often the whole class of three year olds would run after me, laughing and waving. The five year olds would ask me the same questions, but this time I would answer in English: green, apples, the bullet train, roses, etc. Little by little they could identify the English words and later would tell their parents at home what word they had just learned.

When we were thinking of building our new kindergarten in the year two thousand, I got the inspiration to build it in wood. I checked it out and found that building in wood, while impressive and attractive, was extremely expensive in Japan. Then I thought I would inquire how much it would cost to import the wood from the west coast of America where they had very good and durable hardwood trees. I rode over to the American consulate on my bicycle and, naturally, was stopped at a security checkpoint. I told the officer that I wanted to speak with someone in charge of American imports. I was shown into the consulate where a receptionist listened to my request and then made a phone call saying that there was an American in the office who wanted to speak with the person in charge of imports. A moment or two later a striking looking Japanese woman came to the door to usher me inside. When she saw me a surprised look came to her face and she said,

"Dowaiya Shimpu-sama!!" (Father Dwyer!!) And I, absolutely amazed, responded "Mariko." A few years before, I had taught English as a second language at the nearby University and Mariko had been one of my best students. I had lost contact with her and never dreamed that she one day would have such a prestigious position as Director of Imports in the American Consulate. Of course, she invited me inside to her office where we spoke of old times for a little, while she prepared some coffee for me. Finally, in perfect English she asked, "What can I do for you, Father?" I then proceeded to tell her of my dream to build a kindergarten entirely in wood for our parish right there in Fukuoka. She listened intently and then, once again in flawless English, picked up a phone and spoke to an importer of wood. She arranged a meeting for me with a Mr. Robert Yamazaki, an American. The rest is, as they say, history. Bob and I became quite good friends and he did everything needed to fulfill my order and have it delivered on time and in good order. In my estimation, I think the building turned out to be superb. Everything was located on one floor with the teachers' room surrounded by the classrooms. The rest of the story is really too long to narrate here so I will just pass over it at this time. Mariko later introduced me to the two men who were in charge of the American Consulate in Fukuoka with whom I became very friendly. One of those gentlemen, Mark Reiker, came to my farewell party in May of 2010. It was very impressive to hear him speak in perfect Japanese to all my acquaintances. On that occasion he presented me with a special citation from the American Consulate for my work in the education and welfare of the Japanese people.

In March of 2002 we held the official dedication of the new kindergarten. It was a very formal affair with fifteen speeches, toasts and awards, all given in accordance to the details of Japanese protocol. Of course, in preparation for the talk that I would be making, I was coached by the teachers and the parents on the committee for the dedication so that I would not make any gaffes. I had to practice considerably in order to present the formal words of thanks to Bob Yamazaki, to the architect, and to the president of the construction company. These words were written in high class Japanese, but I feel that I handled them well. I had also been coached on the proper way to bow according to Japanese custom which I performed without a hitch. Afterwards I got two thumbs up signs from the teachers and the members of the committee which pleased me very much. In mid-April of the same year we had the formal opening of our new kindergarten, and I can say with much pride and satisfaction that it has flourished ever since.

Throughout my long stay in Japan I tried to build a bridge between our Beloved Church, the Bride of Jesus Christ, and the fine Japanese people and their honored culture. Friendship, I think, is one of the keys to a successful missionary life. Call it love, if you like. That's the story of the second half of my long career in the missions. The Blessed Virgin Mary carried me through just as She had graciously led me since

I was a young boy. "Never was it known that anyone who fled to Her protection or sought Her intercession was left unaided." The *Memorare*, the ancient prayer of intercession to Mary, was my prayer every day of my missionary life. Mary never fails. Never!!

To Nagoya: Our Third Mission

With the opening of our next mission station in Nagoya a certain number of changes took place, some of which are more significant than others, but all of which should be noted here.

First, there were some geographic changes. Both Nagasaki and Fukuoka are cities located on the southernmost island of the Japanese homeland, the island of Kyushu. Both cities are located on the western side of the country with limited port facilities which, of course, has an influence on the type of industry to be found there.

The move to Nagoya introduced us to life on the main island of Honshu. In addition, the city of Nagoya is located on the eastern coast directly facing the wide Pacific Ocean. In fact, Nagoya is listed along with six other major cities as one of the major port cities of Japan. Quite naturally this has had a very substantial impact on the local industry, the occupations of its citizenry, the size and even the ethnic diversity of the people living there, and especially in Japan with its limited size and ever expanding population, and the amount of living space available to families. For instance, whoever among you, my readers, would have thought that in describing the people we would serve in our new mission in Nagoya, I would mention people coming from Peru and Brazil? It would be understandable for me to say that immigrants came to Japan looking for work from the Philippines, an Asian nation itself not too far distant from Japan. But from South America? That's really stretching it. But such is the case. Nagoya is, after all, an international port city, the home of the world famous and immensely popular Toyota Motor Company. Word spread quickly of the need for workers, and in impoverished South America that would be incentive enough to induce many to take the leap and migrate to a land so different from home.

Their settling in Japan would bring success, but also problems of assimilation into a much different culture and spiritual needs as well since many of the South Americans had a Christian background.

Some of the major corporations of Japan, Toyota in the automotive industry, Noritake, a company producing some of world's finest dining china, Brother Industries known the world over for producing office machines and equipment, and many others as well are all located in Nagoya. But Toyota is the one central industry of the region. In fact Toyota and Nagoya and sometimes compared to the American automotive industry and its relationship to Detroit.

One cannot separate Nagoya's history from the devastation of World War II. This city, then as now, was known as an industrial complex, and as such had been heavily fire bombed with incendiary devices which literally burned out large sections of the city. As a result, with the rise of Toyota and other post war industries, living space for the workers became a sought after premium with small houses and restricted space being the norm. It was into this crowded, multi-cultural area of modern Japan that we decided to bring the age old message of God's love for his human family into a new setting framed by the traditions of our Augustinian way of life.

Fr. Tom Purcell had been conferring with the Bishop of Nagoya and had expressed interest in building a church in the port area. There was already one Catholic church in that general area, but the bishop, out of concern for the many Nagasaki Christians who had settled in the area, and knowing of our work in Nagasaki, was open to our establishing another parish to care for the needs of these people. With land prices going at premium rates, we nonetheless were able to purchase a very small piece of land and to build a compact facility. Our new building consisted of a church on the first floor, a Hall and dining room area for the Friars on the second floor, and the actual living quarters of the Friars on the third floor. Such an arrangement left parking space for only one car. It didn't take long for us to realize that we had misjudged our need for space. In short order, with the land around us being rapidly developed, we discovered that we were hemmed in by a lack of space in the parish for parking, with little room for Sunday school classes, and other shortages of usable space. On the other hand, we were there, the people were hearing the Gospel and receiving the sacraments, and the Church in Nagoya was indeed growing.

The next step in the development of the parish has some of the overtones of a Hollywood movie. But it did happen, and we Augustinians have a new hero in Fr. Tom Purcell, the quiet man from Shamokin, PA. Large numbers of Christians from Nagasaki had migrated to Nagoya because of the very favorable opportunities for work in the many industries located there. Finding favorable living space in reasonably comfortable surroundings, however, was another question entirely. Far too many of these people were living in small, rented apartments, crammed next to one another in really unacceptable living conditions. Fr. Tom's great heart went out to them and he determined to do something to bring them relief. He dared to dream of starting a housing project!! The odds against his succeeding in this venture were great since under Japanese law, for any such project to take place, those involved would be required to form or have their own legal corporation. At first, that seemed absolutely impossible. Fr. Tom must have recalled the words the Angel Gabriel said to Mary at the Annunciation, "Nothing is impossible with God." So Fr. Purcell went down to City Hall and sat down with the local officials to discuss his proposal. Simply put, his plan would provide decent housing at a low price for people living in the port area. This would be a no frills, humanitarian gesture. When the city authorities challenged Fr. Tom about creating new corporation, saying in effect that the existing customs would not allow it to be done, his answer was, "We'll make our own new corporation." And he did!! First he spoke to several groups of people to get their support. Then, after endless hours spent in putting together the required paper work, and with dexterous use of his new personal seal, (in Japan signatures on documents are not valid legally because many different Chinese characters that make up the written Japanese language have the same sound), he finally succeeded in creating the new corporation which would pave the way for this ambitious program to go forward.

Fr. Tom next proceeded to buy an adequate amount of land in a section of the port area not far from our church. He succeeded in finishing this first housing project to the great delight of the Catholic people who had risked a lot financially when they agreed to become part of the corporation. Over a number of years Fr. Tom built three more such housing projects in the general area of the parish church, (the last project was a half hour away by car). This vision of Fr. Purcell became a legend in welfare work throughout Japan. Indeed he became an icon to the many people he had helped!!

There was yet more work for Fr. Tom to do in establishing our new parish in Nagoya. A Community of Sisters was needed to come to Nagoya to serve the people in a number of ways that would enable our parishioners to receive the full ministry of the Church in the struggle of the daily lives.

Fr. Purcell solved this problem by inviting the Sisters of the Sacred Heart to come to Nagoya to do parish and welfare work. This they agreed to do. The Congregation sent four of their best Sisters to work with Fr. Tom. They are still active there in the parish and continue doing excellent ministry among the people. Their work entails visiting the sick, teaching catechism classes to the children, and doing welfare work with the foreign workers and the homeless. Through the extraordinary kindness of the Sisters, many indigent people have found food, clothing, blankets and shoes. A most important fact attributable to the presence and the work of these Sisters is that these indigent people and others are welcome at the church in the port. One young Sister in my time stood out not only for her leadership qualities, but also for her command of spoken and literary English. Later when she became principal of a well known high school, she often invited me to speak to the girls on Religion. An American Sister from this same Community proved to be outstanding in many forms of welfare work. We were blessed indeed the day these Sister of the Sacred Heart agreed to Fr. Tom's invitation to come join us in serving the people of Nagoya in our parish at the port.

The remaining reflections to be included here in my Memoirs concern people, five Augustinian brothers, all of whom I admire greatly but whose contributions to the success of our mission in Nagoya I can best treat of in a summary fashion.

Fr. Ed Hattrick followed Fr. Purcell as pastor and did his best to put this small church complex together with its four stations into a more unified and viable parish structure. Children's Catechism lessons, committee meetings and welfare work were virtually impossible to run efficiently in the small building that was at the heart of our parish. He did his best, however, to bring all these activities under one roof. But to do so in a fitting manner proved to be virtually impossible. Fr. Hattrick could only manage to make basic repairs on the roof without really altering the basic style of the building. In the midst of all this struggle he was rather quickly called upon to return to Nagasaki to see what he could do to save the parish school which was failing because of financial setbacks and strong competition from other private schools. Clearly, however, as Fr. Hattrick departed it was apparent to all of us that a new church and parish center was badly needed in Nagoya.

Fr. Liam O'Doherty, a graduate of our Msgr. Bonner High School in Drexel Hill, PA, and a person imbued with a deep love of the Japanese culture, who also had a great command of the language, arrived as Fr. Hattrick's replacement. His would be the task of undertaking the responsible and stressful job of finding new land to purchase and the building of a new church. Fr. Liam and the Catholics who were on the search committee were stunned to learn that there was hardly any land available. All the different sites which they examined proved to be out of their reach for various reasons, financially in many cases, but not exclusively so. I was present as associate pastor to Fr. Liam at the time and I can attest to the strain under which he was forced to work. We were fortunate, however, to be supported in our struggles by the fraternity we shared as Augustinians living according to our Rule and the way of life it bolstered and strengthened. It gave us energy to support one another and to endure whatever trials we were facing at the moment. Looking back, I can say that those were very happy days for me. Fr. Liam and I became close friends and have remained so ever since. But even this was not to last. I received an Obedience to return to Fukuoka where it was thought I could put to good use my previous experience as principal of the kindergarten. Fr. Liam was left alone. This hardship and the continuing weight of the building process regarding the new church eventually took their toll. Fr. Liam, in the end, asked to return to America for reasons of his health. Being a missionary in today's world, even though the parish itself may be small by American standards, can be hard grueling work.

Into this mix stepped Fr. Joseph Masami Yamaguchi, our first ordained native priest, not so much because he was Japanese, but rather because he was available and now was being entrusted with his first pastorate. (I have a separate section in this the book concerning our native Japanese vocations and direct your attention to that section). Almost immediately Fr. Masami discovered there was a great deal of dissension among the Christians concerning the old site, the architect for the new church and, of course, finances. The young priest was at a loss. He did the right thing in contacting Fr. Tom Purcell who was living in semi-retirement in Nagasaki to come up to Nagoya and give him some assistance in resolving his difficulties. He called upon the right man. In the space of but a few short weeks Fr. Tom found a good piece of property and even engaged an architect who was acceptable to everyone. After Fr. Purcell's return to Nagasaki, Fr. Masami then got the necessary documents and building permits from the City and the Prefecture offices needed to carry out the program which Fr. Tom had laid out. Fr. Masami proved to be extremely adept at doing this type of work. Although he had to live alone, he accomplished the task of building the new church complex with great skill and vision. In keeping with its long standing support for the missions in Japan, the Augustinian Province of St. Thomas of Villanova very generously granted the new project a direct gift and also a no interest loan, a grant that went a long way toward the success of the whole project. Back in Japan, even though the parishioners had been divided on several points before construction, later embraced the challenge of paying off the many loans the parish had undertaken. I was very pleased to see that they had carried out these promises with generosity and graciousness.

During this period of directing the construction process, Fr. Masami lived under tremendous stress. The state of a friar having to live alone amid the many distractions and pressures of his apostolate is not encouraged by our Order which, in the spirit of St. Augustine and the Rule of life he left us, is dedicated to our living our lives in a community with our brother friars. When Fr. Masami fell ill from the pressures of his work, I invited him to come and live with us in Fukuoka where I was pastor. After two years of recuperation, he was able to return to Nagoya as associate pastor. In the interim during Fr. Masami's absence, Fr. Peter Tetsuya Hirano, a native of Nagasaki and a graduate of our school, had been named pastor in Nagoya. Fr. Hirano is greatly loved by the parishioners and foreign workers. He shows a deep concern and understanding for the young people who seek him out with their problems, and with whom he spends much time in joining them in their various activities. Fr. Masami, after his return to the parish, dedicated his life and work to helping the seamen and crews from the many cargo ships and tankers that come and go in and out of the port of Nagoya. He is well known to the security guards and often offers Mass right on the ships docked in the harbor. Regarding the apostolic work these two native Japanese Augustinians are doing, as well as their continuing to live a community life with prayer, meals and recreation together is a source of much satisfaction to us older American missionaries as it clearly demonstrates that the Augustinian spirit which we tried to bear witness to in our lives had indeed taken root and was thriving among our young native Japanese Augustinians. Both priests receive frequent requests to hear confessions, preach and give retreats in other churches both in Nagoya and in other dioceses as well. Fr. Hirano is especially popular with students of Catholic schools. He has gained a reputation for connecting with young people. Principals of Catholic schools throughout the country call on him to speak to their students and recommend him highly to teachers of other Catholic schools.

In the spring of 2010 when I was preparing to return to America, I visited the friars in the various parishes we were staffing throughout the country to say goodbye. I arrived in Nagoya just before Easter and celebrated the Resurrection of Christ with the two friars stationed there. I was deeply impressed with the unity of heart which I witnessed among the parishioners. I had been stationed there at a time of great tension and so I was quite touched when I saw the warm signs of peace the parishioners shared with one another. The Korean Catholics are very much part of the parish also and they too were very kind and gracious. The Koreans who live in a continual state of fear of invasion from the North are highly religious and indeed are dynamic Christians. During the Easter liturgy, as I listened to the sermon of Fr. Tetsuya, I began to understand why he was so respected as a preacher. A highpoint in the liturgy came when two children received their First Holy Communion and one infant was baptized.

I remained in Nagoya a week or so. Having been extensively rebuilt after the devastation visited upon the city as an industrial center in World War II, Nagoya is now a totally modern city serviced by subways, trains and buses which provide local and even national transportation. On one of my many walks around the city I returned to view the site of our former church complex. It is now a private home, but just seeing it after so many years filled me with a lot of nostalgia. At the time when I was stationed there, on many an occasion I used to take a walk down to the area of the port which at that time was a very seedy area but which since then has been transformed into a tourist attraction for visitors coming to the city. The boat ride around the harbor is also a very popular attraction. Security, for a number of reasons, was strengthened considerably since the time I was there but still did not take away from the overall beauty of the harbor with its many restaurants, an aquarium, and a host of boutiques and souvenir shops. "Omiyage" is a word that is almost always on the minds of the Japanese people and signifies a souvenir present that one gives to the family and friends after having been on a trip. (This makes Japanese visitors a very welcome sight for souvenir shop owners in all the well known tourist areas of the western world).

There was one event, totally unplanned for, that cast a long shadow over my final days on this Easter visit to Nagoya. Toward the end of my stay I was coming down the steep stairs of the friary one evening at twilight. I thought I had reached the lower floor, but I was only on the second step from the bottom. I stumbled down the rest of the stairs. On the way down I tried to keep my balance to avoid having a serious accident. As any elderly adult can testify, when a person is in his late seventies a bad fall is the last thing he wants to have happen. In my case, I evidently hit the wall with my back, (how I managed to turn around I don't know), and slid the remaining distance to the floor, winding up with my legs straight out in front of me. Fortunately I wasn't seriously injured but I did suffer a rather badly bruised arm. Unfortunately, on the other hand, I was unable to stand up and so had to just remain there in my sitting position at the bottom of the stairs until help would arrive. I must have been sitting there for an hour or so when Fr. Masami returned home and aided me to my room. Imagine his surprise as he entered the house and saw my two legs sticking out in the dim light before him. After an uncomfortable night's sleep, I nonetheless made it a point to keep to my prearranged schedule which called for me to depart the next morning from Nagoya to visit my brother Augustinians in the Philippine Islands.

A Tribute To The Philippines

In my life as an Augustinian I have been blessed in more ways than I can count. Certainly among the foremost is the opportunities to travel which have come my way because of the assignments that were given to me, assignments which opened up vistas into cultures and meeting people that I hardly even imagined I would see as a boy growing up just outside Philadelphia. Having been chosen to go to Rome to study theology while living in the shadow of St. Peter's Basilica and the Vatican was but the first step in my travels. A whole new scene emerged when I traveled to the Far East where I would spend my entire active ministry serving the people of Japan whose lives, culture and language I would share and who became dear to my heart in so many ways.

Now, a half century later as I prepared to return in retirement to Villanova, there was yet one more place I wanted to visit briefly as a kind of side trip before returning to Japan to conclude my final goodbyes and then flying back home to the United States.

I would make a final trip to visit my Augustinian brothers and sisters located in this island nation in the midst of the Pacific Ocean which has a rich historical connection to the Order dating back several centuries to the time of Magellan's voyage of discovery, and a rich modern political history connecting it to the United States throughout the tumultuous days of the twentieth century.

My visit, in no way political in nature, could best be described as a personal pilgrimage in which I set out to visit some very famous and very Augustinian shrines that have connections with the Order. I think it can be said that most people connect the idea of Catholic religious shrines with places of renown found mainly throughout Europe, places such as Lourdes and Fatima. Catholic shrines, places of healing, are to be found elsewhere in the world as well, however, and to one of these, a favorite of mine, the Basilica of the Child Jesus located in Cebu, I was heading. Centuries ago Spanish Augustinians had brought a statue of the Infant Child Jesus, (called Santo Nino) to Cebu where right from the beginning the site became known as a place of healing.

My visit to the shrine, something I had long planned, began with my flying from Nagoya to Cebu, arriving there late at night. Things got off to a rocky start when my driver, who was to pick me up at the airport, was held up at the entrance to the airport for security reasons. As a result, I had to remain waiting there at the baggage return center after all the other passengers had picked up their luggage and departed. A whole hour or more must have passed as I paced back and forth waiting anxiously for his arrival. It is not pleasant, and actually a bit dangerous, to stand around outside an airport late at night in a third world country all alone. Several people, in fact, approached me and offered to take me to my destination. To be perfectly honest, I was kind of terrified as I politely turned down their offers, trying at the same time to appear self assured (which I definitely was not)!! Finally at long last, I was relieved to see my man walking toward me carrying a sign bearing my name upon it, the universal sign at an airport of a driver looking to pick up an incoming passenger to bring him to a pre-arranged destination.

The driver took me to the Novitiate of the Augustinians with whom I was to stay. I was very warmly received and made the most of my stay among them, joining in the life of the community and enjoying the camaraderie that developed between myself and the fourteen young novices, a sizable number considering the times in which we are living. The Novice Master, Fr. Donatus (nicknamed Fr. Doughnuts) was very kind and welcoming and made my stay very enjoyable. I was able to relax and get some much needed rest in the very comfortable guest room made available to me. However, little relief was able to be had from the very oppressive summer heat there in Cebu with temperatures soaring above one hundred degrees each day. The following day I sought out the Augustinian church where the famous statue of the Little Child Jesus was enshrined. When the Spanish friars arrived over four hundred years ago to begin their evangelization of the islands they built a small shrine dedicated to the Infant Child Jesus (Santo Nino) close to the spot where the great explorer Magellan had been killed. Devotion to the Child Jesus developed very rapidly and has continued to prosper down through the centuries. I had visited the shrine two times previously and was always impressed by the simple yet very deep faith of the people of Cebu. Along with many other pilgrims I stood in a long line as we approached the statue, made my reverential touch of the statue, and at the same time offered my petitions to the Christ Child. I also attended Mass twice during my stay and was again overwhelmed by the reverent display of faith at the liturgy with huge numbers of pilgrims participating in the ceremonies. On one occasion I was standing toward the middle of the church. At the sign of peace, the Cebu Catholics engulfed me with their generous smiles. Since I was wearing a Roman collar, they took my hand and touched it to their foreheads in a typical Filipino fashion of showing respect for the Catholic priesthood.

One of the highlights of this visit was the opportunity to visit the family of Fr. J. R. Santos, S.V.D., a native Filipino and a member of the Divine Word Society who had worked with me in Japan as we took care of the spiritual needs of the foreign workers in Fukuoka. Fr. Santos and I had become good friends and we often took our days off together. When he heard that I was to make a farewell visit to the Augustinians in the Philippines, he urged me to visit his family in Domaghetti. I bought a ticket for the high speed boat that ran between the islands, and at Fathers.' suggestion, stopped in Bikol where I stayed overnight with the S.V.D. Fathers. They have a large and well known school there and were very accommodating in their welcome to me. A member of the school's staff, along with a driver from the school took me on a tour of the island which indeed was very beautiful. The next day I took another boat to the island of Domaghetti where Fr. Santos' family was waiting for me at the dock. They in turn took me to a hotel where they thought I would have more privacy than in the more crowded space at the family's home. This did indeed work out as they had planned because after all my traveling I was tired and did relish the opportunity to unwind and relax for a while. Later that day, and for the remaining part of my visit to the island I took my meals with the Santos family and very much enjoyed their hospitality, especially the evening we all went out to well known local Chinese restaurant with its excellent cuisine. The following day they took me on a tour of the island, highlighted by a visit to a four hundred year old church. We also visited the local university where Father's sister-in-law had worked for many years and from which she had just recently retired as a vice president. They also brought me over to visit a Catholic college for women, many of whose students got their degrees in nursing and were known both for their professionalism and for the very personal care they gave to their patients. Together we strolled along the magnificent boulevard by the sea and watched local high school and university students playing sports while others among them gathered in groups as they sang their favorite Filipino songs. All in all I stayed in Domaghetti for two whole days and nights, thoroughly enjoying my stay there and considering it to have been a real blessing to have had this special time with the family of my close friend Fr. Santos.

Now I had to return to Japan, if only to be present at some "good bye" events before I departed for home. I had a lot to think about during the three hour boat ride to Cebu, sitting on the cool deck and listening to the water rushing by as the boat chugged along. I had been privileged to spend four years at the very heart of the Church in Rome, living next door to St. Peter's Basilica at the time when Blessed John XXIII began the Second Vatican Council which has had such a profound effect on the Church and the world. If that was not enough, I was immediately sent by my Augustinian Community to the Far East, to our missions in Japan which were just getting started. That assignment would turn out to embrace the entire active ministry of my life as an Augustinian. Fifty two years, a whole half century I had been privileged to give of myself to the development of the Order and its traditions to the Japanese people whom I grew to love dearly. Nagasaki, Fukuoka, Nagoya, Tokyo; each had its story to tell as I reminisced while the boat slipped through the water until we at last tied up at the pier in Cebu.

Before leaving by plane for Nagoya I had one last opportunity to make a visit I had been hoping to make for some time. I spent some time visiting with the cloistered Augustinian Nuns who had a thriving convent in Cebu. During the visit I had a conversation with the Mother Superior who suggested very seriously that I retire there. "We will take care of you, Father", she said. Indeed I was tempted to accept her invitation, but when I mentioned this to my family, they were dead set against it. After all, I had been away from them for 56 years, including those four years of study in Rome. My Provincial also wanted to welcome me back to beautiful Villanova.

Tokyo Remembered: Our 4th Mission

The final stop in my "Tour of Memories" from the time I spent in each of our missionary locations in Japan is limited to a rather brief description of the events connected with our coming to Tokyo. My words and memories are limited because I really did not spend much time ministering to the people there. I was asked to go to Tokyo to fill in for an Augustinian who was away for one reason or another.

On the other hand, Tokyo has a very unique history, quite different from any of the three other cities in which we Augustinians settled and began our missionary work. I think that it would prove to be very much worthwhile describing the origin and growth of the city that today ranks as one of the top three cities of the world, along with New York and London, as powerhouses in the commercial and financial world.

Tokyo, as a word, didn't even exist for centuries, not until as late as 1869. But the little fishing village called Edo struggled into existence toward the latter part of the 12th century, a tribute to the hardy fishermen who made their living plying the cold waters of the northern Pacific. Life in Edo changed dramatically in 1590 when the Shogun Tokugawa built the Edo Castle and established the city as his base of operations. By 1603 the city had become the center of his military government and its population surged ever higher until in the 1700's it had become one of the largest cities in the world. In keeping with its prominence, Edo was considered the political capital of the country even though the emperor lived in Kyoto, thereby making that city the imperial capital of Japan. All this changed in 1869 when a new leader, the Emperor Meiji left Kyoto, moved both his political base and personal residence to Edo, and in effect created a new national capital. This move was further enhanced when he took possession of the ancient Edo Castle (1457) and made it his home. The building thus became the Imperial Palace, a title and place of residence for the Japanese Emperor down to this very day.

By this time you may be a bit puzzled and ask, "If all this was happening to Edo, where did Tokyo come from?" Good question! In 1869, the same year the emperor united the political and imperial offices into the new capital, a new name was created which followed the oriental tradition of including a geographical reference to the name of the capital. Hence, Edo became "To (east) kyo (capital)." Or as we would spell it, Tokyo! I'll bet you couldn't have figured that one out without some help! After things settled down, the population soared in keeping with the city's new role until today it has become not just the city of Tokyo but an entirely new area with a title befitting its national and international stature: Tokyo Metropolis.

Two tragedies, the first an act of nature, the second acts of war, have marred Tokyo's history during the twentieth century. In 1923 a major earthquake struck the city and left it devastated. It is estimated that the seismic shock reached a staggering 8.3 on the Richter scale. Over 140,000 people lost their lives in the quake. Japan however lies at one end of the "Ring of Fire," an earthquake prone zone extending from lower Chile in South America up through the full extent of the Western Hemisphere, over across the southern edge of Alaska down to the four islands that make up the nation of Japan. That being the case, it was not unexpected that severe earthquakes would hit Japan at different times, something that is true right down to today. The second tragedy was the fire bombings of the city in 1944 and 1945 which took the lives of upwards of 200,00 people and destroyed half the city. A real tribute to the Japanese people and spirit occurred after the war when the city completely rebuilt itself in time to host the world in the Summer Olympics in 1964, just twenty years later.

We Augustinians came to the Archdiocese of Tokyo a few years after we built the church in Nagoya. Archbishop Shiranayagi, who would later become a Cardinal, welcomed us with open arms. He told us that by living out our charisma of community life we would have a great influence on the people. We found him to be very favorable to religious Congregations, something which pleased us very much. He was known and held in high regard for his personal care for his priests, often being seen visiting them in hospitals and caring for their personal needs.

Where exactly in the archdiocese we would be working had yet to be determined. As a community we talked over the various possibilities. After some discussion, I was chosen to request a meeting with the archbishop to discuss and plan for choosing the proper location. I decided that it would be best if I brought along Fr. Tom Purcell for the meeting because he was well known among many of the clergy in the country and someone of his stature would thereby lend a certain quality to our presentation. Our discussion with the Archbishop got off to a good start with Fr. Tom and the Archbishop engaging in light hearted conversation as the social part of the visit began. When the talk began in earnest, the Archbishop suggested that we establish a parish in a district called "shita-machi" (downtown). After our meeting with the Archbishop ended, we met with the Vicar of this territory who advised us to buy a large piece of property down by the new subway. He said that the area was all land fill at that time but in five years it would be an excellent spot for a church. He believed that we would be able to sell half the property right away, and with the resulting funds we would be able to construct a church complex on the remaining portion of the land later. The area was indeed quite large and seemed worthy of our consideration.

After having given the matter much thought, including a discussion among the community, I asked Fr. Joe O'Connor to go along with me to check out and see just what property was available. We took a bus over to the neighborhood of the subway and were greeted by a sight we hadn't expected. There were heaps of dirt piled all around, some piles running about twenty feet high, and the remaining area filled with all sorts of debris. Not a pretty site. If that weren't enough, as soon as we got off the bus we were attacked by flees, mosquitoes and other bugs. Our clothing was soon covered by these insects. Hastily beating an exit from all that, we entered a make shift noodle shop to escape from that unsettling situation. The manager and the few customers stared at us in disbelief when they saw our condition. This, however, did give us the opportunity to speak with all of those present in order to get some local input on the overall situation. They were quite surprised to hear Fr. O'Connor speaking to them in good Japanese and so entered quite willingly into our conversation about the local area. Along with information coming from the customers, the manager and his wife explained what the City was planning for the future development of that area. First, they said, an infrastructure would be set up in order to put into place water and gas pipes, telephone poles, electric wires and a sewage system. Land was certainly available at a low price, they continued, "Yasui yo, Yasui yo" (Real cheap, Real cheap)!! In the next few days Fr. Joe and I investigated the situation throughout the whole City Ward. We checked out the possibilities of buying land with the Prefectural Office and land brokers. This was going to be a big decision and we wanted to "dot all our i's and cross all our t's" to avoid making any mistakes in judgment. We were indeed enticed by many to buy property near the subway, but the thought of having to wait six or seven years to start construction led us to being overly cautious in reaching our decision. Ultimately we came to the decision that it would be too long a time to wait. Instead we decided to look into other properties in the section where there were small family factories where many young workers from around the country were already living. Later, at the Regional meeting of all the Augustinians, the whole issue was discussed at some length. A vote was taken and it was decided unanimously that we should buy land where the people were actually living, rather than wait several years for future development to take place. Fr. Joe and I were sent to purchase a tract of land in the area identified by our investigation. The property we found and later purchased was twice as large as our place in Nagoya, and we all thought it would be sufficient—even though there was not sufficient space for parking.

Now came the time to build a new church on the property we had purchased. Fr. Ed Griffin was assigned this task. Upon examination of the site he determined that given the area in which to work, a dual complex of church/monastery would be most acceptable. This called for some shifting of furniture in the church each day in order to make efficient use of the space needed for both the daily liturgies and the need for a meeting hall to provide space for various groups to gather for discussions. After Mass each day, the celebrant would draw a curtain in front of the Tabernacle, place leather covered benches in a circle, thereby creating an acceptable area for parish meetings. We could work with this, and the parishioners were really happy to be together in a comfortable place that fostered their being and working together. At the dedication of the parish complex, however, the Vicar of the area again reiterated the plan he had suggested when we first met and said that he was sorry we had not followed his advice at the time. My reaction to this lack of protocol on his part was to consider it rather out of place and somewhat offensive. Of course he was right.

Initially our discernment over the choice of this plot of land and the structure we had built worked out well. We had opened a church for the immediate use of the people of the area. The people were very happy coming to our church and at the thoughts of beginning something very important to them and for their children: establishing their own parish community in their new church. With our daily liturgies and Fr. Ed's catechism classes which attracted a steady stream of people interested in the Christian faith, we felt that the parish was off to a very good start.

At this point the joint American missionary endeavor was still heavily dependent financially on our mother Province of Villanova back in the United States. Naturally we were looking to find some additional sources of revenue to supplement our regular means of support. Fr. Griffin, always on the alert to develop potential ideas and to convert them into practical realities, decided to start an English academy for Japanese adults wishing to broaden their language abilities. Given the location of our parish right in the capital city of the nation, there was good reason to believe that people would respond to this opportunity taking place right on their doorstep, so to speak. And respond they did! Fr. Ed charged a low tuition, but with the number of students who came, he was able to make our parish self-supporting almost right from the start. He made many friends also through the school, and ever the missionary, he was always both aggressive and imaginative in also promoting the message of the Gospel along with his other instructions.

After ten years or so of this schedule, the price of doing all this work day after day caught up with Fr. Ed and after suffering a serious heart attack he was forced to return to America to recuperate. To take his place while he was away, I was dispatched to Tokyo to try to fill in for him in the various works in which he was involved. For me this opportunity proved to be an interesting and educational year of ministry. As in our other three parishes, the Christians of Tokyo became very loyal and supportive of us Augustinians in the work of the Church and in what we were doing for them in particular. It was a pleasure to minister to them and to work alongside them. I stayed on for a few months after Fr. Ed returned, but then was transferred back to Fukuoka where I soon got the nickname "Fr. Farewell" because I was going in and out of Fukuoka like a bouncing ball.

It was soon after that when a big shuffle of personnel occurred with Fr. Tom Purcell being assigned as Pastor of our church in Matsue, Tokyo. It was not unexpected that

Fr. Tom would have a new approach to the problems facing us at the parish; that is a common practice wherever there is a change of administration, be in the world of business or even in the church. Fr. Purcell looked long and hard as he examined the situation, all the time trying to make the complex run more efficiently within its given limitations. In the end, however, he found that the lack of parking space available to the parish, coupled with other immovable obstacles to our ministry, were insurmountable. At our next Regional meeting the situation was discussed at length, a vote was taken in which we all agreed to a man that we should abandon the situation at Matsue and seek to buy new and larger property down near the subway. Even here our plans were thwarted because the building boom in both commercial and private land development caused the price of available land to soar well beyond our reach. This new reality forced us to settle on a piece of property which actually was not that far away from the church in Matsue. The name of the new church complex was Kasai (since Christian saint's names mean nothing in Japan, all churches are known by the name of the neighborhood where the church is located.) Here Fr. Tom proceeded to build a church complex similar to the one in Nagoya. A major drawback, however, lies in the fact that there is room for only ten cars on our property. We were really stuck in a bad situation because the price of land became exorbitant and totally out of our reach. To this day Kasai church is totally inadequate. Sadly we are forced to conclude that our initial vision was faulty.

Even though the new site was not quite what we had hoped for, we determined to carry on. After all, our mission was to preach the Gospel, to proclaim to the Japanese people, living in a world society steeped in secular and materialistic thinking and values, that God loves them and offers them a way of life that far excels the material values everywhere around them. So with that in mind and with Fr. Purcell at the helm, we began our Tokyo apostolate in our new surroundings. These would be Fr. Tom's twilight years in the active ministry for he soon reached the age of seventy five, that time when each pastor must retire and allow the burdens of the office rest on the shoulders of a younger man.

This simple transferal of office, no different from similar actions in parishes all over the Catholic world, proved historic in one sense. The new Pastor was Fr. Masami Yamaguchi, and his appointment was significant and an occasion of great joy for both us Augustinians and the people of the parish. He was a native Japanese, and handing over to him the pastorate of the Kasai church marked a high point in the life of our mission to Japan. Our goal as missionaries was to present the Gospel and guide the church through its growing pains until a native clergy could emerge, through God's grace, and lead the church into the future. Fr. Yamaguchi was assigned to do just that.

In due time Fr. Masami's tenure as Pastor was over and he moved on to work elsewhere in one of our missions. I want to spend a while describing the person and work of the priest who succeeded him, Fr. Maurice Mahoney, because he has both a different background and a very dynamic approach to his missionary work.

Fr. Moe, as he is called by just about everyone, like Fr. O'Connor, comes from the city of Lawrence, Mass., a "mill town" north of Boston. However, he hails from a different local parish, St. Augustine's on Tower Hill. That parish has a rather singular history regarding its contribution to the missions. St. Augustine's is the native parish of no less than three Maryknoll Bishops: Bishop Raymond A. Lane, Bishop John W. Comber, and Bishop William J. McNaughton who retired after serving some 35 years as Bishop of Inchon, South Korea. Bishop McNaughton in fact is linked to the Augustinians in yet another and even more singular manner. Some years ago, remembering his roots in both Lawrence and with our Augustinian Order, he invited the Augustinians to come into his diocese and begin apostolic work in South Korea. At the time, we American Augustinians were too committed to our work in Japan so we sent on his invitation to our brothers in Australia. They were happy to oblige and began, as we did in Japan, by sending a small group of men to Inchon to begin the mission. Many of my readers may not know this, but the Church in South Korea is thriving more than elsewhere in the Far East with the result that many converts have been made. Even beyond that, a very respectable number of young Korean men have entered the Augustinians and have laid the foundation for a permanent place in the Augustinian family. God bless Bishop McNaughton who in such a significant way remembered his roots in that small Augustinian parish in Lawrence.

Fr. Moe assumed leadership of the parish once Fr. Masami's term ended and he left for another of our parishes. Fr. Moe, as Fr. Masami before him, did much to unite the parishioners to the changing needs of the Kasai parish. Fr. Mahoney's warm and friendly personality, along with his missionary zeal, motivated him very much in the direction of social work among the many foreign workers who, along with an increasing number of young students from many nations, had moved into the parish. The number of these foreign Catholics increased dramatically shortly after Fr. Moe's arrival. Along with them came large numbers of homeless people in need of food and other necessities on a daily basis just to survive, especially during the winter months. Facing the many demands that such a situation thrust upon him, Fr. Moe's talent was to delegate work for these different ministries. This proved to be a blessing indeed because it led people to rely on their own sometimes undefined and hidden abilities to achieve results far beyond what they thought possible. Fr. Moe's famous response to someone's hesitant suggestion about an idea was: "ii ja nai desu ka" (that's okay with me), and launched many a person to do things he thought were beyond him. With complete trust in his parishioners, Fr. Moe encouraged them to find their own way to engage the people coming to the church. Meticulous organization is one of the key factors in Japanese society. In the Kasai parish the people, thus energized and motivated, established a network of Catholics to engage the Japanese spouses of the foreign workers. Their objective was to integrate the parish and not allow it to drift into different communities.

To aid in accomplishing that, Fr. Moe also invited into the parish an outstanding Filipino Nun who had a superb command of the Japanese language, and strengthened by that ability to communicate, proved to be absolutely fearless in carrying out her ministry to the Filipinos, Koreans, Indonesians and Indians. As a sign of solidarity with those to whom she ministered, she stood right along with them before the immigration authorities and pleaded that they be allowed to stay and earn a living. She began the practice of having a priest come and offer Mass frequently, in the morning for the native Japanese in their own language and in the afternoon for the foreigners in a language common to most of them. Sensing a special need, Sister also instructed the children of the workers who often were entangled with the Japanese mafia (called the "yakuza"). Sister was a woman driven by apostolic zeal and personal courage in her drive to serve the needs and raise the hopes of countless confused and frightened immigrants who were seeking only to find a better future for themselves and their families. In their drive to fulfill the social message of the Gospel, Sister and Fr. Moe together visited the inmates in prisons, especially those holding foreign women arrested for dealing drugs. Fr. Moe also went to visit other prisons where male foreign prisoners were confined.

The unity that grew up between the Japanese Christians and the various other nationalities living together with the Kasai parish did not go unnoticed by others. In time our program came to be a model for not only the Archdiocese of Tokyo, but throughout the country. What distinguished our work and set it apart from other parishes was the unity for which we became known. Other parishes were indeed kind to the many foreign workers living in the area, but at the same time they maintained a strict division between the foreigners and their own native Japanese people.

Fr. Mahoney's mind was already moving in another direction: how to care for the homeless who were constantly appearing at the church door? Once again he gathered around him his faithful followers, asked for suggestions, and uttered his now well known byword: "ii ja nai desu ka" (that's okay with me) to many of the several suggestions that were put forward. That was all that was needed to light the fire of Christian charity to bring the required food and clothing to those poor people. The Japanese love to form committees and to work together in attacking a problem so they took to Fr. Moe's green light suggestion and got busy right away. Soon they were working smoothly and before long they were serving thirty, forty, then fifty or more people each day and also were distributing clothing and shoes when needed. Well, what can I say? The church at Kasai, without much space or facilities in which to work, and with a minimal amount of equipment as well, soon became a model community of faith and good works throughout the area. I tip my hat to my old buddy from our seminary days in Rome! Even with all the activity and people swirling around him and with constant demands needing attention and decisions needing to be made, Fr. Moe maintained his good humor and vision even under all the stress. I consider him to be a great Augustinian missionary. His aptitude in finding the right people he could trust and in delegating authority is remarkable and much to be admired. He led the way in outreach to those in need and in welfare work to bring assistance to the poor and the disadvantaged. He is an Augustinian treasure!! He recently celebrated his Golden Jubilee of Ordination and is living in Nagasaki, still taking his preaching very seriously. His humble personality and way of life together with his good humor constantly wins the admiration of people everywhere.

After Fr. Mahoney went back to Nagasaki to continue his ministry, Fr. Thomas Shibata came to Tokyo, and once he was settled in he began a program to refurbish the Kasai church and Monastery. In the present difficult times facing Japan along with so many countries, Fr. Thomas and the people faced the fact that it would be only with much sacrifice, great effort and generosity that the plan could be carried out. As they did in the past, however, showing once again that they are indeed a united community, the parishioners have closed ranks and are working to accomplish this great endeavor.

Time inexorably moves on, and after Fr. Thomas' term as Pastor was finished, Fr. Jesse Dano became Pastor of the Kasai church with Brother Masaya Ide to assist him with ministry. Fr. Jesse is a Filipino who is a member of the Cebu Province of the Order. His Province has been very unselfish in offering Friars to help out not only in Japan, but in other areas of the Augustinian world where there are shortages of personnel. The Province of Cebu is in difficult straits itself and can hardly meet the costs of training and feeding the candidates from the Philippines who are applying for admission to our Order there. I would like to commend Fr. Eusebio Berdon, Provincial of the Cebu Province, for the great spirit of sacrifice he and his Friars are making for the work of the Order.

With that, my dealings with the church in Kasai comes to an end and I can say with much affection "Sayonara" to our apostolate in Tokyo!!

Priestly Ministry

Before bringing these memoirs to a close, it is important, I believe, to acquaint you with in insight as to how we "did our job," so to speak. As you will see, it will not differ that much from what you have observed of your own clergy doing their parish work here in the United States. But there are differences, many of them small external matters that seem of little importance, except that in an Oriental culture with its centuries old traditions that imply politeness, personal respect, deference to age, etc. these assume greater importance than many of us in our Western tradition realize. It is important for us then to be aware of the fact that we are learners, that these customs have deeper meanings than we may be aware of, that the many bows in meeting people or before proclaiming the Gospel in the liturgy teach a level of respect that we in the West sometimes neglect. The same can be said about seeing symmetry and elegance in the art of flower arranging, or listening for the rhythm or meaning in the beauty of Japanese haiku poetry. We have much to learn from a number of Oriental customs.

When I first went to Japan in 1959, the Mass and the other Sacraments were all celebrated in Latin. In Nagasaki, I remember, many people said the Rosary during the second part of the Mass, i.e. from the Offertory on. This manner of attending Mass, so common with Catholics throughout the world at that time, was spiritually inadequate and needed to be corrected so that God's people could be open to and enjoy the full richness of the Mass. The Second Vatican Council set about correcting this and many other deficiencies in the way the Liturgy and the Sacraments were celebrated, and the results have benefitted the Church in many significant ways. In Japan, as the time for the introduction of the changes approached, the Bishops, rightly I think, chose not to hurry into this new era without proper preparation of the people. We had problems in Japan that were far different from what was common in the English speaking Western world. Besides the difficulty of the Japanese spoken language with its many nuances, it was equally difficult to incorporate the changes into the Japanese written language which had been taken over from its original Chinese base with the many characters that make up whatever words one wants to use. Since the new Liturgy of 1965 was meant to be heard, it was imperative to make the translation both clear and literate. The work was not going to be easy, but the Japanese Bishops tried to engage the Catholics throughout the country in the process of translation. Simply put, the first version was considered to be inferior and calls for revision arose. After much work and intense efforts to achieve a blending that satisfied both the spoken and the written language, a final version was approved and implemented and was considered to be very good and was well received by the people. Now the whole process has to start all over again, for as all you readers know, a new and major revision of the words of the liturgy in use since November 27, 2011.

The Japanese Bishops, right from the beginning, urged that the whole Mass be sung. This, of course, is far different from what we Americans experienced here at home. In the end, the new national hymnal contained music of a very high caliber, was in keeping with Oriental tradition, was theologically correct, and was well accepted by the people.

A new national hymnal was published which contained music akin to the Japanese ear and was theologically correct. The priest celebrating the liturgy was given the freedom to choose whether he would sing the words of the Mass or simply speak them. When the Japanese Liturgy is celebrated in the complete musical form it is very moving and satisfying to Japanese Catholics. Many native priests sing almost the entire Mass. Since the Japanese put great emphasis on singing in all stages of their educational system, the people followed instinctively and participated enthusiastically. When a Japanese priest sings the Mass with the peoples' participation, it is a beautiful act of worship. Personally, I was very touched and impressed by the solemnity of the Japanese liturgy. The Japanese tea ceremony is a long standing tradition and was certainly a model for the Catholic Mass. I have visited Korea, Hong Kong, Taiwan and the Philippines and have found that the Asian people participate well in this dramatic supper recalling the Death and Resurrection of Jesus Christ. They dislike casualness or triviality in any type of ceremony. The faithful watch the deportment of all those actively engaged in the ceremony, and this is true of the liturgy as well as for any secular ceremony. Our Japanese Friars, I might add, are exemplary in their celebration of the Liturgy.

One of the most important functions in the life of any priest is his role in proclaiming the Good News: in a word, preaching. Daunting as this challenge is to any priest as he prepares his Sunday homily or sermon, it is of cardinal importance in the life of a missionary. It is of the very essence of his work as Our Lord himself said "Going therefore, teach ye all nations…." (Matthew, 5) Almost always, fulfillment of that command from the Lord requires a knowledge and ability to speak the language of the people to whom the missionary has been sent to serve. With the grace of God to help us, this was not an insurmountable task, just a very challenging one. We American Augustinians understood the importance of this work and labored with great diligence to succeed to the best of our abilities.

Personally, here is my account of how I approached this great task. I always read my Sunday homilies. At times I questioned myself as to whether this was the better approach, but in the end I justified my way by realizing that I had made sure that I had no grammatical errors in my text and that the phrases were all carefully nuanced to conform with proper Japanese grammar and expressions. To achieve this result, I must admit that I had spent a good deal of time writing and rewriting my text. In my early years of preaching I had my sermons corrected for grammar and phrasing by experts in speaking Japanese. Then I would practice delivering the finished homily over and over. Try as I might, I couldn't erase from my thinking the thought that my sermons lacked punch because I had read them. This is a general criticism, and accurate to a point, in regard to most speakers—when speaking of someone delivering a talk in his own language. It is very different, however, when speaking of someone who is attempting to address an audience on an important matter in a foreign language, especially a language as difficult as Japanese. And preaching the Gospel to prospective converts is indeed an important matter. I also feel, as a matter of faith, that the Holy Spirit can and does override these feelings of inadequacy I felt by his power to touch the souls of my listeners and lead them to accept the Gospel message and seek conversion in many cases.

At weddings and funerals, I would try to center my homily on Japanese customs and how they relate to our Catholic liturgy. For many non-Christians who were attending these liturgies, it frequently was the first time they had entered a Catholic church. Non-Christians were always deeply impressed by the Catholic wedding ceremony. Young women often choose a Christian ceremony for their own weddings after having been moved and impressed by the dignity and personal touch of the ceremony on one of their Catholic friends. In both the funeral and the wedding services, we used a Catholic ceremony director to explain the background and meaning of the Mass as we went along. This, of course, is something not seen back home in the United States, but if done properly, the addition of a person well versed in his faith who calmly focuses everyone's attention to what is taking place in the liturgy can be of great assistance and importance in the mission field. At funerals, the Bishops permitted us to integrate the ending of the Buddhist rite directly into the Catholic ceremony. Again, this was done in keeping with the ecumenical spirit of the missions, and was quite pleasing and acceptable to non-Christians.

I first learned the common practice of pastoral ministry in Nagasaki where it was the custom of taking Holy Communion to the sick and the disabled once a week. In our parish, we Augustinians each had areas or blocks in the city where we would visit the sick in their homes early in the mornings. Later in the day, during the afternoon hours, we would visit the sick in hospitals across the city. This custom of personal attention to the sick or disabled was very effective pastorally, and also contributed to holding the priest in high regard among the people. Serving one's parishioners is this manner is, of course, one of the first obligations of priests and is recognized and appreciated by the faithful all over the world.

Regretfully, the Sacrament of Reconciliation is not used as frequently today as was true in the past. There are many reasons for this, reasons which are beyond the scope of this book, but all of which in one way or another have an effect on a person's faith. At the very least, infrequent use of this sacrament, especially for long periods of time, interrupt a person's special contact with Christ and the healing effect of the grace that comes from regular confession of one's sins and failings. In Nagasaki, as in many parishes back home in America, the recent post Vatican II practice of Penance services in which there are hymns, Bible readings and a homily, is growing in acceptance and serves as well as a function in bringing the parish together. Outside the city of Nagasaki, where the number of Catholics is much less, private confessions and Penance services are less frequent. In the United States, Msgr. Stephen Rossetti, a very compassionate and successful spiritual director of priests has urged his fellow priests to make continued use of this sacrament themselves . Otherwise, he says, there will not be the urgency to exhort the faithful in going to Confession regularly.

On Sunday afternoons I set aside time to do home visitations in a more organized way. In so doing, I was able to find people who needed special pastoral care. For example, I might discover a situation where children of a Catholic couple were not baptized, or a couple who did not have a Catholic wedding, or someone who was seeking an annulment from a failed marriage. These were problems not unlike those found in parishes everywhere, but because they were in our parish they were of special concern to me. Naturally after visiting families a couple of times, I began to know and remember their names, and the names and nicknames of their children. Later, after my transfer to our parish in Fukuoka, I continued the same practice of Sunday afternoon family visitations, but with special emphasis directed toward the non-Christian families who had children in our kindergarten. I must admit that even though this work was ongoing and seemingly without end, I never considered it a burden. Indeed, I enjoyed doing it very much because I found it to be very fulfilling in my life as a parish priest.

Right from the very start of our missionary apostolate in Japan, we Augustinians made use of a sometimes little known movement in the Catholic Church, the Legion of Mary. The Legion is an organization of Catholic lay people who serve the Church on a voluntary basis by openly practicing the Spiritual Works of Mercy, i.e. visiting the sick, giving catechism instruction to prospective converts, seeking out the homeless, the prostitutes, prisoners in jail, etc. The Legion was founded in Dublin, Ireland in 1921 by a man named Frank Duff and is organized strictly according to the divisions of the Legions of the ancient Roman army with Latin names for its various subdivisions. Even though there are Praesidia active in the United States, it is not as well known as it is in missionary countries or nations with few priests. It is, for example, very prominent in South Korea, the Philippines, Brazil and Argentina where the majority of its 10 million members are to be found. It's power as an aid to the Church is testified to by none other than the Communists when they were overrunning China in the late 1940's. It is well recognized that as they entered one village after another, the first group they arrested were the members of the Legion of Mary. These little cells of active Christians and the impact they were having in the villages was considered extremely dangerous by the Communist officials. Our Friars in Japan, however, find them to be a very valuable asset to our work there. We have two Legions of Mary in Nagasaki, one in Fukuoka and one in Tokyo. God bless them for all the work they are doing to assist the Church.

Teaching catechism to non-Christian adults is a very delicate and challenging work of pastoral ministry. People, for instance, would come to the door of the Friary or call on the phone and say that they would like to study the Bible. A request like that would not itself convey the idea or the hope of an imminent conversion. In a land of so few Catholics and so many people yearning for the truth and for peace of soul, yet living in a nation steeped in Buddhist and Shinto religious beliefs and centuries old traditions, not to mention the whirlwind of modern materialism and secular values, a missionary must respond gently and with an open mind to whatever is motivating this person who is knocking on the rectory door. This is far different from what might be the case in the United States where the majority of people share a background of at least some acquaintance with Christianity of one denomination or another.

There are other differences as well. In general, Japanese people like to be instructed individually or in small groups so that they can interact with the priest or catechist. Still another difference is that many of the people that I, for one, instructed were not baptized at the end of the period of instruction, but often only many years later. Every now and then I would hear that someone was recently baptized whom I had instructed at some earlier date. This is not uncommon, and to understand this, one must keep in mind that it is not easy for a Japanese to leave the family religion and take up another religion which most people considered to be of Western origin. In dealing with such very delicate and personal matters, one must realize that perseverance in evangelization together with a great deal of patience is a must for all missionaries in their apostolate. One must develop a long range view in order to understand and deal successfully with people of another culture. Some of our own well known and most successful missionaries have left us models of their success in dealing with people of Asian cultures and religious beliefs. St. Francis Xavier himself marveled at the sense of prayer and the kindness of the Buddhist people he encountered. Fr. Robert Di Nobili, S.J., tried to use the Hindu religion as a basis for the teaching of Christianity. A statue of Fr. Matteo Ricci, a Jesuit missionary internationally renowned for his scientific scholarship and the respect he had for the Confucian ethic, still stands in that country as a tribute to him.

Therefore, it is a must to take a long range view of evangelization. After all, it took a thousand years before all Europe had accepted the Christian faith. Great missionary endeavors arose in the great age of world exploration when the new world and the distant Orient were discovered. Indeed early predecessors of our missionaries today, Spanish Augustinians, accompanied Magellan on his around the world voyage in which he discovered the Philippine Islands. Another fact that must be remembered when one examines the growth of the Church, is that countries such as Korea, China, Japan and Vietnam all have a long history of cruel persecution of attempts to bring the message of Christ to those lands. The truth of the saying, "The blood of martyrs is the seed of Christians," is well attested to throughout history. The sufferings and the blood shed by all those martyrs has not been lost in vain!!

At the present time, the Church in Japan is highly respected especially for her educational and welfare work. In South Korea, the Catholic faith is flourishing in an especially strong manner. Indeed, the Church there, through the grace of God, is attracting new members and having such growth that it is being perceived as a threat by the government, though no open persecution has occurred. Who knows what will happen in China? In that huge country, the Communist government and the Catholic Church stand in direct opposition to one another. The government is oppressing the Church very openly, to such a point that it has established a kind of parallel Catholic Church controlled by the government. All the information we have received is that Christianity, and the Catholic Church in particular, is very much alive and even growing, although under very difficult circumstances. Indeed, the Communist government perceives Christianity as an ever present and dangerous threat. The resulting situation is too complex to go into in this booklet, but your prayers are needed to aid the brave Chinese Catholics loyal to the Holy See in Rome, in their ongoing struggle to practice their faith.

As I conclude these reflections on the Church in Asia, I see a new dawn coming for the Church in these far off lands. One of the amazing things about the dawn of this new day is that its leaders will be native Bishops, Archbishops and Cardinals. Few would have thought this possible in the early years of the twentieth century. Tremendous strides have been made in the last fifty or sixty years, spurred on surely by the Holy Spirit in the aftermath of the Second Vatican Council which convened in the early 1960's. There is no doubt that the conversion of Asia will come through the work of the Asians themselves. And the Church will be richer for that as the people of Asia bring their beautiful qualities of prayer, respect for others and their kindness into the Church which is always open to all cultures. In the truest sense, the Church is becoming more and more Catholic, a word which means universal or all inclusive, as it embraces and welcomes into its midst new races and cultures from Africa and Asia.

As the curtain comes down on my priestly ministry, spent entirely among the peoples of Japan and the foreign workers of many Asian nationalities, I can truly say that it has been joy-filled and graced by God in many ways. I am the richer for it. I love being a priest. I love mostly being an Augustinian priest. I ask all my readers to never tire praying for an increase of vocations.

Preparations For Coming Home

In December, 2009 the thoughts of possibly drawing to a close my missionary commitment to the people and the Church in Japan first began to emerge in my mind. I prayed over it for some time because it would be a tough decision to make. After all, I had experienced such a joyful, fulfilled life as a priest and missionary in Japan. I had been very warmly accepted by the Japanese people to whom I had ministered, and over the years I developed many close friendships with so many of them. They would understand; I could assure myself of that, but leaving would indeed be difficult on everyone concerned.

However, health issues were concerns which weighed heavily upon me, and in the final analysis they were the deciding factor. Even though Japan provides very high quality medical facilities and has an equally fine welfare system, I thought it more appropriate to retire to my native land while I still had the ability to share a semi-active but meaningful life with my Augustinian brothers. Also, such a retirement would offer me the opportunity to be close to my family who had seen me only briefly during the rather infrequent vacations I had at home over a long fifty six years. (I had studied four years in Rome prior to going directly to Japan in 1959).

Going through the proper channels is a regular procedure when one is part of a closely knit team and at the same time feels that the time has come for him to make a major change in his life. We Augustinians, both at Villanova and here on the missions in Japan, are a closely knit team dedicated to our life's calling to proclaim the Gospel. I spoke first with our local Superior here in Japan, Fr. Thomas Masaki Imada, and then after getting his approval I wrote to our Provincial back in the United States. Both were in agreement that it was time for me to come home and, as the expression goes, " to come in from the cold."

It turned out to be more difficult for me to handle when I spoke with my many Japanese friends in the parish church and as well with the teachers in the kindergarten to let them know of my decision to leave. Over the many years that I had worked with them in the schools and in our several parishes, many of us had formed deep and lasting friendships. As one might expect, when I informed them of my decision, the meetings became rather emotional both for them and for myself. However, as we talked and discussed everything, they began to see that the time had indeed come for me to return to America. Back in the Philadelphia area, my family, as one might expect, was overjoyed at the thought of my returning home after so many years abroad.

Attempting to change one's residence from one country to another is not exactly for the faint of heart. A whole host of often minute and infrequently consulted details can lie hidden and only surface when a person thinks he has everything ready, all his i's dotted and his t's crossed, only to discover something very important has gone unnoticed. After having been in Japan for decades, and having held various important positions pertaining to both the Augustinian Order and to kindergartens and church offices, I knew I had to do this right or risk embarrassing mistakes arising at just the wrong moment. To begin with, there were two big safes in my room filled with many documents, all in Japanese. Contained within each safe were legal papers concerning our property, bi-laws, financial statements and other matters pertaining to our two corporations, i.e. the religious (O.S.A.) corporation, and the corporation under the Japanese government. It was absolutely necessary to resolve any confusion and to establish procedures that would ensure an orderly and error free future.

One of the first things that came to our attention and which was worthy of preservation was a professional survey, done by experts in the field, with photos of all our property which had cost thousands of dollars to have made. Another item of some significance was a set of documents having to do with our turning over to the government a small portion of our property some years ago. Fr. Michael Stanley then engaged a lawyer who specialized in dealings with Religious Corporations to work along with us in this whole process. Fr. Michael was an ideal person to have working on all such matters, looking out for our interests while at the same time making sure that all legal matters pertaining to our missions were solidly established on a secure footing. Fr. Michael himself had a superb grasp of the Japanese written language and could handle with confidence the many legal details. Our Order and Province has always been deeply grateful for Fr. Michael's ability and vision. Another person to whom we owe a great deal of thanks was our very talented Japanese accountant who went through all the documents referring to our kindergartens and the establishment of the new corporation according to the government regulations. She then placed them in correct order so that if ever there were an investigation by the government, our records would be found to be accurate and all in proper order. I, for my part, took one of the two safes from my office and had it placed in a corner of the teachers' room in the kindergarten, and into which I stored all the documents referring to the kindergarten. After that, I then filed all the documents referring to the Augustinian Order in the other safe and had it placed in a secure place in my office. Needless to say, I was deeply relieved to know that I could return home with full assurance that all these precious legal documents were properly accounted for and in good order. My deep appreciation is extended to all who assisted me in this very important matter.

The next item on the agenda was to turn my attention to the task of sending all my personal effects back to America. All of you, my readers, who have had to cut your ties to a location and to the memorabilia associated with a half century's worth of life with all its myriad details, will understand the complexity I faced as I looked it all over and said: "Where do I start?" It would turn out to be a two month operation in which I would receive much assistance from a number of women parishioners in my church who rose to the occasion and to whom I am greatly indebted. First, very wisely, they persuaded me to buy a paper shredder which we used to destroy unneeded papers, magazines, photos and other materials that could not be simply placed in the trash as such. After the shredding process was complete, the resulting material was put into special bags approved by the city. With very great thought fulness and respect for my privacy, these Japanese women of every age group then went on to separate my effects into groups of what I could ship, what I could dispose of, and what I could give to the poor.

As far as my effects that had to be sent home, the women planned every detail precisely and discussed minutely with me the separation I wished to have regarding my clothing, CD's, albums, photographs and other items, and how they should be handled.

Three of these wonderful ladies went to the local post office and had a private meeting with the postmaster, who by the way, was a personal friend of mine. Together they determined what would be the most economical way to send the packages, the kind of tape that would be necessary, and how to address the packages according to both Japanese and American standards. They even, in their determi nation to do all things correctly, put all the directions in writing to avoid having any mistakes or glitches occur in the final packaging.

The shredder, by this time, was being put to good use. I was ready to shred just about everything in sight, but the young women hesitated to destroy my old sermons which I had retained since my early priesthood days in Nagasaki. There were drawers upon drawers full of these discourses, some old and yellowed with age, others were of more recent origin. "Omoshiroi wa" (these are interesting), they kept saying as they looked over many of the old homilies, and refused to give them back to me. (I kept wanting to feed that shredder!!) "No, we are going to check these out, find the appropriate ones, and edit them. We will get back to you," they insisted as they carried my sermons out in a large trash bag. Later they formed a committee whose object it was to narrow down the number of sermons they wanted to preserve, after which they arranged them in order according to the Catholic Liturgical Year.

It is important for me to interrupt the narrative at this point to explain something that my American readers might otherwise miss. Where did all these written sermons come from? Why go to the time and effort to write out one's Sunday sermons? There are, undoubtedly, many American priests who follow this same practice of writing out their homilies and keeping them in some kind of order as they store them away. On the other hand, I would dare say that a greater number of priests in America would preach either from an outline or in an ex tempore manner without any written text.

In the missions, however, especially in countries like Japan and Korea where the written and spoken languages are so challenging to the Western tongue, it is absolutely imperative for the missionary priest to approach making a homily in a much more complex manner. First he would have to write out in English the message he wanted to deliver. Then, with the aid of a bi-lingual native Japanese interpreter, the sermon would be re-written using English letters to capture the thought as it would be expressed in everyday Japanese usage. (A better and more direct way would be to eliminate the second step and have the interpreter write the homily directly in Japanese which we would then read from the paper as we delivered our Sunday sermons.) This latter procedure is what we learned in language school, as I mentioned earlier in my Memoirs when speaking of our introduction to Japanese in the Franciscan language school I attended in Tokyo. Personally, I always read my Sunday homilies. I forgave myself for taking this easy way of preaching by thinking that at least I had no glaring grammatical errors in them and that the phrases were carefully nuanced. I spent a good deal of time writing and rewriting my text in what I believed to be acceptable Japanese. In my early years, I then had my sermons corrected for grammar and phrasing by experts in Japanese. After that I would practice the finished homily over and over. I always thought that my sermons lacked punch because I was just reading them rather than speaking sponta-neously. I received almost no feedback from the people of the parish and I thought to myself, that try as I might, I really didn't really touch them in the heart as a good homilist should do. Many a time I came away doubting my own success, and accepting the fact that it is indeed very challenging to preach in a foreign language, especially one as difficult as Japanese. Such was my thinking, but a ray of sunshine broke through those clouds of doubt as this touching little story continues to unfold.

Let's get back now to continue the story of what an outstanding thing these ladies did by taking my old sermons, and with a lot of ingenuity as well as some technical help, transformed them into a whole new medium of communication which ensures that the work I did in the 1960's and 1970's will go on proclaiming the Gospel for an indeterminate future. One morning, shortly after they had marched out of the Friary with my old sermons in a trash bag, three young women came to the Friary and told me that they had decided to put some of my talks on CD discs. It was kind of like an order I couldn't refuse. The chosen sermons had already been edited by experts in the Japanese language. After some discussion, they and I decided on an agreeable schedule which called for me to present myself to yet another lady, a professional in making CD's, who had me practice the talks time and again in Japanese until I could read them without hesitation. Much to my surprise, I discovered that I had completely forgotten many of the old sermons. Following the pattern of the Liturgical Year, we recorded sermons for Advent, Christmas, Lent and Easter seasons. Over a period of a few weeks we finished recording four discs. These ladies were really something else. Even after having done so much to enhance my old sermons, they took their work to a higher level still. With some technical skill and assistance from one woman's husband who worked in television, they edited the tapes and added music to them. Imagine that!! Still there was more to come. They topped it all off by taking the now enhanced CD's to our church bazaar where they sold them for five dollars each and made $700.00 for the church!! And so, long after I have left the scene, those old sermons of mine will still continue to live on, reaching a new generation of listeners as they continue to proclaim the Gospel message anew. Meanwhile back at the church, other women were sorting through what remained of my belongings and were placing my clothing and other effects into boxes for shipment back to the United States. They took pains to weigh each carton several times, just to make sure that each one would come in under the weight limit. Doing this work was considered by them to be a big honor, and so everything had to be just right, down to the last detail.

There was one funny incident. I had asked the women to not send my long johns back to America. In Japan, where there are many buildings and homes with little or no interior heating during the winter months, the buildings can and do become quite chilly, and that means that wearing long johns becomes very advisable, especially for Americans who are used to the comfort of warm housing. "Do NOT send these," I printed on a large handmade sign next to the long johns so that there would be no confusion on the matter. Later in the day I had gone out on a sick call, and upon returning I dropped into the hall to see how the ladies were doing. There was no one there; they had all gone home. I searched and searched for the pile of long johns but could not find them. The only thing I could think was that they had sent them against my wishes. So I stomped over to the telephone, called the woman in charge and asked just WHAT had happened to my long johns. She paused for what seemed a long moment, and with a troubled and perplexed voice she replied, "We…thought…you…would…be…happy…to…know…that…we…took…them home to wash them…before giving them…to the catholic center down town…to be given to the homeless." Sheepishly I apologized and hung up the phone berating myself for having carelessly jumped to the wrong conclusion. I thought that would be the end of it, but such was not the case. Evidently the story went all over the parish that Fr. Dwyer had shouted over the phone, "Where are my long johns?" The following Sunday after Mass many women passed me and asked "Find your long johns?" "Find your long johns?" "Find your long johns?" The story had gotten blown way out of proportion, but in the end we all got a good laugh out my frantic search for my missing long johns!!

By March, 2010, with my belongings all shipped home and my office and bedroom all but stripped bare, I felt that I should show my appreciation to all the ladies who had done so much for me in the way they organized and accomplished the very time consuming task of helping me close out my time as I prepared to leave Japan for home. Everyone likes to go out for lunch or dinner. It's for the camaraderie and to mark good times that draws us to the table. So it was for me and these very loyal parishioners. I divided the ladies into small groups, which meant that I would have the opportunity to spend some time with each of the three or four groups to give individual attention to all. We really enjoyed ourselves at these lunches, with good food, a good supply of green tea, some ice cream, much light hearted conversation and laughs all around. A nearby luncheonette was the ideal location for our midday meetings. It proved to be a very opportune time for my friends also, with the kids all in school, no dishes to wash and a few moments of leisure time to enjoy. They loved to sit and talk with their close friends while at the same time teasing me about one thing or another. When four or five Japanese women all attack you at the same time, you don't stand a chance. We used to go to this one local tofu restaurant which was well known for its lunch specials. They used to joke, "let Father sit on the outside because at his age he has to get up frequently." When I actually did get up for a bathroom break during the meal, three of them had to help me stand. This may sound very odd to American readers, but in Japan the normal arrangement is for people to cross one's legs and sit practically on the floor around a very low table which rose only a few inches off the floor. That being said, it is not surprising that with my enlarged anatomy and creaking bones I couldn't sit on the floor any more as I had been quite accustomed to do when I was a much younger priest.

So in the end, all my effects were gone, shipped correctly to the United States (I hoped), my sermons had been transferred to CDs and the women parishioners who had been such a help to me were very well satisfied for jobs well done. "When are you going to take us out again?" they asked, but I pretended I didn't hear. All my effects, by the way, arrived safe and sound at Villanova in early June, 2010.

Last Farewells

Notice that I start this final chapter of my Memoirs by using the plural. My saying goodbye and leaving Japan one final time occasioned a number of farewell gatherings in my honor. They all were quite memorable and understandably very emotional as well. While they remain fixed in my memory, I will mention here only the two largest.

The first and larger of the two farewells took place on May 2, 2010 in a hotel in downtown Fukuoka. Two hundred and eighty people came to wish me well and Godspeed. About half of those present were non-Christians who had attended our kindergarten, or parents whose children were already enrolled there. A professional photographer had been hired to record the event. His works included many photos with my friends and me posing in small groups that were especially meaningful to me. In all, his work enabled me to put together a very beautiful album which I have shown to many after my return to America.

Preparations for this party were made well in advance with traditional Japanese organization and precision. In Japan, formal ceremonies such as this one should not have any glitches associated with them, and this one certainly did not. The intimate details of a dinner such as this were planned mostly by young Catholic women who had some contact with my non-Christian friends. The cuisine featured a combination of Chinese and Japanese dishes which highlighted the best of both cultures. In order to keep things running smoothly a buffet style dinner was provided for those seated at unreserved tables. My special invited friends and closest associates were served personally along with myself at the main table.

Among those who attended were fifty people from Nagasaki who made the two hour bus trip to Fukuoka just to be part of this testimonial. Many of them were graduates of our school in Nagasaki where I had taught Religion and English for many years. Also present were many parents from Fukuoka whose children were in our school, some who had already graduated from the school and, of course, a good number of parishioners from our church in the city of Fukuoka where I had been associate pastor and pastor for many years. For me it was an especially emotional experience to meet once again with the group from Nagasaki where I had been stationed for a number of years when I was a young priest and had just newly arrived in Japan. Even in the Japanese "no-touch" society, many people hugged me and actually cried on my shoulder. It was a very emotional experience!! Many of the graduates from our school in Nagasaki, now in their fifties, told me how much of an influence I had been in their lives. "Shinkou senba" (keep the Faith) was a phrase I had said over and over again in their local dialect when they were young. Thanks to my Irish memory I was able to remember most of their names which made both them and me feel very good.

After the initial greetings were finished and everyone had been seated, the formal Japanese ceremony began. On cue, I entered the dining room formally while music was playing in the background. I bowed and waved to everybody as I entered. After winding my way through the guests, I reached my place at the main table where I remained standing as the applause continued. I must admit that I did get a bit choked up amid all this spontaneous emotion from those in attendance. Finally we all sat down and the MC greeted us on behalf of the hotel management, after which he explained briefly the program that my friends had planned for the occasion. First, one of the elders of the parish gave a welcoming speech. Then Fr. Maurice Mahoney, one of my Augustinian brothers, and a close friend from the many days we had spent together in Rome, gave a short and very humorous toast. "Kampai, Kampai" (A Toast, A Toast) the people all responded as they touched and drank from their glasses of champagne in their salute to me.

The MC then announced that dinner was set up on tables on either side of the room which enabled the guests to serve themselves and gave them opportunity to eat leisurely while chatting with the guests seated at the same table. When I started to stand and go to the food tables, two kindergarten teachers hurried over, told me to be seated, that they would get me whatever I wished. To tell the truth, however, I wandered about instead from table to table and greeted my old friends while pouring beer into each glass as is the Japanese custom. They all had memories of some incident that had we had many years before. Again, many stood up and embraced me as a sign of affection and honor. All the while, my two kindergarten teachers kept running over to me saying, "Father, sit down and eat." But my heart was caught up in the emotions of the moment and I continued the rounds of the table until I had met and talked with just about everybody. This was an occasion that I did not want to forget or be diminished in any way. The parish organist reminded me one more time of my tin ear and how I was always off key in the liturgies. Others spoke of the many farewell parties I had had over the years. Indeed, one of my nicknames among the people was "Father Farewell." Others recalled that I had been the priest who married them, or in other cases, had taken care of Mother and Father when they were sick or had passed away. Some, of course, recalled my many faux pas in trying to master Japanese, and how many giggles and smiles they provoked among the parishioners and the students in the school. Still others reminded me of the various skits we used to put on at the New Years Parties. Some commented on sermons I had given which they liked while others mentioned my jokes and puns (which can be very easy to do in Japanese). All in all, it was a very nostalgic time we spent together that day, an occasion I will long remember.

By the time I got back to my table, the program was just beginning. The first presentation was by a group I had formed to sing at our liturgies and other special occasions, such as the very one we were engaged in that very day. I gave it the name "The Laudare Group" because the name "Laudare" in Latin means "to praise," and was chosen to identify a group of singers who would praise God by their melodious songs.

This choral group is composed of Christians and non-Christians alike, women in their twenties, thirties and forties who had come together a few years earlier at my request. After repeatedly gathering for practices and presentations, they have established a deep bonding and lasting friendships, which was my primary reason for starting the group.

The Laudare Group walked up to the stage in perfect order and began to sing my favorite hymns in Japanese. Then to my surprise, they sang a song written by the director of the chorus group, and dedicated to me. They sang it twice, after which the children and some of the guests were invited up on stage. Then they invited me to come up and join them on the stage so we could have pictures taken which I now treasure.

After this small concert, three short skits were presented. I was the main character in all three. First we did the last scene from the film *Casablanca*. I was Rick and one of the teachers played Ingred Bergman. Mr. Bill Fish, a close friend of mine, sang the song "As Time Goes By" all the while pretending he was playing a piano. Two Gestapo agents, played by the teachers, enter, but Rick deceives them and they leave. "Play It Again, Sam" Rick says, and then, after taking a long puff on his fake cigarette, he exits.

There were no curtains so we changed scenes and props right there before the guests. This second skit was the last scene from the Alan Ladd movie *Shane*. Yours truly was Shane. The teachers reappeared, this time cast as Jodie, Jodie's mother, and the gunman. In the duel, Shane "takes out" the gun slinger who promptly goes off stage. Shane, however, is "winged" by a bullet in the shooting, but his faithful horse, (disguised and played by two teachers), comes onto the scene. Shane takes the bridle and walks beside the horse (it looks like I'm actually riding the horse) as we exit the scene. Jodie then shouts out the famous words, "Shane, come back, Shane! Come back, Shaaaaaane!"

Again the props are changed. The next scene takes place in the teachers' room in our kindergarten. The teachers, all wearing aprons (as is the custom in Japanese kindergartens), are talking to each other about how sad they are that Fr. Dwyer is leaving for America. Then I, acting the part of the protagonist, enter wearing a French beret, and stand in the middle of the teachers. One by one they say how much they enjoyed working with me and go on to relate more colorful stories of me and the children. At that point they hand a mike to me and I pause a long time before saying "Au revoir." The teachers answer as we have practiced, "Au revoir," "Au revoir," "Au revoir," "Au revoir." With that, I exit as the teachers wave goodbye. They pretend they are sad until one teacher says, "Let's sing the song Fr. Dwyer taught the children." They sing My Bonnie with big gestures that I had taught the little ones to make. They then sing it again and direct everyone's attention to the program where the song is printed in English allowing the whole audience to sing "Bring back my Bonnie to me." At that point, I suddenly reappear without my beret and I say to everyone, "Tadaimaaaaaa." (I'm baaaaaaack)!! We all joyously greet each other again. Then all the teachers who had taken part in all three skits take their bows, Finally, from among the guests Hiromi Akutagawa, the head teacher at the school, comes up on stage to award me an Oscar for best actor.

Mr. Mark Dicher, a fervent Catholic and head of the American Consulate in Fukuoka, came on stage and spoke in perfect Japanese (his wife is a native Japanese), as he presented to me an award from the American Government for my work in welfare and in education. For this I was very surprised, and very deeply moved as well.

The MC, just before my final greetings, informed the people that as a going away gift from me to them, they should pick up a book of fiction that I had written. The young women in the parish and kindergarten had translated what I had originally intended to be a series of essays from English to Japanese, edited them in a superb way, designed the cover themselves (one lady is a designer by profession) and found a high technology publisher who gave us a phenomenal price of two dollars a copy for one thousand copies. Basically, in the essays my intent was to convey to my readers my sentiments regarding both the Japanese culture and the Japanese people as well. However, in the long run, I thought that in such a format of essays I could not maintain the interest of my readers. That meant changing the whole format of the book. I accomplished this by creating eleven characters through whom, in several short stories, I tried to convey my sentiments and impressions as they developed during my fifty two years of working in Japan. I had estimated a year or so to publish my short stories, but all the estimates I received from publishers were far beyond my limited budget. The women in the parish (God bless them!!) once again persuaded me that they could do the work cheaply, within my budget– which indeed they did. The stories themselves were, I believe, simple but interesting naturally enough, but certainly not up to the caliber of professional Japanese literature. In the end, however, I complimented the women for a work well done, which provided me at the same time with a personal touch of their farewell.

Now it was my turn to say a word of thanks to conclude the celebration. To prepare for this moment, I had been coached well in advance by the young women of the parish to insure that I would say everything appropriate in typical polite and thorough Japanese custom. However, true to form, for me in pressure moments, and in light of all the excitement of that day's celebration, I forgot just about everything I had memorized the night before and kind of stumbled through my response to all the tributes paid to me that day. Afterwards the ladies saw me and, throwing up their hands in jest, said, "We knew you'd forget. That's what you always do." Well, at least I tried!

Later, a parish elder, a gentleman well respected in the community, sensing my embarrassment, graciously stepped forward and brought the evening to a close with a few choice and complimentary words.

After closing things out at the hotel, and having gathered up all our props used in the skit, my good friends the teachers at the kindergarten drove me home in a van owned by one of them. Along the way we laughed and joked about the three skits, how well they all went off and how much they added in their unique way to the celebration that evening. These young women were great, and I called them my "gekidan" (theatrical company). I thanked them again and again. There was so much bowing going on that my back hurt. I have parts of the party saved on a DVD and show it frequently to my family and friends. It was truly a night to remember!!

Really Last Farewells

A few days after my farewell party downtown, I had two other farewell affairs that were memorable as well. The Laudare Group which I mentioned above held a small recital in my honor. To begin with, they sang some of the songs they had practiced for a concert they gave a few days earlier. The highlight event of this evening's concert came when they introduced the well known Japanese violinist, Ms. Haruko Daigo, who performed some of my favorite classical pieces. Haruko is a personal friend of mine whom I had invited to play at several of our parish concerts. She is a lovely person and a fervent Catholic. Although I had listened to her perform many times, never had I seen her play with such heart as she did that evening. In our conversation at the end of the recital, she recalled how I had invited her, for her first ever performance in our church, to play at the Christmas Mass, a custom she continued to observe for the next ten years. Many non-Christians come to Mass for the feast of Christmas, and upon hearing Haruko playing, they later said how they were quite overwhelmed by the dignity and high quality of the classical music she played in conjunction with the liturgy. The Japanese have a deep appreciation for Western classical music, and the exquisite "Ave Corpus Meum" by Mozart is especially well known and loved. Haruko's rendition of this piece after Communion at the Christmas Mass is, well, breath taking. On the day of this personal concert, presented as a tribute to me and to honor the work I had done over the years for the people of Japan, was very moving and emotional for me.

After the concert had ended, we went over to the parish hall for a simple lunch. To open the remarks, the directors of the Laudare Group took a moment to greet all those who were present. When it was Haruko's turn to speak, she mentioned that she appreciated the way I used the talents of the parishioners and the mothers of the kindergarten children, encouraging them to step out of their usual passive roles and to pitch in and get involved in different parish activities. I was touched by this remark by Haruko because it endorsed one of my central practices as a pastor. My parish in Fukuoka was filled with people who had hidden talents which they were unaware of. With some prodding and encouragement on my part, many of them cautiously and then very generously responded to my requests to use their gifts for the good of the community. Could it be that, for those who were recent converts to the Christian faith, this new way of interacting with their new found friends served to strengthen and even enhance their new life in Christ? I don't know the answer to that, but I always felt that the parish enjoyed a strong bond of unity and brotherhood. This generous remark by Haruko was something I valued very highly because it validated something very important to me in my role as pastor.

The meeting continued with the more formal time devoted to drinking tea, eating "o-nigiri" (rice balls), salads and other dishes that made up this pot luck lunch. As we were eating and drinking and enjoying our lunch together, the DVD of my farewell party just a few days earlier suddenly appeared on the television screen in the parish hall. The women were really delighted to see themselves on the screen and they made funny comments and got a lot of laughs from what they saw. As the afternoon luncheon progressed the ladies of the Laudare Group, who had become fast friends in the course of their group's frequent gatherings, began to entertain us with songs and many humorous stories. As a sign of my appreciation, and in keeping with proper Japanese etiquette, I went around to each woman, poured another helping of tea into their cups, and thanked each of them personally. Most of the women of the Laudare Group were non-Christians which made me feel that my forming this group had been a great success. The women had all benefitted in their singing from the frequent professional hymns we were able to provide, and that along with their growing friendship truly made this a win-win situation all around. Our Catholic women from the parish had also developed in leadership roles in our parish activities which likewise gave me great satisfaction. In the end, as the years of my missionary experience in Japan grew and developed, I really came to believe that the process of evangelizing begins by building bridges with people of other cultures. I call it my "Theology of Mission." Although I cannot claim a great number of adult Baptisms, I pray that these bridges will become in time pathways leading those I instructed to finding and accepting Our Lord Jesus Christ as their Savior as they received the Sacrament of Baptism from some other priest who has succeeded me. I pray every day as well that the little people, the dear children I knew from their time in our kindergarten would also find their way to Jesus Christ who is the way, the truth and the life.

The following Saturday night it was time for the staff of our kindergarten to present their farewell party for me. This event would be different from the ones which preceded it as was hinted at when they wouldn't tell me where we were going. My only guess was that it would be something big and something of a surprise party. At any rate I was game for whatever they had in mind, because our work together over the years had served to build a deep friendship between us. I got into a van with five teachers who I could tell were all dressed up in evening finery, another indication that this was indeed going to be something very special. The remaining members of the staff, altogether twenty people in number, were scheduled to arrive in other cars. Clearly this was a well-planned takeover and my mind was racing to try to find out what was going on. "Well, where are we going?," I asked. There was silence. "Where are we going?" I repeated. "You'll see," "You'll see," was all they would say. On through the evening traffic we sped as I looked around at the buildings passing by, vainly trying to determine my fate. Where are they taking me? More silence. Finally I could see that we were headed for that area of the city near the dome of the big baseball park. That was interesting–but there was no game scheduled for that night. Whatever. At last some clues began to come together. It was early evening, and I, like the others, was hungry, so when some fine restaurants near the ballpark appeared I thought I had put all the pieces together. Not so fast, Yankee boy, not so fast! We drew up at the famous Sea Hawk hotel in downtown Fukuoka which had a first floor buffet style restaurant, an ideal spot for us all to enjoy a nice meal together. One after one the other cars arrived until we were all assembled into one group, more or less, as we approached the front desk. At that point we were greeted formally by the manager of the hotel's dining rooms who shook hands with me and started bowing in true Japanese fashion to all the staff from the school. The manager's elder children were all graduates of our kindergarten, and his youngest child, a four year old boy, was presently a student at our school. Both the manager and his lovely wife were avid supporters of our kindergarten and were very anxious to show us a good time in the hotel that evening. Beaming with evident pride and honor that we had chosen his restaurant for our testimonial dinner, the manager led us to the elevator and brought us up to the fourteenth floor where he showed us to the most expensive room available. There were windows on both sides and the view was spectacular. I knew that the cost for the use of this room would be far in excess of our means, but I was told that when the teachers had asked for a private room and who would be the guest of honor, the manager used his influence to obtain this fashionable room just for us. I was stunned!! The manager proceeded to welcome us officially and went on to explain the details of the French cuisine menu. When we had all been seated, Hiromi the head teacher at the kindergarten, rose to offer a toast, after which we all sat down to enjoy a deluxe dinner. In true Japanese fashion appropriate for an occasion such as this, the manager, wearing a serving apron, with the aid of several waitresses, personally served each one of us. After the initial shock at all the extravagance had worn off, I was able to relax, laugh and enjoy the many stories that were shared among us, reminders of all the good times and happy days of the past few years.

From either side of this grand room, one could look on to the grandeur of Fukuoka Bay, still busy with ships and smaller boats moving about as they prepared to dock at the end of the day. This was the same bay where, several centuries earlier, the Mongol fleet of warships intent on invasion and war, had been turned back by the force of an awesome hurricane. The ancient Japanese attributed their survival to the god "Kamikaze" (the god of the divine wind), a name they resurrected in their futile attempt to thwart the Allied forces at the end of World War II.

What can I say? It was simply a delightful night!! At the end of the meal we paused to take many pictures to carry away the many memories that this evening's celebration was sure to offer all of us in years to come. Before departing for their respective homes, the teachers all gathered around me and presented me with a beautiful gift as a remembrance of this most special evening and all the memories that made it so special. I was urged to open the box so that everyone could see my reaction. The gift was a beautiful winter sweater (they had heard that Philly is cold from November to March—which indeed it can be and often is.) The elevator then took us down to the lobby where we tarried some more, talking in small groups as we exited the hotel and returned to our cars for the return ride home.

It is difficult for me to explain in a few words my relationship with the staff of our kindergarten. Overall I had been principal for some twenty six years, and throughout all that time I had made it a point to work in a harmonious way with both our young, and sometimes inexperienced, teachers and other members of the staff. My American readers may not realize the idea of harmony and the very special importance that virtue holds in Japanese society. It may be that it has it origins in the native practice of flower arranging, or bowing to one another as a sign of respect for the other person, or listening attentively to the flowing beauty of haiku poetry, or maybe something else. But whatever its roots may be, great attention is focused on harmony, especially as it pertains to kindergarten students and their teachers. That can be seen and appreciated by reflecting on the importance it held in the everyday running of our little school.

Our head teacher was a good example of someone who believed strongly in the importance of harmony in the setting of a kindergarten. She was a firm believer that communication among the staff members was key to a harmonious work place. Every morning the teachers gathered together for a formal meeting in which the programs and objectives for that day were discussed and planned. Later in the day, towards evening after the children had gone home, we would reassemble to discuss the problems we had met. The head teacher, Hiromi, did not say a word until everyone had spoken. Finally Hiromi herself spoke. Always in a gentle manner, Hiromi would comment on the events of the day and gave her advice, especially directed to the new teachers who had just recently been employed by our school. It is my own opinion that when teachers can have their say and are respected for their opinions, little by little, that spirit of harmony arises. In general, this is how the Japanese work place operates. Communication, consultation and mutual respect are among the ingredients that produce a happy work place. I felt that we were especially blessed in that we had such a wise and kind lady at the helm of our school. Her calm and gentle attitude reached into every classroom and did much to bring about the right environment for our little children of such a young age.

Right about now I think it's time to close the book on my life in Japan. It's been a great ride, alongside some really fine and decent people. They have mattered a great deal in my life, and I hope I have in theirs. Saying "good bye" is not easy. Those words in English, however, sound too cold and too impersonal. The Japanese have a word that is much more expressive of the feelings I have right now. "Sayonara," when you say it for the last time to people who have been especially close to you, looks back with a smile on what has been, and with a look of confidence and satisfaction on what yet might be. Literally it means "If it must be so…." That has a fitting sound to it, somber yet filled with hope. I like that. My days in Japan are now numbered, yet my days back home in the States beckon me forward to relish new experiences amid old and new friends. God has been good; God is always good. The warm farewell parties I've described for you in these past few pages are but some of many remembrances that will go through my mind as I sit under a tree on the beautiful campus of Villanova University.

Sayonara "If it must be so…" Sayonara

Passing On The Torch

The ritual occurs every four years. With great fanfare the Olympic torch is lit at the site of the original Games in Greece and then passed from runner to runner through almost every country en route to its final destination in the host nation for the next Olympic Games where it will light the flame that will burn throughout the Games.

Many metaphors have arisen over the years that try to capture the drama of that Olympic torch and all that it symbolizes as it is handed from one runner to the next. Some are connected with one generation succeeding another. Others are connected with sports achievements or the drama of political changes.

A case can also be made to apply that metaphor of the Olympic torch being handed on to what is taking place right now in our missions in Japan where the American presence of the post war era is giving way to native Japanese Augustinians being handed the "Torch of Faith" to burn brightly in their homeland for years to come.

The "Torch of Faith" image is enhanced as well by recalling the events of the first Pentecost where St. Luke uses the symbol of fire over the heads of the Apostles to illustrate the dynamic presence of the Holy Spirit transforming those same Apostles into being the first missionaries bearing the Good News to all the world.

Certainly one can look back on the first half-century of our work in Japan and see the imprint of the Holy Spirit in so many different ways. Standing out among all of them is the number and the quality of those native Japanese who have been drawn to the Augustinian way of life and who are now taking their rightful place in assuming the direction of our Vicariate in Japan. I would like to use this opportunity to introduce to my American readers our brothers from Japan.

Native vocations are always on the minds of missionaries. In the past, pre-Vatican II era, it was thought that native Catholics in a mission field could not be responsible for the affairs of the Church. The focus in our time is to search for native vocations from the very beginning of new missions. Presently native Bishops in Asia and Africa are leading their flocks in a superb way. Many Religious Orders and Congregations are now led by Superiors from those same mission territories. The formerly Irish Augustinian mission in Nigeria now has a native Provincial, and most of the Friars are Nigerians.

In Japan we have always searched for native vocations. Over the years we have had many candidates, but only a few persevered, took Solemn Vows or were ordained priests. We are very proud of our Japanese Friars who have continued and are now in important positions in our Vicariate.

Our first vocations in Japan were natives of Nagasaki, two sibling brothers, Minoru and Takeshi Akakura. Neither had finished high school, and upon entering the Order had expressed a desire to be Brothers, not clerics. In Religious Orders, like the Augustinians, Brothers have often been the backbone of the Province. In Villanova's first years Brothers from Ireland worked on the farm, did excellent carpentry work and carried out highly skilled maintenance of buildings. In more recent years, however, our Province has become more or less a clerical society with most new vocations going on to the priesthood.

Minoru Akakura was sent to the newly established Friary in Fukuoka to complete his years as a candidate and Novice. In later years Minoru would recall how both Fr. Griffin and Fr. O'Connor had encouraged him so much. After his Novitiate year, Minoru served in our parishes in Nagoya and Tokyo. Fr. Griffin encouraged him to continue his education by correspondence courses. In a short time, he received his high school diploma and decided to continue this manner of study in the university. With great perseverance, Minoru did all the necessary work, went to summer school at Keio University and did his thesis for graduation. We were all delighted when Minoru graduated from Keio. He then decided to study for the priesthood. His brother Takeshi continued in Nagasaki as chief sacristan in the parish. He is retired now and is remembered for his great sense of humor.

While Minoru was doing his training as an Augustinian and studying at the University, Masami Yamaguchi, a high school student from Omuta in Fukuoka Prefecture, joined our Order as a clerical candidate. After finishing high school in Nagasaki, Masami entered the Diocesan Seminary in Fukuoka where he studied Latin and took other courses. In these early years of training our men in Formation, it was decided to send Masami to America for his Novitiate year and then on to Villanova and Washington for his studies in Philosophy and Theology respectively.

Masami then returned to Nagasaki where he was ordained as the first Augustinian native Japanese priest in over two hundred years. In the years following ordination, Masami ministered in all four of our parishes in Japan, becoming pastor in Tokyo and Nagoya. While in Nagoya, he built the large church complex (church, parish hall and Friary). Continuing to develop his education, Masami then returned to the United States where he enrolled in Catholic University in Washington D.C. from which he went on to receive a Master's Degree in Philosophy after which he returned to Japan to continue his work in the ministry. Masami is known for his great kindness and for his astute knowledge of Japanese civil law.

While Masami was studying in America, Minoru continued his studies for the priesthood at the Archdiocesan Seminary in Tokyo. At the conclusion of his training and studies he had the honor and distinction of being ordained a Priest by none other than Pope John Paul II in Nagasaki in 1981. Later he worked in parish ministry, especially in Fukuoka and Nagoya. In Fukuoka he was noted for his diligence in caring for the buildings and grounds. He is remembered for his Nagasaki-type piety and his prayer life. Sadly he succumbed relatively early in his life to what is known locally as "atomic bomb sickness" while still laboring in his last assignment to the parish in Nagoya. A man of great faith, he is still missed. Fr. Minoru Akakura is buried alongside Fr. Tom Purcell, his mentor, who had urged Minoru to enter our Order in Nagasaki.

When Fr. Tom Purcell was Pastor in Nagoya, he was asked by the SVD Fathers to teach English as a second language in their University. Not long after Fr. Tom had begun his classes, he met a Catholic student whose mother had been born in Nagasaki and they became close friends. Her son, Thomas Masaaki Imada, later became an English teacher in a prestigious public school in Shizuoka Prefecture. In planning for his future as a teacher of English, he thought it would be wise to attain a Master's Degree from an American University. When he asked for advice in selecting the right school, Fr. Tom suggested Georgetown University in Washington D.C. Fr. Tom then called the Prior of the Augustinian Seminary in Washington and asked if Masaki could live there while attending Georgetown. Getting an affirmative answer, Masaki moved in and began his studies. At this point something unplanned and unexpected began to take shape. Masaki began to attend Mass and entered into the prayer life of the Professed students which in turn gradually enveloped him with a love of the Augustinian way of life. Upon graduation from Georgetown with his Master's Degree, Masaki returned to Japan where he returned to teaching in the public schools as well as becoming a track coach.

At the same time he and Fr. Purcell met frequently, during which discussions Fr. Tom asked Masaaki to enter a period of serious personal discernment about whether he might have a calling to an Augustinian vocation and priesthood. Masaaki complied with Fr. Tom's urging which ultimately led to his entering our Novitiate in Fukuoka. He then continued his studies at the Jesuit Seminary in Tokyo where he earned a Master's Degree in Theology. After ordination, Fr. Masaaki began his ministry by serving in our school in Nagasaki where he ultimately became Principal. In matters Augustinian, he was elected to become the first Japanese Vicar Provincial of the members of the Order serving in Japan. Fr. Masaaki is known for his outstanding knowledge not only of the spoken English language but of its Literature also. He is an excellent preacher and truly touches the hearts of his parishioners. In addition to his work in the parishes, he is also called upon frequently to give retreats to Sisters, other parishes and to young people. He has a great heart with a deep Japanese love and sentiment for his people and his country.

The first baby to be baptized in our parish in Nagoya was Hiroyuki Shibata. His full Christian name is Thomas Kozaki, named after one of the young boys who was crucified in Nagasaki in 1598. His mother is a devout Catholic who became the cook in our Friary at the parish in Nagoya. Hiroyuki (nicknamed Hiro) grew up in our parish in that city and was very faithful in attending Mass and to his prayers. After attending local public schools, Hiroyuki entered Nanzan, the SVD University right in Nagoya. After graduation he was accepted in one of the large companies that dot the city of Nagoya and began the grind of Japanese men in the work place. He is remembered by the Augustinians who ministered in Nagoya as a man of prayer. He often came to the church in the evenings directly from work, before going home for dinner, to make a holy hour before the Blessed Sacrament. Such was his personal piety. In time he entered our Order and made his Novitiate in Tokyo. After pronouncing his Vows, he continued his seminary studies at the Jesuit University in Tokyo. He then flew to the United States where he spent a year at Villanova to perfect his already excellent English. Upon returning to Japan he was ordained to the Priesthood and has ministered in our parishes in Fukuoka, Nagoya and Tokyo. In matters pertaining to the Order, he has also served as Director of Formation for those candidates considering a possible vocation. At the present time, Fr. Hiroyuki is the Vicar Provincial for the Order in Japan and is known for the thoroughness of his work and his knowledge of Japanese law as it pertains to Religious Corporations. He also has put his considerable talents at the service of the Community as Accountant for the Vicariate . Fr. Hiroyuki is also known among his brother Friars for his calm nature, his dedication to prayer and his easy going way in community life.

Peter Tetsuya Hirano comes from our parish in Nagasaki. Peter began his education by attending our parochial school in Nagasaki from kindergarten through ninth grade after which he went to a private high school where he starred as a tennis player. He often says that some of our Friars invited him to enter our Order which he did after graduating from high school. Peter spent his Novitiate year in Tokyo after which he continued to study Philosophy in the Fukuoka Diocesan Major

Seminary. He then went back to Tokyo to acquire a Master's Degree in Theology. Following in the footsteps of our other Japanese Friars who preceded him at the Jesuit run Sophia University in Tokyo, Tetsuya did extremely well in his studies. After ordination, Fr. Peter taught in our school in Nagasaki, was associate pastor at our parish in Nagoya, and later became Director of Formation in our community in Tokyo. Fr. Tetsuya has a deep religious faith handed down from his beloved Mother and Father who were devout Catholic Christians. Father Peter is well known for his ability to minister to young people and high school students. In a word, he connects with them. He is frequently called upon to preach to youth groups and Catholic high school students throughout the country. At present he is Pastor of our church in Nagoya where his sermons are greatly appreciated. Fr. Tetsuya reaches out quite easily and successfully to youth and has a strong following among young workers and students. His gentle nature serves him well, and he is very thoughtful and considerate with his brother religious in our community life.

Father Peter Mitaru Toyama has a very interesting and quite touching background, revealing how God is ever present in our lives, drawing us closer to Himself as he prepares us for a calling to a life of fulfillment in ways we never thought possible.

Peter was born and educated in the castle town of Kumamoto on the Island of Kyushu. After high school, he studied Education at the prestigious Kumamoto University. At the time he graduated, he had earned enough credits to teach on every level of Japanese schooling from kindergarten through high school. During his years at the University he had a steady girlfriend, but all the while he was not happy about his life and very uncertain about his future neither of which seemed fulfilling or satisfying. It was an empty future that he was looking at, he now says as he looks back on it. In his search for something that would give meaning and fulfillment to his life, Mitaru joined a group somewhat equivalent to the American Peace Corps and was sent on a mission to Honduras in South America. This proved to be an eye opener. For the first time in his life he was living among people who were destitute and in dire poverty. For someone whose life had been unfulfilled and empty of purpose, Mitaru was deeply impressed by the way the poor people shared their food, water, and other necessities of life. Wanting to contribute in some way, he started to do some welfare work at a Catholic church. The priest there gave him some assignments to attend to, one of which was teaching little children. This work, teaching the children, living among the poor and seeing firsthand how the Church cared for the lives and welfare of these people, the poorest of the poor, inspired him to become a Catholic himself. After finishing his term of service with the organization, he returned home to Japan and began thinking about joining a Religious Order. He came across a publication which listed Religious Orders and Congregations and under the heading "A" he read about the Augustinians which led him to write to this group seeking advice. With God's grace prompting him, in time he applied for admission as a candidate, was accepted and later was sent to make his Novitiate and do his seminary studies in Tokyo. After ordination to the priesthood, Mitaru was sent back to serve in our church in Tokyo which serves many foreign ethnic groups. Fluent in Spanish from his time in Honduras, he was able to have an immediate impact among the many foreign nationals, many of them from different nations in South America, who had come to Japan seeking work they could not find at home. Fr. Mitaru later worked in cooperation with the Diocesan Vicar to provide care for foreign workers in the Tokyo area on an even wider scale. After providing this service for the foreign workers for a long period of time, Mitaru was sent south to our parish in Nagasaki where he taught in the parish school and was associate pastor in the Shiroyama church. After a few years he was appointed Principal in the kindergarten school in the parish. When I retired from active ministry in Fukuoka, Fr. Mitaru was made Pastor of the church and was given the heavy burden of finishing the construction of the new church complex in that parish, a job that he carried out with great distinction. Fr. Mitaru is very quiet by nature and is very conscious of his Buddhist background. He is very much at home in understanding the Buddhist culture and makes good use of it in addressing the needs of prospective converts in his sermons and in teaching catechetics where he can meet the needs that others might miss.

Fr. Antonio Kiyotsugu Yamano was born in Nagasaki and is a product of our school and our Youth Club. As a young man he became a candidate for our Order. He was accepted, did his Novitiate and seminary studies in Tokyo at the completion of which he was ordained to the priesthood. Fr. Kiyotsugu has spent his whole ministry thus far in Nagasaki where he teaches in the school and is associate pastor in the church. He has gathered around him a flourishing group of high school students from the parish with whom Kiyotsugu works very closely in various church related and social projects. He knows them well since most are graduates of our school where he is very popular as a teacher. One interesting aspect of Fr. Kiyotsugu is that he can trace his ancestry back to the period of the persecutions in the Nagasaki area. He comes from a family which has a decidedly Christian background. His grandmother was a very fervent Catholic as are both his parents. His easy going manner and warm personality makes it easy for him to succeed in his work with the youth of the parish. He is an excellent preacher, especially with the children who enjoy his Liturgies. Fr. Kiyotsugu will be a leader in the Japanese Vicariate in the coming years.

Brother Francisco Masaya Ide was born, grew up and was educated in Tokyo. He, as Fr. Mitaru before him, was searching for some meaning in life. The rich opulence and the secular and materialistic atmosphere of the Tokyo scene proved less than fulfilling for Masaya. He turned to the Church, became a fervent Catholic and developed a healthy life of prayer. Masaya became one of the thousands of office workers laboring in the metropolitan area. A life-changing moment came his way when he heard about an end-of-the-year retreat being given at the Augustinian Seminary in Tokyo. He signed up and was so taken by the experience that he extended his attendance to three retreats in a row. Masaya soon afterwards entered our Community as a Brother candidate, did his training and Novitiate in Tokyo and shortly thereafter pronounced his solemn vows. One of his more immediate assignments was to take advantage of his earlier work in the business world and become bursar of our house of formation in Tokyo. Bro. Ide is currently stationed in Tokyo where he is a very busy catechist. He takes Communion calls to the sick, teaches catechism classes to children and is sacristan of the parish. Bro. Ide has a gentle sense of humor and is dedicated to prayer and community life. With the number of priests decreasing, an Augustinian Brother is invaluable in the church as a catechist. Bro. Ide is greatly loved by the parishioners in the Tokyo parish, especially by the children. Bro. Ide works well with the Pastor, Fr. Jesus Mernillo Dano, an Augustinian from the Cebu Province in the Philippine Islands who is on loan from his mother Province in the Philippines and has worked for us in Japan for over ten years.

The Cebu Province Comes To Our Aid

Of those first American missionaries who came to Japan shortly after the end of World War II, most are deceased and others are living in retirement. Only two American Friars are at present ministering in Japan, Fr. Maurice Mahoney and Fr. Michael Hilden. Ten years ago it became apparent that quite soon we would find ourselves handicapped by a lack of personnel. In our attempts to grapple with the implications that would come when this shortage of manpower became a reality, we contacted different sources that might be of help as the problem developed. We were all greatly relieved when the Cebu Province from the Philippine Islands offered immediate assistance by sending some Friars to assist us. The area around Cebu where Augustinians had been serving for many years had grown to be a full Province just about twenty five years ago. At the same time they had been graced by God with many native vocations, sufficient for their own needs and abundant enough to provide assistance to other areas in the Augustinian world where there were urgent needs for priests. They had already sent men to help our missions in Korea and in South Africa, and were generous enough to send some Friars also to Japan.

The first Friar from Cebu to arrive was Fr. Jesus Mernilo Dano. In Japan he is known as Fr. Jesse by all. He came to Japan in 2003 after his ordination in Cebu. Shortly after his arrival, Fr. Jesse was sent to language school where he faced the daunting task of learning the Japanese language with all its complexities. Since I spent time earlier in this booklet describing my time in language school, I want to mention that Fr. Jesse studied the language in a different manner and school than we early missionaries had experienced. To his credit, Fr. Jesse did so well at the language school that he was commended by his teachers for the excellent record he had achieved in reading, writing and speaking this very challenging language. This was no small accomplishment, and he is rightfully to be commended for all that he accomplished in language school. After finishing language school in March, 2006, he was sent to Nagasaki to be associate Pastor in the parish and to teach in English in our school there. The people of the parish and the students in the school took to Fr. Jesse immediately for his gentle nature and good humor. In 2008, to broaden his experiences in adjusting to life in parish life, he was transferred to our parish in Tokyo where he became associate Pastor. His talent in speaking the language became immediately apparent and he is known as an excellent preacher with a very good command of the language with all its challenging nuances. In recognition of his abilities, in 2010 Fr. Jesse was appointed Pastor of the parish. In March of that year he got the scare of his yet young life when he got caught up in the after effects of the huge earthquake that occurred in Fukushima. Although the epicenter of the earthquake was some eight hundred miles north of Tokyo, the tremors were so severe that Fr. Jesse feared for his life. That, however, is part of life in Japan, and after checking all the buildings and being reassured that all was well, he went on with his work in the parish. Besides ministering to his Japanese congregation, Fr. Jesse also serves the many Filipino workers in the Tokyo area where he celebrates a Mass on Sundays for foreign workers and students.

Fr. Charles Barnuevo Pomuceno came to Japan in 2010. Upon arrival, the first task set before him was to master the challenge of learning the Japanese language. As I write this, Fr. Charlie is stationed in Nagasaki. Fr. Charlie preaches in English at the Sunday liturgies when he celebrates Mass for the foreign workers and students. He has a very calm way about things and fits in very well in community life and activities, even the routine activities of daily life: cooking for the community when it is his turn, cleaning around the house, doing the dishes, and of course the final step of putting out the trash. Both Fr. Jesse and Fr. Charlie were high school teachers before entering the Order. Fr. Jesse taught Mathematics while Fr. Charlie taught Chemistry. Even though both those subjects will not play a direct role in their ministry, we hope that they will both find happiness and fulfillment in ministry and that by their example others will be inspired to enter our Order.

We cannot bring this salute to the Cebu Province without recalling another Filipino Augustinian who spent many years in the 1960's working alongside us in Japan. Fr. Pedro Ferrer volunteered to come to Japan and spent ten years with us in the early days of our missions. We are so very grateful to Fr. Pedro for his dedication to ministry and all the good that his presence, gracious good will and good example brought to our ministry and to our lives as Augustinians. Fr. Pedro is retired now and currently lives in California.

And so, with this final tribute to our Filipino brothers who were and are of such assistance to us in Japan, we bring this part to a close. You have learned some facts about how it was that our mission to Japan had its beginning, gotten to know, however sketchily, the men who left their work in America to labor in Japan. You have witnessed the growth of our mission parishes from one single parish to four thriving parishes, each with its own special characteristics. We have introduced you to our newest Augustinian brothers, the Japanese Friars who are assuming leadership in carrying on the presence of the Order in their native country. Finally we paid tribute to some very generous fellow Asians, our brothers from the Philippine Islands who so graciously have offered to assist us in recent years. As one who was privileged to be part of this story from its earliest days right up to the dedication of the new church in Fukuoka, I can only say that it was a journey well worth taking. Sayonara!! my friends, Sayonara!!

The Early Years

Photos on page 99 clocklwise from top left:

1. Departure from St. Denis Church, Havertown, PA. Fr. Thomas P. Dwyer, September 1959.

2. From Left: Fr. Edward Robinson, Bishop Paul Yamaguchi, Fr. Thomas Purcell, Fr. George Krupa.

3. Reception of missionary crosses, Fall 1954. From left: Fr. Edward Griffin, Fr. Provincial Joseph M. Dougherty, Fr. Gerry Ryan (Midwest Province).

4. Nagasaki, 1959. First row from left: Fr. Edward V. Griffin, Fr. Thomas P. Dwyer, Fr. Thomas Purcell, Fr. Joseph X. O'Connor. Back row: Fr. Edward V. Hattrick, Fr. George Krupa.

5. First Augustinian Church, Shiroyama Church Nagasaki, 1954.

6. Family of parishoners in our church in Nagasaki, 1966.

7. Arrival of the Congregation of the Sisters of the Infant Child Jesus, April 1966.

昭和56年7月12日堅信

Along The Way

Photos on page 101 clocklwise from top left:

1. Memorial Mass for Fr. Thomas Dwyer's deceased parents, November 1968. Left to right: Fr. Peter Ferrer (Philippine Province), Fr. Maurice Mahoney, Fr. Thomas Purcell, Fr. John McAtee, Fr. Thomas Dwyer, Fr. Joseph O'Connor, Fr. Edward Hattrick, Fr. Edward Griffin, Masami Yamaguchi (seminarian).

2. Ordination of Joseph Masami Yamaguchi, November 1975 (first Japanese Augustinian priest since the middle ages). Fr. Labelle (Father's former teacher and mentor), Joseph Cardianal Ssatowaki, Fr. Harry Cassel (Prior Provincial).

3. Thursday night basketball, Nagasaki, circa late 1970s. Youth of the parish, mostly graduates of our school.

4. Weekday Mass for Junior High school students, circa 1985. Celebrant Fr. John McAtee.

5. Vicariate Retreat, circa 1983. First row from left: Fr. Maurice Mahoney, Fr. Arthur Ennis (Retreat Master), Fr. Peter Ferrer, Brother Andrew Takeshi Akakura, Fr. Thomas Dwyer. Second row: Fr. Michael Hilden, Fr. Liam O'Doherty, Fr. Edward Griffin, Fr. Gerry Ryan, Fr. Thomas Purcell.

6. Ordination of Fr. Joseph Minoru Akakura by Pope John Paul II. From left: Fr. Liam T. O'Doherty, Fr. Maurice J. Mahoney, Fr. Thomas P. Dwyer, Fr. Edward V. Hattrick, Fr. Joseph Minoru Akakura, Prior Provincial Fr. Joseph Duffy, Fr. Hamada (diocesan priest from Nagoya, alumnus of our school in Nagasaki), Fr. Thomas Purcell, Fr. Michael J. Hilden, Fr. Joseph Masami Yamaguchi.

7. Confirmation, Nagasaki, July 1981. Auxaularfy Bishop Joseph Matsunaga.

8. Entrance to Primary School, Nagasaki, April 1981.

ヴィラノヴァ管区日本分管区　第1回総会　1996年10月17日

Mass in the Shiroyama Catholic Church in Nagasaki

Minato Catholic Church in Nagoya

Along The Way

Photos on page 103 clocklwise from top left:

1. Vicariate Retreat, October 1984. Front row: Fr. Maurice Mahoney, Fr. John Rrotelle (Retreat Master), Fr. Thomas Dwyer, Fr. John McAtee, Bro. Andrew Takeshi Akakura, Fr. Joseph Minoru Akakura. Back row: Fr. Joseph Masami Yamaguchi, Fr. Michael Stanley, Fr. Liam O'Doherty, Fr. Michael Hilden, Fr. Thomas Purcell, Fr. Edward Hattrick.

2. Provincial Visitation, 1991. First row from left: Bro. Andrew Takeshi Akakura, Fr. Thomas Purcell, Fr. Michael Hilden, Fr. Thomas Dwyer, Fr. Joseph Minoru Akakura, Fr. Maurice Mahoney. Back row: Fr. Joseph Minoru Akakura, Fr. Michael Stanley, Prior Provincial Fr. Donald Riley, Fr. Liam O'Doherty, Fr. Maurice Mahoney, Fr. Frank Horn (Bursar of Villanova Province), Fr. Anthony Burrascano (Director of Missions Villanova Province), Fr. Thomas Masaaki Imada, Fr. Edward Hattrick.

3. Sunday Mass in Nagasaki.

4. Kasai Church in Tokyo.

5. Fiftieth Anniversary to the priesthood of Fr. Maurice Mahoney with Fr. Michael Hilden.

6. Minato Church in Nagoya (inside).

7. Minato Church in Nagoya (outside).

8. Provincial Visitation, 1996. First row from left: Fr. Michael Stanley, Fr. Thomas Purcell, Fr. John Deegan (Prior Provincial), Fr. Thomas Masaaki Imada, Fr. Thomas Dwyer, Fr. Anthony Burrascano. Back row: Fr. John Rotelle, Fr. Patrick McStravog, Fr. Peter Tetsuya Hifrano, Fr. Joseph Akakura, Fr. Maurice Mahoney, Fr. Edward Hattrick, Fr. Joseph Masami Yamaguchi.

Present Day

AUGUSTINIANS SERVING IN JAPAN, AND PETER JONES FROM THE PROVINCE OF AUSTRALIA. FROM LEFT TO RIGHT: JESUS M. DANO, O.S.A., FRANCIS MASAYA IDE, O.S.A., JOSEPH MASAMI YAMAGUCHI, O.S.A., PETER TETSUYA HIRANO, O.S.A., PETER JONES, O.S.A., JOHN FUTOSHI MATSUO, O.S.A., MICHAEL J. HILDEN, O.S.A., THOMAS HIROYUKI SHIBATA, O.S.A., CHARLIE B. POMUCENO, O.S.A., ANTHONY KIYOTSUGU YAMANO, O.S.A., ANDREW TAKASHI AKAKURA (OBLATE), MAURICE J. MAHONEY, O.S.A., PETER FRANCIS MITARU TOYAMA, O.S.A., THOMAS MASAKI IMADA, O.S.A.

Present Day

Photos on page 105 clocklwise from top left:

1. New church in Nagasaki, Dedicated in 2000.

2. Simple Profession of John Futosh I. Matsuo, February 6, 2013.

3. Parish Women and Kindergarten Mothers. Chorus called "laudare group" 2010.

4. Fukuoka Parish Community inside new Church. Dedicated September 2011.

5. Japanese Augustinians, 2010. First row from left: Fr. Perter Mitaru Toyma, Bro. Andrew Takeshi Akakura, Thomas Kozaki Hiroyuki Shibata. Back row: Antonio Kiyotsugu Yamano, Bro. Augustine Masaya Ide, Fr. Thomas Masaaki Imada, Fr. Peter Tetsuya Hirano, Fr. Joseph Masami Yamaguchi.

6. Mitsuyo Uchiyama: My unpaid secretary, 2010.

創立50周年記念誌

1961年〜2011年

1 カトリック笹丘教会

2

3

4

2013/4/16

Present Day

Photos on page 107 clocklwise from top left:

1. Sasaoka Catholic Church, Dedicated Sept. 2011.

2. Filipino Augustinian Missionaries 2012. From left: Jesus M. Dano, Charlie B. Pomucino.

3. Sasaoka Kindergarten Staff, 2011.

4. New Primary School in Nagasaki. Dedicated April 16, 2013.

Fr. Thomas P. Dwyer, Retired Villanova, June 2010.

PART II

A Glance At Comtemporary Japan
Through Fiction

Introduction

Father Thomas Dwyer knows that there is much more to the Japanese people than other people's stereotypes of them. Father Dwyer is an Augustinian Missionary to Japan and has lived behind "the bamboo curtain" for more than half a century–since 1959. Through his work as a priest at a church and his teaching at a parochial school, he met and got reacquainted with innumerable people in Japan in local communities in Tokyo, Fukuoka, Nagasaki, and Nagoya, including taxi drivers, owners of sushi restaurants, kindergarten teachers and children, Catholic priests and sisters, policewomen, school children, and so on.

The stories in this book are fiction, but the author wrote them to express the goodness of Japan by sharing his experiences with Japanese people with his readers. In fact, he wrote, "I love the Japanese people very much and I am very grateful to them for accepting me. I have had a wonderful, fulfilling life in Japan and I look back with happiness on my long career there. " In this book, Fr. Dwyer shows us that the Japanese, like all of us, are imperfect human beings with their own unique worries and cares, hopes and inspirations. He introduces us to individual Japanese whose characters have been formed by the often battling forces of culture, family, history and personal needs, desires and fortune (and misfortune) –in other words, he shows us the *kokoro* ("heart") of the Japanese people.

He wants to show the bright side of the Japanese, and especially to show some faces of contemporary Japanese life, of individual human beings who, like people all over the world, try to deal with the swirl of forces in their lives as best they can. He writes about the strong character of Japanese women; dropouts who had to deal with bullying in school but reclaim their lives in later years; Japanese who acted kindly to Americans during the war; people dealing with family life and the incredibly competitive Japanese school system; the wonderfully progressive Japanese kinder gartens; and about sushi shops and cabbies, relationships and weddings, the atomic bomb from the victims' perspective, and other subjects that help us see the human side of the Japanese.

Just as Father Dwyer helped encourage his Japanese parishioners to be rich in spirit and full of love in their hearts through the teaching of Augustinian spirituality, he wrote these stories with a loving heart, for as he puts it, "I wanted to show that I think love is looking for the good points in every person (and the Japanese have many fine qualities)."

And the final lesson of these stories is that although they are about Japanese people, they are first and foremost about people who, like all of us, do the best they can to travel the perilous path we call "life."

Masako Hamada, Ed.D.
Associate Professor of Japanese Studies
Institute for Global Interdisciplinary Studies
Villanova University

Kiyoshi and Masato

----- Two Brothers -----

There were thirteen years between Kiyoshi and Masato. Their mother was a nurse who worked shifts and their father was a busy business man in a large company. Kiyoshi suspected that Masato's birth was both unexpected and resented. Kiyoshi felt instinctively that his baby brother was a burden to his parents. Kiyoshi was in first year Junior High School when Masato was born.

Kiyoshi had failed the entrance examinations at two private Junior High Schools much to the disappointment of his parents. They reluctantly sent him to a nearby public school where he was bullied from day one. The main attacker was a third year Junior High School student who wore his collar open and swaggered like a gangster. His method was to punch a weak student in the stomach, and when the student collapsed with the wind knocked out of him, he got a kick in the back for good measure. The brute would then demand to be given money on a fixed day each week. Otherwise there was a punch and two kicks. Kiyoshi was terrified to tell either his parents or his homeroom teacher (a young woman who also taught English) about the hoodlum's extortion. However, he avoided contact with this hood by running as fast as he could the long way home. On two occasions he outraced the hoodlum and made it safely into his home where he quickly locked the door.

After that, Kiyoshi was afraid to go to school and often told his mother that he was sick. He played computer games at home while his parents were at work. Once when his homeroom teacher visited his home, he answered the door in his pajamas. Since Kiyoshi was alone, the teacher did not think it was appropriate to enter the home. So she questioned him in the "genkan" (entrance way) about his attitude, "Is someone bullying you?" she asked. "You seem to be afraid of something or someone." "No, absolutely not," answered Kiyoshi. "I just get fevers." "But your mother's a nurse. Doesn't she take your temperature?" insisted the teacher. "Yes, she does and it's always high," Kiyoshi lied. "I think you're hiding something from us. I can tell," the young teacher said with great sympathy. "No, I would tell you about it. I'm not hiding anything and I am not afraid," Kiyoshi was obstinate.

Kiyoshi missed school frequently and became addicted to software games. Fortunately he did fairly well at school and managed to pass his examinations. He loved English and felt close to his teacher. He passed the English proficiency test for the third and fourth level even while he was still a first year junior high school student.

His English teacher would often whisper to him, "Who are you afraid of?" Kiyoshi was thought to be a weakling by his male classmates, but the girls thought he was cute. The girls called him "Kiyoshi - kun" (Master Kiyoshi) a term used after a boy's name to indicate his youth, and they would often tease him. He helped the girls with their English and carried their book bags from school to their homes, all the while looking over his shoulder for the appearance of any hoodlums. The girls' mothers often invited him in for tea. The girls would tell their mothers that Kiyoshi could run like a deer because he was afraid of the hoods. "You can't always be running away," one mother told Kiyoshi. "Sometimes you have to stand up and fight. Just stand tall." "Are you kidding?" answered Kiyoshi, "You can't just stand up to these guys. They will surround you, punch you in the stomach and kick you when you are down. Some of them even carry switchblades. It's better to stay away from them."

One time a policeman came to Kiyoshi's homeroom at school and showed them a picture of the hoodlum who had attacked him. He had been arrested for possession of drugs, violence and extortion. He was awaiting a hearing at a juvenile detention facility. "If this hood is bothering you, or has been acting with violence against you, just let us know and we'll use it against him in court," the policeman said. A girl raised her hand and said, "Ask Kiyoshi. He's already been attacked." Kiyoshi was led out of class to the principal's office where he was questioned at length. "Yes, sir," said Kiyoshi, "I saw that boy out on the field, but no, sir, he never bothered me." "Well, why do you run home so fast if you're not afraid?" questioned the principal. "Everybody knows you run home." "Oh, I run for my health," said Kiyoshi while looking at the ceiling. The policeman laughed sarcastically. Kiyoshi knew that the other hoods would take revenge on him if he talked. This time it would be more than a punch and a kick in the back. It would be a cut on the face. The policeman leaned over and took Kiyoshi's hand. "Son, you can trust us. Nobody will hurt you," he said. Kiyoshi still wasn't talking. He continued to run all the way home, sometimes in record time. On some days he would still carry the girls' book bags for them. The girls agreed on two things: Kiyoshi could run like a deer, and he was cute.

Kiyoshi noticed his mother was pregnant when he was in his first year junior high school. "I'm going to have a baby, Kiyoshi. Will you be happy?" "Oh, yes," answered Kiyoshi. "I always wanted a baby brother or sister." And so, Kiyoshi looked forward to the birth of the baby with great interest.

Kiyoshi held the baby in his arms in the hospital. "His name is Masato," said his smiling father. "Ma-kun, Ma-kun," answered Kiyoshi. "Yes, I like that name." Kiyoshi tickled the baby under his chin. "You be good to your little brother, you hear," his mother admonished him from her hospital bed. Kiyoshi loved his little brother and vowed always to protect him.

Kiyoshi went to a private high school in his town when Masato was still a little toddler. They were inseparable. "Niichan," (affectionate word for older brother) "Ma-kun's bike broke down. Can you fix it?" Masato would ask when he learned to speak. Kiyoshi always found a way to fix Ma-kun's bicycle. "Niichan, my friend Mu-kun's bicycle is broken. Can you fix it?" Masato would ask in behalf of his friends. "Niichan, Sa-chan's chain came off her bicycle. "Can you fix it?" Kiyoshi became very adept at fixing bicycles.

During his university years when Masato was in primary school, Kiyoshi worked part time in a bicycle shop. The manager was amazed at Kiyoshi's ability to fix bikes of any range, even those with complicated gear shifts. "That kid can fix anything," the manager said in praise of Kiyoshi. Meanwhile Kiyoshi continued to fix Masato's bicycles.

Kiyoshi lived a normal carefree life. He always had girl friends in high school and university. He often had Masato accompany him on dates when he went hiking or swimming. His girlfriends spoiled Ma-kun with chocolates and cookies, something that was directly opposed to his mother's philosophy of education. "Sweets give you bad teeth and make small children hypersensitive," she would say with a nurse's authority. His girlfriends, however, continued to give Ma-kun sweets.

From Ma-kun's early childhood, he and Kiyoshi loved to go cycling. Kiyoshi would peddle slowly so that Ma-kun could keep up with him. Ma-kun gradually progressed from a tricycle to a small bicycle and from there on to an adult bike. Their mother, ever the nurse, made them both wear helmets.

When Ma-kun was in kindergarten he loved his homeroom teacher. He often told her about his bicycle rides with his Niichan. "We ride along paths through rice paddies. Niichan doesn't like wide streets with lots of cars," he would tell her. "You like your older brother, don't you, Ma-kun?" she would reply with wide eyes and a big smile. "Oh, yes, I love Niichan. He's my best friend," Ma-kun would answer with enthusiasm.

Their parents considered Kiyoshi to be a baby sitter. They had the utmost confidence in his discretion and love for his little brother. "I work in the hospital as a nurse and my husband is often away from home on business. We both feel that Ma-kun is perfectly safe with Kiyoshi," his mother would tell Ma-kun's teachers at the primary school which he attended. "They seem inseparable," one teacher observed.

Kiyoshi had received special permission from school principal to meet the kinder-garten bus, and later when Ma-kun entered the primary school, Kiyoshi tried to be home when school got out. He would often give Ma-kun cookies and milk as an afternoon treat, and then they would go cycling through the rice fields. A favorite practice was to stop on a bridge overlooking a beautiful stream. While they rested and relaxed, Kiyoshi would often teach Ma-kun how to throw flat stones so that they bounced two or three times across the water. Ma-kun practiced and practiced until he too could make the flat stones bounce. Then they would laugh out loud as they continued on their ride. Cycling and throwing those flat stones were a part of Ma-kun's childhood, and as he grew older he treasured those precious memories.

When Ma-kun advanced to higher grades in primary school, he sometimes went cycling alone. Kiyoshi cautioned him, however, to stay on the paths through the rice paddies, and also to avoid cars and hoodlums. "Just tell me if anyone bothers you and I'll take care of him," Kiyoshi said. Once when some junior high schools boys ran Ma-kun's bicycle off the road and into a water filled rice paddy, Kiyoshi was enraged when Ma-kun told him what had occurred. The next day he waited to encounter the boys, but they never showed up that day or again. Kiyoshi next taught Ma-kun to ride very fast by standing up as he peddled. Ma-kun became so good at this that he seemed as fast as a bike racer. Even the junior high school students couldn't catch him. No one ever bothered him again.

Ma-kun went his own way when he entered junior high school. Occasionally the brothers would go on bike rides together, but more and more Ma-kun sought out his own friends. He was growing up. Ma-kun liked school, took his studies seriously and progressed so well that he was always among the top students in class at the private junior and senior high schools he attended. He set his goals high, and when asked what he would later do, he would always reply, "I want to go to medical school at Kyoto University." All his grades seemed to indicate that he could and would achieve his goal.

Kiyoshi had studied Economics in a private university but could not get a job in that line. Instead he was recruited out of the university to a position in an insurance company. His salary was determined by how much insurance he sold. He spent long hours calling on and visiting prospective clients. Kiyoshi hated the job with a passion. His mother advised him to seek another job or line of work, but Kiyoshi felt that he had better stick with something he knew rather than learning a new trade. His days were indeed dark and glum. Kiyoshi was extremely unhappy but convinced himself that life was just tough, and that this was his lot in life. It didn't necessarily follow that he would find happiness in a new job. At least that is what he felt. And so the days passed.

When Masato was on vacation from Kyoto Medical School, he and Kiyoshi would cycle the same paths and throw stones over the water into that same flowing stream. Twenty years of his life had passed in what seemed to be a fleeing moment. Kiyoshi was thirty five and still unmarried even though he had many girlfriends. He was looking for the perfect girl of his dreams. "I cut up a cadaver," Masato said, "it was gruesome. I hope to be a surgeon one day." "You'll do well in whatever you choose," Kiyoshi said with encouragement. They rode on and took turns passing each other on the bike paths. "This is where those hoods ran you off the road," Kiyoshi recalled. "Yes, you waited for them but they never showed," Masato answered. "You always protected me." Unexpectedly, Kiyoshi's life took a turn while Masato was an intern at Kyushu University Medical School in Fukuoka. One day as he was cycling, he noticed a strikingly beautiful young woman standing on the same bridge from which he and his younger brother had thrown stones into the river. He stopped beside her and said, "Isn't this just beautiful? I used to stop here often when I was younger." "Yes," she replied. "I really love Kyushu. I was raised in Tokyo. I got a job in a hair dresser's shop. Later, I had my own business but it fell through." Kiyoshi felt his heart thumping. Would you like to cycle together sometime?" Kiyoshi asked. "We could meet right here on this bridge." The woman hesitated a long time before answering. "Excuse me, but are you married?" "No," answered Kiyoshi, "but I date."

Her name was Mari. She smiled and gave Kiyoshi her name card with her work place and her personal phone numbers. "I work long hours, but you can give me a ring. I have to work until nine o'clock at night," she mentioned shyly. "I'm thirty two, by the way. Is that alright?" "Perfect," Kiyoshi answered, "I'll call you." They met frequently on her day off and cycled through the rice paddies. Kiyoshi taught her how to throw stones that skipped over the water two or three times. Kiyoshi thought he had never met a lovelier person. Kiyoshi proposed on the bridge and gave her an expensive engagement ring. In truth, Kiyoshi had never felt so happy. "Thank God," said his mother, "I thought you'd never settle down. You're almost forty."

On the day they registered their marriage at the city office, they went out for some sushi, drank beer and just looked at one another lovingly as they shared their family backgrounds and planned for their future together.

Their wedding was solemnized at the Shinto Shrine with the san-san-kudo ceremony (the nuptial exchange of cups). Afterwards, there was a small hiroen (wedding reception) for the families and a few friends. Masato gave a formal greeting and proposed the kampai (toast). He recalled how his niichan had often taken him cycling when he was still a little boy. He went on to recall his happy times as a young boy, and how niichan had fixed his and all his friends' bikes. "Niichan, arigatou" (Elder brother, thank you), he said with affection and with tears in his eyes. The brotherly bonding was clear to everyone and was very emotional for everybody in the room. It was a case of Japanese "moriainaki" (everyone crying together in sympathy).

As part of their honeymoon, Kiyoshi and Mari took a trip by train around the large island of Kyushu. At the various stops in Miyazaki, Kagoshima, Kumamoto, Unzen and Nagasaki, they cycled all around the areas enjoying the scenery and, of course, one another's company and love. It was indeed the happiest time of Kiyoshi's life.

When they returned to their new apartment, Kiyoshi carried Mari through the threshold in keeping with the long standing tradition. There in the kitchen, right before their eyes, were two expensive mountain bikes. Attached to one of the bikes was a note, "Older brother and Mari, I pray you will find much happiness riding these bikes," signed, "Masato." The newlyweds straightaway took their new bikes out for a ride, making sure to follow the same route that the two brothers had used so often while they were growing up.

Kiyoshi and Mari decided to open up their own bicycle repair shop. Mari kept her old job in the hair dresser's shop, but used her expertise from the business world to keep the books and manage the finances behind the scenes as her contribution to Kiyoshi's new enterprise. They advertised in the newspapers and distributed printed flyers both to let the public know about them and to let people know that they would take old bikes that otherwise might be thrown away. "We'll take your old bikes," was the message. It turned out that many people were anxious to get rid of bikes that were old and in dire need of repairs. Kiyoshi would fix them, paint and polish them until they gleamed like new. Under Mari's supervision, they would sell the refurbished bicycles on weekends. Some Sundays they sold as many as ten bikes, bringing in a tidy income. As word of their shop and Kiyoshi's skill spread throughout the community, little kids came in frequently and asked to have their bikes fixed. If they were not accompanied by their parents, Kiyoshi never charged them.

When Masato brought his own children's bikes in for repair, he would call out, "Niichan, it's me, Ma-kum." Kiyoshi looked forward to these family visits, and would then fix his nephew's and niece's bikes as Masato looked on with pride.

One day when Mari was off from work, she asked Kiyoshi if they could ride out to the bridge and stand in the place where they had first met. "I've got something to tell you," she said. When they reached the bridge, Kiyoshi threw some flat stones across the water for old times' sake. "Kiyoshi," Mari said with a shy smile, "how would you like to become a Daddy?" Kiyoshi was at a loss for words. He embraced Mari for a long time, and then fumbled for the right words as he said, "That's, that's, that's great, Mari, that's just great." He closed his eyes and was overwhelmed with joy as he began to realize all that those few words meant. As they were getting ready to return home, who pulled up but Masato along with his wife and children! He greeted Kiyoshi and Mari and exchanged some pleasantries. When he was told the good news, he just beamed with happiness for his brother and sister in law. "Congratulations, Niichan. Congratulations, Mari," he repeated again and again. Masato's own two little children were busy all the while, trying make their stones skip over the water. Kiyoshi and Mari stayed chatting for a little while longer as they watched the children playing. Then when it was time to go, they all got on their bikes and started for home, taking turns passing each other as they rode through the rice paddies.

Sweetie

----- The Guard -----

Eddie and Edie were the names by which they were known among their close American friends. The Japanese faithful in the Evangelical Church, and the Japanese students who they taught at the nearby University, called Eddie "Edwaado Sensei" (teacher) or "Edwaado-san" and Edie they named "Edisu-sensei" or "Edisu-san". Back home in America they were known as Edward Johnson, an eloquent preacher who spoke superb Japanese, his wife Edith Johnson, who was the church organist, Sunday school teacher and teacher of music at their denomination's college in Sendai, Japan.

Eddie was deceased for some time now, a massive stroke had taken his life in a few minutes. And a good man he was, thought Edie, as she waited on the platform of the Tokyo railway station for the bullet train that would carry her to Hiroshima to visit with old and dear friends whom she had taught in the University. Her purpose in returning to Japan after so many years was to celebrate and commemorate the hundredth anniversary of the founding of the college. Her former students by now were scattered throughout Japan. Many years before, at the time when the war broke out interrupting their lives so severely, she and Eddie had been married only a few months. Like all other non-Japanese citizens, they had been arrested and interred in a special camp until they were repatriated in late 1942.

Edie was holding a non-reserved ticket that was a little cheaper than the reserved ticket. Always the preacher's wife, she had kept a sharp eye on the family's finances. "Old pinch penny," Eddie had called her in his gentle, reproving way. Her white hair was pulled back in a bun, and she wore a white glove on her left hand which she held close to her breast. A slight stroke had paralyzed her arm a few years before. That, of course, did not hold back Edie. Determination: Thy name is Edith.

Then she saw him, standing in the front part of the line. My goodness, she thought, that's "Sweetie." Instinctively she worked her way up through to the front of the line, tapped the man on the shoulder, and said, "Aren't you Mr. Suzuki?" "Chigai-masu, Chigai-masu," (No, I am not,) he answered, and in a huff, picked up his suitcase and moved to the line for the next car. "Sumimasen," (I'm sorry), Edie replied, thoroughly embarrassed.

The bullet train was moving along now at a fast pace. They crossed rivers, went through endless tunnels and soon, there it was, the sacred mountain, Fujisan, (also

121

called Fujiyama), majestic and magnificent. Eddie and she had climbed it before they were married.

Her memory too was racing back to the days in the internment camp at Mito during the war where, along with some foreign missionaries, they had been imprisoned. Catholic priests, Catholic Sisters, Protestant families of all denomi nations lived together in barrack like structures which were steaming hot in the summer and very cold and damp in the winter. Nonetheless, they all shared the primitive facilities as best they could. In a sense, to borrow a phrase from current times, it was an ecumenical community. Jan McPherson, a Protestant minister from Scotland, had been the leader, chosen so by universal acclaim from among the camp detainees. Jan did most of the negotiations with the guards and was adept at keeping peace in the barracks. As so often happens in the strained circumstances which everyone was undergoing, tempers flared sometimes and there were petty jealousies and a continual desire for food.

Among the prisoners was a Canadian Catholic priest, nicknamed "Hey" for his Canadian manner of speaking. His proper name was Joseph Grant, and he was a very gifted violinist who had a love for Mozart. With Fr. Grant on the violin and Edie on the piano, they had given many concerts together, especially at Christmas and Easter. Fr. Grant had died in the 1950's while teaching philosophy to Japanese students preparing for the ministry. As Edie remembered him, he was very shy, especially among women, but seemed to have a very simple but vibrant faith. He could be seen day after day, walking up and down behind the barracks saying his beloved rosary.

Ed, her husband, and Jan took turns preaching in English at the camp liturgies. For those two gifted missionaries, Edie would say in a pun, it was like speaking to a "captive" audience. Because the confinement and the harsh living conditions of the camp were so pervasive and oppressive, the message of the Gospel took on an added importance of keeping alive one's faith and sustaining one's morale in an otherwise bleak existence. That being the case, both men, strong in their own faith, spent long hours preparing their sermons even though their listeners were few in numbers.

There were some Catholic Nuns there in the camp also. The Sisters had different style habits and came from a number of different countries in Europe as well as from the United States. Their common language was Japanese. It always appeared a bit strange to Edie to see two foreigners conversing in Japanese. As the miles on the train ticked by and the countryside slipped into a kind of blur, Edie began thinking of how greatly the world had changed in the years after the war's end. "I wonder whatever happened to those Sisters after the war and with all the changes that took place in the Catholic Church?" One Sister's name stood out in her memory, Sr. Mary John, who had given the young camp guard, Suzuki, the nickname, "Sweetie."

We never once spoke to Suzuki, Edie remembered. He had stood at his post at the gate of the camp and had little contact with any of the prisoners. One thing stood out, however, something that she would never forget. Whenever Suzuki was on guard duty, the next morning they found a big bag of sweet potatoes behind the barracks. At first, they did not know where this "gift from God," so much like the manna in the desert that kept Moses and his people alive, came from. But, oh how delicious those sweet potatoes were, and how much flavor and nourishment they added to the weak soup they were given each day. There was no doubt in Edie's mind that those sweet potatoes had helped them survive.

No one ever saw young Suzuki leaving the gift of potatoes behind the barracks, but whenever he had been on guard duty, the sweet potatoes were always found the next morning. Jan said it would be better to not mention what was happening to either the guard or especially to anyone else. Suzuki could get into serious trouble for giving precious food to the prisoners. Just where Suzuki got the potatoes, or just when he managed to leave them behind the barracks, no one knew, but there was no doubt in our minds that Suzuki was our benefactor. After saying grace before meals, someone would always add, "Thank you too, Sweetie." We were indeed deeply indebted to Sweetie, but because of the very tense and dangerous circumstances under which we were living in the prison camp, it was impossible for us to have expressed our gratitude to him, she reflected.

Then one day Suzuki did not appear at his post. Had his kindness to us been discovered? Had he been transferred to a war zone? Had he been moved to a similar position in another prison camp? No one knew. The sweet potatoes abruptly stopped coming also. Sweetie was out of their lives, but no one could forget his courage and his quiet kindness.

Eddie and Edie returned to Tennessee shortly after they were repatriated through Canada. Their church had asked Eddie to become a teacher in the Theological School in Memphis. They left Japan with heavy hearts, even though their time in the wartime camp had been a crucible of suffering. After Eddie died in the mid-sixties, Edie went to live with their son, David, and his family in the suburbs just north of Memphis. Edie often told her grandchildren about her life many years before in Japan. "And, you see, there was this guard whom we nicknamed Sweetie because he secretly gave us sweet potatoes," Edie would say and the children would respond, "We heard that story, Grandma." But one day, little Janice who was only five, said something remarkable that made everything from the past come rushing back into the present for Edie. "I think that guy Sweetie was a good man—all he did for you."

Tears came to Edie's eyes, and she hesitated a while before responding as all the tensions of life in the prison camp came rushing forward. "That he was," she said, "that he was."

The bullet train pulled out of Osaka and continued its journey south after making a very brief stop in that city. After the train was fully underway, a woman attendant came along with a cart full of food and drink, calling out as she walked down the aisle, "Bento, Bento." (Box lunch, Box Lunch). She stopped in front of Edie and offered her a Bento. "I did not order that, Miss. There is a mistake," Edie said. "No, the man who got off in Osaka said to give it to you and that you would understand," replied the attendant. As the full impact of the message hit home, Edie was startled, realizing that the stranger she spoke to back in Tokyo really had been Sweetie after all. The wonder of it all, and the warmth of that last gesture by Suzuki swept over her and was tinged only with a moment of sadness by the realization that she would probably never see him again. Wherever he would go, however, his life might end, she thought, here was one fine man who walked straight and true to his ideals in extreme danger with great kindness.

In the suburbs of Osaka, Suzuki turned into the Zen Buddhist Temple he had inherited from his father. His wife, dressed in a Japanese style long sleeve apron, was sweeping leaves away from the entrance to the Temple. "The roof is leaking again," she said as he was entering the building. "Well, it's six hundred years old," Suzuki answered, and went straight into the Temple where, in Japanese fashion, he took off his shoes and sat on the mat floor in a "seiza" position, with his legs tucked under his body and his back upright. He breathed slowly in and out as his father had taught him as a child. Then he picked up the wooden stick and rang the bell with it. After finishing his prayer, Suzuki returned to his office which was situated right next to the entrance of his home. He called to his beloved wife, whom he called "Kaachan", (Mom, an intimate word that husbands used for their wives after so many years together). She entered the room carrying a stack of mail that had arrived earlier that day. "It's here," she said in an excited voice. She handed him a letter with the words "Minister of Justice "as the return address printed on the envelope. "I can't wait to see it," she continued as she adjusted her eyeglasses. He picked up the letter opener which he had purchased in Spain when they were visiting there with a tour a few summers before. Ever so deliberately and slowly, he slit open the letter from side to side. He read the letter, but his face showed no emotion. He handed the letter to his wife who read it very carefully and with great emotion. With tears of joy in her eyes, she took his hand and held it to her breast. "You deserve it," she said, "You deserve it."

The letter from the Ministry of Justice read as follows:

Dear Dr. Suzuki:

It is with great joy to inform you that you have been nominated to be President of the Chaplain Corps working in prison ministry. Your affirmation will be a matter of course as all the background work for your promotion has been examined with great care.

It may be of interest to you to know that you were highly recommended for the post by the Protestant Christian minister, the Reverend Paul Somerson, born in Alabama in North America, and a long time minister in many prisons across our nation. I understand that you and he are close personal friends. The video clip about you and your work has been viewed in places around the world. It is narrated in English by Dr. Somerson himself. He told us with admiration your benevolent work with death row prisoners. We thank you especially for your compassion toward Jiro Nakamura who died with dignity. His deep bow to you in his last moments was witnessed with great emotion by those present. Our records show that over the years you have ministered to ten prisoners at the time of their execution. With deep respect for your dear wife children and grandchildren, I urge you to accept the nomination. Your reluctance to accept any kind of adulation or publicity is well known. Still, we urge you to accept.

Signed:
Konishi Watanabe
Minister of Justice

Suzuki Sensei turned away from his wife for the moment and stared out the window. Slowly he told her something he had never revealed to anyone. "When I was drafted into the army and had just finished the terrible ordeal of basic training, just before I was sent to fight in China, I was assigned to a prison camp as a guard. The foreigners interred in the camp were all Christians. I was very much touched by their unselfishness and their spirit of prayer. I never thought of them as enemies, just human beings like ourselves. After the war I continued in prison ministry. I've studied a lot about prison systems throughout the world. No country's handling of crime is completely just. Japan's system is not completely fair either. The police here have too much power to coerce confessions. That is a lot easier than searching for evidence to a crime. The judges often bow to the police even though 95% percent of the defendants have already pleaded guilty. In the west they have what they call 'Habeus Corpus' in which you cannot imprison a person without going before a judge. This law, I think, comes from their Christian tradition. I think it is a very good law. Some Japanese want to have the jury system over here, but what's the point if everybody pleads guilty?" "Now, now," said his wife, "You take everything so seriously. There will never be a completely just world. We Japanese do not like to incarcerate people on small charges. We have one of the lowest rates of incarceration in the world. Here you have to be a repeat offender or do something very cruel to be put in prison. Our low crime rate is something to be proud of, don't you think?"

125

"Kaachan," he answered, "you usually have the last word, good Japanese wife that you are." They went to dinner, both sitting on the mat floor. She served raw fish, pickles and a fish style casserole. They rarely if ever ate red meat. She poured him a little cup of sake. In return, he poured a cup for her also. "I hope the carpenter comes and finishes the roof on the Temple tomorrow," she said. Suzuki Sensei said nothing. He was thinking of his early days in the army when he guarded a prison camp. That woman on the train, he mused, must have been in that camp. He wondered if they ever knew that he had provided those sweet potatoes.

Minoru

----- The Dropout -----

As the taxi slowly pulled up to the primary school in Atsugi, a town close to Yokohama, the children excitedly ran out and encircled the vehicle. Some of the children were carrying placards which read in Japanese, "Welcome home, Takeuchi Sensei," (the word "sensei" is used for almost everyone in authority or respected who is well known). Takeuchi, the world renowned orchestra conductor, was coming back to the primary school from which he had graduated many years before. In keeping with this very special moment, the principal of the school had set aside time for the school to have a special program of introduction with questions and observations being made to their famous guest by the students and the faculty.

Takeuchi was traveling with his American wife, Kay, and Fumiko Murakami, a renowned Japanese violinist, who today would be acting as interpreter for Kay. Kay herself was a musical artist of some prominence, having played the cello in both European and American orchestras. She was introduced to Minoru in an interview which blossomed into a beautiful relationship and their marriage about a year later. For Kay, traveling from continent to continent in keeping with the demands of her career, the real joy and happiness of life seemed to have eluded her, but with her marriage to Minoru, she had achieved all that in the love she shared with this gentle man from Japan.

When the visitors stepped out of the taxi, the children swarmed all around them, the little children hugging Takeuchi's legs and the older children reaching out to shake hands or simply to touch him. Takeuchi was carrying an old trumpet which he held up in the air, and with it he waived to the group of teachers who lined up along the wall near the entrance to the school. Among the teachers was his old music teacher, Yukiko Mizuura, who was often called "Naki mushi Sensei"(Miss Cry Baby) because she cried on all occasions. Takeuchi went over to the teachers and shook hands with the principal. He then bowed to each teacher individually, while they returned his greeting with even deeper and more profound bows. When he stopped in front of Mizuura Sensei, the children began to chant, "Naki mushi Sensei, Naki mushi Sensei." Without a doubt, she was still much loved by everyone. Takeuchi invited Kay over to meet Mizuura Sensei, who by now was "doing her thing," crying away with joy. "Minoru-kun" (Master Minoru), she said, and fell into more tears. "But behind the joyous occasion of this day," Fumiko, the interpreter explained to Kay, "back many years before when Takeuchi was just a little boy beginning to study music in her class, that now elderly teacher saw Takeuchi Sensei's potential as a musician and gave him a trumpet he could call his own, and he has been very

127

grateful to her ever since because that trumpet had been such a force for good in his life." All this was news to Kay, and she was eager to hear all the details Fumiko was telling her as the entire group filed into the school's auditorium to hear Takeuchi speak to the assembly.

The great musician himself was very hesitant at the thought of returning to his old school to make this presentation. He was well aware that many on the faculty, and perhaps some of the older students also, knew of his past history, how in his Junior High School years he became a school dropout, cutting classes and becoming an outright truant. Minoru himself could not pinpoint the exact reasons for his behavior, only that he had become sullen, angry, withdrawn, and yes, even suicidal. It had been a horrible two years, enraged in nasty and shouting arguments with his father, and the constant tears of his mother as she witnessed all that. Now, not that many years later, he was returning to his former school, a success in life with thousands of fans in the music world, and yet deep within himself was the haunting realization of how close he had come to personal disaster right after leaving this very school. As he stood there on the stage, listening to the principal introducing him and praising all his accomplishments, he was all too aware of how very close he had come to losing it all during those troubled filled teen age years he had struggled through.

Fortunately for Minoru, the end of his ordeal came, not from anything he did on his own, but from a business decision in his father's company which called for him to relocate the family to the United States, specifically to New Orleans, Louisiana. In so many ways this was the opening to a new world which allowed Takeuchi to leave behind the black morass that had held him fast and to step out into an astonishing new life. For Minoru, life began when he was enrolled in an American Junior High School. Shortly after the school year began he met and became close friends with an African American classmate, Charlie Tucker, son of the famous Jazz musician, Tiny Tucker. Tiny was a man of immense musical talent, equaled only by his physical size of some 300 pounds. Tiny had become one of the greatest clarinet players in the world, even though he could not read a word of music. Minoru took his trumpet over to Charlie's house one day and Tiny taught him how to "pucker up" and to keep time by tapping his foot. Right from the start it was apparent to Tiny that this young Japanese kid had quite some talent for music and so he began to teach Takeuchi the fundamentals of jazz music. Tiny was later to tell Minoru's parents, "That boy was nasty as a cornered moccasin at first, but after I taught him to 'pucker up' he changed into a warm spring breeze from the Bayou." Minoru's parents also saw the change and encouraged him to continue to play the trumpet every chance he got with Charlie and his group over at Tiny's house. Minoru already could read music because his mother had sent him for extensive piano lessons from his earliest kindergarten years. Tiny Tucker often said about him, "That Japanese kid must have some black blood in him. He's got rhythm, man, he's got rhythm." Back at his own house Minoru always kept up the practice of tapping his foot to some rhythm he could sense within him. "Minoru, why do you keep tapping your foot like that?" his mother asked him? Minoru answered her in his New Orleans English, "I'm improvisin', Mom, I'm improvisin'."

After a few years in America the family returned to Atsugi, home city of Sony, Inc. As they settled back into the activities of their former life in Japan, Minoru asked if he could attend a private high school in Yokohama, a school well known for its band and its music program for its students. His parents considered this request, and thinking back on how much music had changed Minoru's life while they were in New Orleans, they gladly consented. It didn't take long for Minoru to become a leader among his fellow band members and to teach them how to "pucker up" and to keep time by tapping their feet as Tiny Tucker had taught him.

As graduation approached, Minoru's counselor and mentor at the high school recommended that he take the examination for the Tokyo University of Fine Arts, arguably the finest musical school in Japan and was highly respected and recognized throughout the world. Besides the very rigorous written exam, there was also a personal interview at which the student had to sing or play a musical instrument of his choice. Minoru seized on the special opportunity this presented to him by lighting up the room with his renditions of American Jazz, a la Tiny Tucker style that he liked so much. One of the more serious teachers on the examining board asked Minoru, "What's the name of that song that you're playing, son?" To which Minoru responded in his New Orleans English, "I was just improvisin'", Sir, "I was just improvisin'."

At the University, Minoru chose to learn the classical flute, and because it was his own choice, he truly mastered it, practicing over and over again and playing with musical groups every chance he could get. His great talent for music and his desire to embark on a career as a professional was now very apparent to everyone. Minoru's love for Jazz turned to an even greater love for western classical music in the religious tradition of Mozart, Bach and Beethoven. "I don't' know anything about Christianity," Minoru would say, "but I am a Protestant when I play Bach and a Catholic when I play Mozart."

In time, Minoru began to direct the University orchestra and chorus. Just about everyone agreed that Minoru would one day become a famous conductor. After playing for a few years with various Japanese and foreign orchestras, he made his professional debut in directing the orchestra of Kyushu Symphonic Orchestra in the Sun Palace theater in the southern city of Fukuoka. His success there propelled him into national and later international fame.

Returning now to Minoru's visit to his old primary school, and to the talk he gave to the students in the school assembly, he agreed to respond to questions from the children for a few minutes. "Minoru Sensei," asked one young boy," with all the talent you have, why did you become a junior high school dropout after you graduated from this school?" "Well," answered Minoru, sensing the importance of that question for these kids, "there was no one reason. I guess that I just hated myself most of all. I really don't know why, but I did. I hated myself. Don't any of you become dropouts. It's no fun; it's dangerous, and most of all, it can wreck your life. Believe me; I came close to losing everything." "What saved you, then?" asked a sixth grade girl. "This," said Minoru, holding up his trumpet. "This gift from Mizuura Sensei changed my life!!" That statement captured the attention of the audience, and all the students and faculty were in rapt attention as Minoru continued. "Now I am going to play for you a song I learned from a famous jazz player in America." With that, he played for them a rousing rendition of "When The Saints Come Marchin' In." After the applause quieted down, Minoru then left the stage and went over to the area where the teachers were standing. He handed the trumpet to the principal and asked him to put it into the trophy case. Addressing all who were in the assembly, he said it was his hope that as the students looked at the trumpet, they would remember an old dropout who made it all the way back, right to the top of his profession, using this trumpet. With that, and to the cheers of everyone in the room, he took Mizuura Sensei on his left arm, and with his wife Kay on his right arm, strolled up the aisle and out of the Hall.

As they were chatting in the taxi on their way back to their hotel, Kay said, "Oh, Minoru, you are so sentimental. I did not know the Japanese were like that." Fumiko, the interpreter, broke into the conversation and said, "Oh yes, people everywhere think we are the inscrutable Orientals who never show our emotions." Kay then turned to Minoru and asked, "You kept saying "Oh-chi-ko bo-re" and you bowed each time you said that. What does that mean?" Fumiko answered, "Minoru was apologizing each time for being a dropout." Kay kissed Minoru on the cheek and said, "Oh, my Minoru, 'Oh-chi-ko bo-re', a high school dropout." Minoru himself broke in and said, "Back in New Orleans, when I started improvising with my music, suddenly everything kind of came together. Where would we be without the Mizuuras and the Tuckers of this world who somehow show love to a disturbed child and point out a way to success and happiness? Without Nakamura Sensei's trumpet and Tiny Tucker's encouragement, I simply would not be here today. I very possibly would be dead!" "Oh, no, Minoru, countered Kay, "God was watching over you. He had other plans for you. He allowed you to go through all that suffering in your childhood for a purpose. You met those people who saw something special in you, and they said and did just the right things to bring you around and paved the way for you to succeed. Now it's your turn to take the extra steps to reach out to the troubled kids of this generation." "OK, then," said Minoru, "that's what we'll do."

From that day on, there was a new dimension to Minoru's life. Every chance he got, he'd tell and re-tell his story, especially to audiences of children. He would tell the children that he understood their pain. Truancy, dropping out of school, etc. had become a major social problem in Japan. Something had to be done. Minoru's answer to the kids was simple and direct: "Don't do it. I've been there. It just doesn't work. Stay in school. Develop your talents the right way. It'll be tough, sure. Life is tough, but there is no other way. Trust me, there is no other way!!"

Hanako

----- Wife and Mother -----

"Hmm," Hanako Yamaguchi mused to herself as she put down her recent issue of TIME and pondered one of its leading articles which she had been reading. "It may be all right for her, but I'm not so sure," she said referring to the writer's article heralding her post-modern position that women should 'put aside their aprons' and step out into the world where they were needed and belonged.

Hanako Sasaki Yamaguchi was a dedicated wife and mother who followed closely her husband's career at the hospital. Dr. Kenji Yamaguchi, an eminent doctor known throughout the Tokyo region, was an esteemed Gastroenterologist teaching at the Hospital of the University of Tokyo, a position of great prominence, but also one which carried with it great responsibility. Hanako realized the pressure he was under every day at the University, and so she made it a point to give him constant love and encouragement at home, caring for all his needs as she saw them. In the long standing tradition of Japanese housewives, she saw him off at the gate in the morning and was there to meet him in the entrance hall of their home when he returned each evening. "Did you have a good day?" she would ask as she placed his slippers in a convenient spot on the step.

There was just the two of them living at home now, since Atsuko, their fourth daughter, had recently married and moved to Nagoya to follow her husband there in his work as a project engineer for Brothers International, known worldwide as a maker of business machines. Hanako and Kenji's own marriage, an 'arranged marriage,' in the ages old Japanese tradition, had developed into one of deep love and affection which led to a happy home life for Hanako, her husband and their five daughters.

Even though Hanako was devoted to her role as a mother and housewife, she herself had a good education and was intensely interested in the academic achievement of her children. She prayed to God that they would do well in school and ultimately would find happiness in their own lives. This respect for the values of a good education and the impact such an education could have in a person's life was at the root of Hanako's disagreement with the article from TIME that she had been reading. She shook her head in silent opposition to what was said in the article, saying to herself, "No, there is something to be said for parental involvement in choosing a growing girl's education, and even in the choice of her future husband." "Be open to the wisdom of your father and your mother in planning, but not ordering, your future," Hanako would maintain, "Let them guide you, trust them. This is the Japanese way."

As they were growing up, Hanako encouraged her daughters to attend Christian mission schools. Her own mother, Sachiko Sasaki, had encouraged her to do the same years ago when she was a child. Hanako had attended Christian mission schools all the way from kindergarten through high school and on through college and university levels. Looking back she felt very satisfied with the education she had received in the Christian mission schools she had attended. Hanako recalled especially those teenage years when she had boarded at a convent school during her junior and high school days. It was a time of great happiness and peace for her. She felt very close to God as she walked through the woods observing the different species of birds, often in the company of one of her favorite nuns, Sr. Elizabeth. There was a quiet peace and serenity in Sister's demeanor which would reveal itself as they strolled along talking quietly about life and God and about the beauty of nature all around them. God was so much a part of Sister's life that soon a yearning for a similar relationship with God began to grow within Hanako herself. In her heart she often considered herself to be a Christian, even though she had never been officially accepted into any Christian denomination.

There were more immediate plans for Hanako's future that were foremost in her mother's thinking during those same years. Sachiko Sasaki had encouraged her daughter to go to Christian mission schools with the hope that this would lead to a good marriage for Hanako. Mrs. Sasaki, as with so many other Japanese mothers, had the fixed idea that women graduates of Christian mission schools stood a better chance to meet and win the heart of a man coming from some well known university or high ranking business firm. Indeed it was all part of her own mother's plan for Hanako. "Good marriages are not made in heaven," she would often tell Hanako, " they are made in a good school."

Naturally Hanako herself had adopted the same motives for the education and preparation for marriage for her own five daughters. This way of looking at one's education and future life choices was all but in Hanako's genes. Her grandmother had paved the way in this regard by being one of the early graduates of Kassui University in Nagasaki. Because of the connections she made as a graduate of that school she went on to marry a diplomat and lived abroad for many years as he fulfilled the demands of his career. Hanako's mother, Sachiko Sasaki, was a graduate of the Jogakuin University, a Christian mission school in Fukuoka and later married her husband, a local doctor.

As the hours of the day slowly slipped by, Hanako's thoughts returned time and again to the article from TIME that she had read that morning. She kept thinking that left to her own devices she really would never have met Dr. Kenji Yamaguchi, her much loved husband, the father of her five daughters, whom she had wed in a traditional Japanese arranged marriage brought about largely by the efforts of her mother, Sachiko Sasaki. Mrs. Sasaki had read in the Society pages of the local paper that a brilliant young doctor with an outstanding record from the Medical School at Tokyo University had recently accepted a teaching position at the same University. She learned still more about this young physician by discreet inquiries among her own friends who confirmed for her the fact that Dr. Yamaguchi was still single and unattached. These lady friends of Sachiko also let her know that the new doctor was intending to settle down in the area and was interested in finding someone of marriageable age. Working through the good offices of her husband, Dr. Sasaki, a welcoming reception for the new doctor was arranged during which Hanako was introduced to him. Almost immediately both were attracted to the other and their mutual respect grew and developed into personal love. In short order they were often seen together rooting for the Giants, attending the theater in downtown Tokyo, and in the winter months traveling on skiing trips up to Hokkaido where also Hanako and Kenji's family got to know and like each other very much.

One of their favorite pastimes during this period when Kenji was courting Hanako, was to go down to the area called Shinjiku where so many of the young people around their own ages could be found, enjoying the music and talking over their own futures and interests. They often went to one particular coffee shop because they knew very many of the young people who used to hang out there, and the atmosphere of the place was especially attractive. It was right there, in the midst of their friends, that Kenji surprised Hanako one evening when he proposed to her, on bended knee and with great flair and cheers from the crowd, "If you don't marry me, I'll jump off a bridge and it will be on your conscience." Hanako laughed as she answered, "Yes," extending her hand so that Kenji could slip the ring on her finger, much to the delight and applause from the students gathered around them.

Even though they were both non-Christians, in deference to Hanako's many years in the Christian mission schools and her close association with the Sisters, they were given special permission to have their wedding in a Christian ceremony on the grounds of Sacred Heart University in Tokyo.

After their wedding, the reception for the newly married couple was held in a downtown hotel in Tokyo. Hanako's immediate superior in the American bank where she worked made a short toast in English in which he praised Hanako's ability to speak English so very well and praised her dedication to her work and her loyalty to the company. In turn, Kenji's department head at the hospital lauded this brilliant young doctor from Hokkaido. He also reminded Hanako of the long hours and constant pressure under which Kenji would be working, and he admonished her in the spirit of a loyal Japanese housewife to always make the home a center of tranquility and harmony, and to always have a smile ready when she met her husband when he arrived home late from his work at the hospital.

Their honeymoon trip took them to the United States with a brief stopover in Hawaii to savor all the delights of that island paradise. Then it was on to the United States proper where they visited both the west and the east coasts. San Diego and Boston were Kenji's favorite cities, whereas Hanako loved San Francisco which she had already visited on other occasions with her parents. During their travels from one state to another, it gradually became more and more obvious to Kenji what a remarkable person Hanako turned out to be. Nothing seemed to phase her, adjusting travel arrangements, making (and changing) hotel reservations, arranging rental car times, noting time zone changes, etc., etc. He, the medical scholar, was not nearly so adept at making the many changes that their travel schedule forced upon them. Kenji found himself becoming more and more dependent on Hanako's good judgment in everyday affairs. Happily, as it turned out, this led to his calling her by the pet name "Boss," which amused them both and at the same time drew them closer together. This bonding which became a strong fixture in their relationship was not lost on Mrs. Sasaki, Hanako's mother, who so craftily had engineered the whole thing: an 'arranged marriage' which had developed into a happy marriage to everyone's delight.

In due time, as the years went on, the family grew with the birth of five daughters in the first fifteen years. All the girls were healthy and gave their parents great delight as they grew, with all the laughable antics, petty jealousies and warm affection that five young girls can bring to a family. Hanako loved babies and never seemed to be distraught with the closeness of their ages. She was forever playing with them, singing to them, reading books to them and constantly talking to them. On the other hand, there was a certain strictness about her and Hanako reprimanded them whenever it was needed. Kenji too had a deep love for his daughters and took great pride in their accomplishments, whether at home or at school. The atmosphere in the Yamaguchi household was one of love and discipline which the girls themselves would testify to approvingly in later years. Kenji too, much more than he realized proved to be a loving and caring father. Even though the demands of his work at the hospital put many restrictions of his daily activity, Kenji had time set aside in his weekly schedule to be at home with his family. On those occasions, when the weather and the seasons permitted, he would take one or more of the girls with him to a nearby amusement park, much to their delight and to his own pleasure because these excursions gave him time personally to relax and especially to bond closely with his dear children. At home Hanako was not adverse to teaming up with the girls to outmaneuver Papa in family discussions of everyday matters. She would pretend in mock seriousness to be one with them as she would say, "Remember, if we stick together, six to one, Papa does not have a chance. No defections." Poor Papa, with Mama and the girls against him he went down to one defeat after another. "Even Miki, the baby, votes against me," he told a colleague at work, "I don't have a chance."

As the girls grew older, Hanako registered them in Christian kindergarten and primary schools. However, the girls were free to choose their own junior and high schools. Most of them continued on in the private Christian schools Hanako had recommended. All through their school years, early morning life at home was rather chaotic with the girls teasing and arguing among themselves as they hurriedly got ready for school and quickly downed the morning breakfast. After they had all gone and Dr. Yamaguchi had set off for work at the hospital, Hanako finally had a few moments for herself. In the quiet, those moments afforded her, she would pour herself some tea and then watch the morning news on television.

Three of the girls applied to and were accepted by Sacred Heart University in Tokyo, the same University from which Hanako herself had graduated. One of the girls, Yoshiko, later went to Keio University which featured courses and a degree in communication. She excelled in that field, in part because she had done so well in the study of English while at Sacred Heart University. Yoshiko went on to have a distinguished career as a television reporter and announcer. Miki, the youngest of the girls, chose to have a career in architecture. She was gifted in design even as a child, and even though this field was largely dominated by males, she achieved notable success in the contracts she was awarded.

Hanako was understandably proud of her daughters and at the academic and professional achievements they had attained. Now as they approached marriageable age, Hanako's thoughts focused on how she would influence their choices of suitors, just as her mother had done years before in her own case. Education would be the key. Hanako always had "marriage" in the back of her mind regarding her children. She remembered her mother saying so often when the subject came up, "Remember, your Prince Charming is not going to be found by accident. He is going to be found in or through some school."

The relationship Hanako had with her daughters, the orderly elegance of her home, and also the warm relationship Hanako had with her husband Yamaguchi Sensei was not lost on her neighbors and close friends. Often as they sat sipping coffee in one or another's homes, she would be asked how she had done it. "When they are small, hug them and when they get older help them make the right choices in school. It is important that they think they are making their own choices, but you have to gently guide them to what you think is best for them," she would reply in response to their questions. She always remembered what one lady said admiringly, "Education is an art and Hanako is a Picasso," with the others all nodding in agreement. At the time Hanako had raised her hand "Just a moment," Hanako admonished, raising her hand in caution, "Don't forget, the ultimate plan is for them to have a good marriage. That is the last and most important step."

Even as Hanako led the discussions on child rearing with her friends, she also liked to dwell on her own background and the important events of her own life growing up. She had boarded at a Christian convent school during her junior and senior high school years. It was a time of great peace and happiness for Hanako. The steady rhythm of the classroom contrasted with the beauty of the trees and gardens around the school combined to create a spirit of harmony which tugged at the spirit of Hanako in those teen aged years. But there was more to it than that. There was a spiritual harmony that she sensed among the Sisters, especially in her close friend and confidant, Sister Elizabeth, a feeling that drew her close to God as she and Sister strolled through the gardens together in the late afternoons. Such thoughts, spiritual and comforting as they might be, were at the same time quite challenging because of their life-changing implications. These thoughts were also tough stuff for a teen age mind to grapple with unaided by one's parents, so Hanako brought them up for discussion during one visit home . Neither parent was open to the idea. "We have our own religion," was all that her father would say. Her mother likewise was opposed, especially regarding Christian marriage. With that, the subject was shelved and the discussion ended.

However, when it came time to discuss which University to attend, both parents had words of advice and encouragement. "Papa and I would like you to go to the Sacred Heart University," her mother advised her. "This is the school the Crown Princess herself attended as a young lady," a feature they counseled, which added luster and prestige to the school's name. The school itself already possessed a sterling reputation for academic excellence, with the added feature that it emphasized spoken English in its curriculum. All this pleased Hanako herself to no end leading her to apply for admission, which with the needed recommendation from her own high school counselor was easily realized.

Hanako excelled in her studies at Sacred Heart, especially in her ability to speak fluent English. Her excellent scholastic record, coupled with her outstanding ability to speak and understand fluent conversation in the English language, helped Hanako achieve her greatest award in all her college years: her address to the Crown Princess when she visited the school. Crown Princess Michiko was a graduate of Sacred Heart University and periodically returned to the school for a visit. The highlight of her official visit was an assembly at which the student considered to be most proficient in languages would address the Crown Princess in English. Crown Princess Michiko was very much impressed with Hanako's talk and with her graciousness as a person. She invited Hanako to tea with her at which they held a prolonged conversation in English. This meeting with the Crown Princess would, if properly done, embellish any resume Hanako would later submit in a search for future employment. At home, Mrs. Sasaki was ecstatic and proudly showed to all her neighbors and relatives pictures of Hanako taken with the Crown Princess.

With Hanako's proficiency in English to match with her academic record, it was easy for her to obtain a position with an American bank right in the heart of Tokyo. Not only did the position pay well, but the employees were given long vacations, American style, which Hanako took to with great gusto; a whole new world opened up to her. Along with her new found friends Hanako backpacked through India and China. She also loved to visit vacation spots in Japan. The inland sea and Miyazaki Prefecture were among Hanako's favorite places. She was enthralled with professional sports too and became an ardent fan of the Tokyo Giants, spending many an evening sitting out in the bleachers cheering on her beloved Giants. Her social life took her to the cinema and to dance parties frequented by many of her friends.

All these things, this seemingly never ending and fast paced life style, and Hanako's thorough enjoyment of it all, was viewed with some alarm by her mother at home. Sachiko Sasaki, Hanako's mother kept beckoning her to return home to prepare for marriage in a proper way. "You should learn cooking, the art of flower arrangement and calligraphy. These are the things people look for in a prospective bride," Mrs. Sasaki would admonish her. "Oh, Mama," Hanako would reply, "My man will zoom in driving his new Mercedes and just sweep me off my feet." Her mother was ready with her answer, "No, you've got it all wrong. Look at yourself. You're twenty five and I don't see any big limousine at the door."

Now that the girls were all old enough to think seriously about dating and marriage, they began to question seriously some of Hanako's early decisions and life style which she had enjoyed so thoroughly after her university studies and before her marriage to Dr. Yamaguchi. They had learned much about their mother's early days from Grandma Sasaki which contrasted quite a bit from the way they were being raised at home. In many discussions they would attack Hanako using Grandma Sasaki's stories about Hanako's youthful exuberance.

"Grandma Sasaki says that you were a world traveler, had many boyfriends and did not want to settle down," was the gist of their argument. Hanako, however, was ready for that and was able to counter-argue with facts of her own. Her days as a member of the debating team in college had prepared her well for these quite serious questions coming from her own daughters. "What you say is true. I did indeed enjoy myself in the days before I married. Those are the facts and I won't deny them. However, let's focus on what is the situation in your own lives right now. Did I ever say that you couldn't travel? Did I ever say you could not have boy friends? Did I ever say you could not go ball games? What you are forgetting is that I was only doing things my parents had planned for me and how they were checking to see that I did not go overboard or behave recklessly in all the things I was engaged in. Actually I followed exactly what my parents had planned for me." She followed this up by continuing her rebuttal, "I went to a convent school for six years. Would you like me to put you in a convent school where you would have to go to church every day and to study the Bible? Would you like that? They chose my University too, not that I objected to that. When Mama set up a meeting with Papa at that social gathering where we met, I did exactly as she said by following the set rules for such an occasion. Did I hesitate or want to do it my way? Did I come right out and say that I could find my own husband? No, I did not. And everything worked out wonderfully. If I had not listened to Mama I would never have married Papa. It was all arranged." Of course, the moral of Hanako's arguments was that you disregarded Mama's hints at your own risk. The girls, at least some of them, reluctantly agreed that Mama had made her point. "Mama should have been a lawyer," they said.

The next few years passed rather quickly. Before one knew it, all five daughters had left the nest and married, the last one to do so being Miki, the youngest. Hanako was pleased with all their choices. Three of the girls had found their own husbands, and the other two daughters were "matched" by Hanako with great success.

Life for Hanako had been, from her earliest recollections, a series of blessings even from her childhood. She came from a good family, had received a fine education and married Dr. Yamaguchi, man of sterling character with whom she had five lovely daughters. She would need all the strength she had from that background to help her through the trauma that she was about to undergo, the tragic death of Manami, the second of her five children. Manami, was a bright energetic young woman who enjoyed life and sought to taste and enjoy its blessings while she had the opportunity to do so before settling down to raise her own family. With great joy Manami had told her mother and her sisters that she was pregnant with her first child, and that she and her husband decided to take this opportunity to enjoy a winter vacation in Canada and the northwestern part of the United States. The young couple had been enjoying the area around Vancouver in British Columbia, but they had heard of the beauty of the skiing area in the United States, in Vail, Colorado and decided to take a side trip to experience its beauty before leaving to return home to Japan. They rented a car and set off on their trip south to Colorado. Everything went well for a while, but then they ran into snow and high winds in the mountains of southern Idaho. The exact cause of the accident has yet to be determined, but the basic fact was that the car slid off the road and overturned a couple of times before stopping in the middle of a big snowdrift. Manami, her husband and the baby she was carrying, all died in the accident. The news was, of course, devastating when the family was told. Hanako and the girls who had been so very close all their lives felt that their world had been shattered and their grief was very hard to bear. Kenji, perhaps because he was a doctor as well as Manami's father, could understand the details of the accident more pointedly, which only increased the depths of his pain. He took the death extremely hard and found it difficult to return to his practice for two weeks.

Not too long after Manami's death, and as some might say, because of her daughter's death, Hanako began spending many long hours pondering many thoughts. She often went back to the high school from which both she and her late daughter had graduated. It was comforting to walk through the pathways among the flowers, bushes and trees she had admired so much as a young girl. She also spent long hours conversing privately with her old friend and mentor, Sister Elizabeth. Sister, now retired from teaching, was a spritely and energetic 75 years old, wizened from her many years of listening to and counseling her young charges. Sister Elizabeth had ready answers and a clear explanation in response to Hanako's questions, but what intrigued her more was that the same spiritual harmony and inner peace that was so much part of Sister's life so many years ago was still there, prompting Hanako to probe even further, asking even more questions about God, the meaning and purpose of life, and so on. Where was all this leading her…?

One day when Hanako was especially quiet and very pensive, Kenji finally sat down with her and asked her to share with him what was troubling her so. "Mama, something is disturbing you; I can tell. After all these years together, I know you well enough to realize that there is something disturbing you. Won't you share it with me?" Even then it took a while for Hanako to sit down and discuss with Kenji all that was on her mind. "Papa, I need your frank opinion on what I am about to say. Yes, this has been on my mind for some time now, but I didn't know just how to bring it up for discussion. We have been together now for many years and I have always thought that we have had a very happy marriage. I don't want to disturb the beauty of our relationship in any way. So, yes, I have been troubled on how to approach you on this. But I am pleased now to realize your concern and your desire for me to share my thoughts with you. Yes, let us talk."

Hanako first prepared some tea and cookies so they could both be relaxed, and then she began her story. "For some time now I have been thinking of receiving Baptism and becoming a Christian. You know that as a young girl I went to a Christian convent school, boarding there during my junior and senior high school years. We even agreed to send one of our own daughters to that same school because the education was good and the atmosphere and way of life was very good also for young girls." Kenji was paying rapt attention to all that Hanako was saying which pleased her and bolstered her courage to continue.

"After Manami's death we were both terribly distraught, as you know. It took some time for you to get the courage to return to work. My own life was filled with all kinds of conflict, and I faced all sorts of questions about life, its meaning, our destinies and so forth. To help me resolve these conflicts I often went back to that convent school seeking the peace and serenity I once enjoyed there, just walking around its beautiful grounds, looking at the shrubs and flowers, listening to the birds as I tried to

141

understand and resolve all the thoughts that were troubling me so. I also visited the convent itself and spent many hours talking with my old friend and teacher, Sister Elizabeth. She is retired now, and so had the time to speak with me. We talked at length and visited their chapel to pray for a while. Each time as we parted, she told me that she would remember me and all my family each day in her prayers. All those visits consoled me very much. Gradually I desired to share the peace that was so much a part of Sister Elizabeth's life, and had been ever since I first met her. Finally I decided that I would take the step and seek Baptism. But first I would have to seek your approval because I love and respect you so. That is my story."

Kenji, although very much surprised at her story, was relieved both for her sake and his own, that her troubles had been resolved. He took her hand and calmly looked her in the eye as he quietly responded, "Hanako, my dear, our life has been everything you mentioned and more. You have given me much happiness, more than I can express, and I am so very grateful to you. Your strength has carried me through many tough times and your good humor has warmed my heart. Unfortunately I do not understand much at all about the Christian faith you are speaking of, but if it has helped you so much and given you such peace, I will not stand in your way. You do have my approval, and I will attend your Baptism ceremony myself. I wish you complete happiness."

Hanako was overjoyed and so relieved at Kenji's response to her story. Upon seeing the change in their mother's life, her daughters also were happy for her, but understandably somewhat perplexed because becoming a Christian was another world to them.

At the Easter liturgy the following year, Hanako Yamaguchi received Baptism and entered the Catholic Church. She took the Christian name, Elizabeth, the name of her sponsor and long standing friend who had had such an influence on her life from the days of her youth and had helped her so much in the dark days of pain and confusion after the tragedy of Manami's death. Present at the liturgy were her husband, Dr. Kenji Yamaguchi, just as he had told her he would be, her mother Sachiko Sasaki, her four daughters and their families, and of course, her dear friend Sister Elizabeth.

At lunch in a nearby restaurant, Hanako, very much relieved and beaming with joy, told her family that her conversion was not just something that happened late in her life, but something that she had always wanted to do. "God has always been with me, even from the time I was a little girl. I thank Mama Sasaki for allowing me to attend the Christian schools where I found God for the first time. I am convinced now that God was with me all through my life in ways I did not realize. When we lost Manami I was forced to face some hard questions about life and its meaning.

Those were very difficult days, but I especially want to thank Sister Elizabeth for helping me so much in coming to grips with my sorrow and in leading me through my pain to a loving and compassionate God."

Ultimately much of life is wrapped up in a series of choices we are all forced to make along the way. Sometimes those choices are made for us, hopefully by wise adults who are sincerely concerned with what is in our best interests. At other times there are generational conflicts such as in the "arranged marriages" which figured so prominently in the time of Hanako's youth. More commonly today are the choices which we must make individually, whether for good or for ill. It behooves us all to think things through, to seek the help of wise relatives and friends as Hanako did with Sr. Elizabeth when she was in the throes of conflict after the tragic death of her daughter. Taking it one step further, it is better still to turn in prayer to a loving and compassionate God who, more than we realize, is with us every step of the way throughout our lives.

Dr. Yamaguchi

----- The Country Boy -----

Kay and Minoru Takeuchi arrived at the office of Dr. Kenji Yamaguchi, head of surgery at the Hospital of the University of Waseda identified themselves to the receptionist and sat down in the spacious area for visitors to await their turn to be seen by the doctor. They had seen the doctor just two weeks earlier for a routine yearly examination for the famous conductor. What had started out as a quite ordinary routine examination, however, had turned into something ominous that revealed a spot on Mr. Takeuchi's right lung. That finding prompted today's return visit to the doctor to discuss whatever further procedures might be advised or necessitated.

As they waited, a secretary got up from her place behind the front desk and cautiously approached them, bowing respectfully before addressing Mr. Takeuchi and said, "I saw your magnificent performance the other night at Suntory Hall. Would you be so kind as to sign my program from the performance?" Director Takeuchi smiled as he signed her program in sweeping roman letters, "M. Takeuchi." The young secretary turned to Kay and said in English, "You too, please." Kay also signed the program directly under her husband's name, "K. Takeuchi." The secretary thanked them both profusely, then backed away all the while bowing profoundly. After returning to her desk she showed her program to the other secretaries who then shyly pointed out to one another the famous couple sitting across from them.

Not long afterwards, a nurse clutching a large brown manila envelope approached and said, "Dr. Yamaguchi will see you now." The nurse led them into the office where Dr. Yamguchi was standing ready to greet them. The two men shook hands. "Minoru, it's good to see you again," the doctor said. "Kenji," answered Takeuchi, "It's been a long time since our student days." "Yes indeed," said the doctor, turning to Kay as he replied, "we were in the orchestra together at the University. Even then you were a brilliant director." As if embarrassed by this adulation, Takeuchi turned and said, "You know my wife, Kay. She and your wife Hanako are friends. She teaches the cello to two of your daughters." "Yes, I know her. The girls speak very highly of her," answered the doctor. "I understand that she is, like you, a great artist." "Yes," answered Takeuchi, "she not only has great technique, but she also has the heart and insight of a great musician which are qualities which only the finest of artists possess."

As if on cue, the nurse placed the x-rays from the manila envelope on the lighted viewing screen and stepped back so Dr. Yamaguchi could examine them. With a pencil in hand, Dr. Yamaguchi pointed directly at a black spot on Takeuchi's right lung and said, "See that black spot? That disturbs me greatly. After your routine visit and chest x-ray last month, the technician who took the x-ray informed the resident doctor who in turn asked you to come in for a biopsy follow up. Fortunately, given your extremely busy schedule, you did come in as we requested." The office was quiet now, everyone's attention focused on the x-ray and the black spot. Dr. Yamaguchi continued, "The biopsy is inconclusive, which is both good and bad. It is good insofar as it indicates no full blown cancer is present there. But it is bad in that the spot is located in an area which often fosters the growth of a virulent or rapid growing cancer. Take a look over here at your x-ray from last year. See, the area is clear, no trace of a tumor. This year's x-ray shows, in that black spot, the presence of a small but growing tumor. My advice is to act now. When can you come in for surgery?" Takeuchi took out his cell phone and looked up his calendar for a free date. "How about the middle of next month?" was his response. "How about the first of next week ?" shot back the doctor in a firm and decisive manner. "No, that's not going to work," Minoru replied, "I have a rehearsal for a major performance the week after next and a conference with my agents in Kyoto following that; a week's delay won't hurt." "No," Kay broke into the conversation, speaking in her native English. "This is not the time to put things off just for business. We'll be here next week." She understood Japanese well enough, but in serious matters she fell back into her native tongue for emphasis. Before Minoru could raise an objection, she repeated. "No, no objections. Doctor, we will be here the first of next week."

When Kay and Minoru left the office, the nurse, ever observant of small details, said to the doctor, "You seemed like old friends." "Yes, we go way back," answered the doctor. "I was just a young kid, fresh from a Hokkaido fishing village, just entering the University, and thought I would try my skills with a musical instrument. I joined the University orchestra and that is where I met Takeuchi. He was, for all practical purposes, the head of the club. He was so brilliant even then that the teachers in charge deferred to him in musical matters connected with the orchestra. He directed most of the performances. I tried the clarinet and after constant practice, Takeuchi allowed me to play at a performance in my third year at the school."

After the nurse left his office, Dr. Yamaguchi sat back in his chair and allowed himself some time to reflect on his coming to the University and his meeting and friendship with Takeuchi. Even though he had come from a small village in the northern island of Hokkaido, Kenji Yamaguchi was brilliant enough a student to have passed all the requirements and entered the University on his first try. It was, however, the first time away from home for Kenji and he found himself very lonely. So mostly searching for companionship and friendship, he decided to join the orchestra. A secondary motive was to find out if he had any musical talent and could learn to play a musical instrument. One afternoon he went over to the hall where the orchestra practiced and shyly took a seat way in the back. Minoru Takeuchi, on the other hand, noticed him sitting way back there while paying strict attention to everything the orchestra was doing. So during a break he walked over and approached him. "Are you interested in joining the club? We're always looking for new members. We'll teach you to play an instrument, and if you are good enough you can play at one of our performances. Come on. It's lots of fun." Kenji accepted the invitation, and began taking lessons on the clarinet. As was the custom in the orchestra, a senior member began teaching him the basics, and in fact became his mentor, introducing him to more difficult pieces and supervising his progress. Kenji practiced very hard and his habit of total concentration in mastering both the intricate key work of the instrument itself and the demanding musical scores he was challenged to learn proved very beneficial to his progress. In his third year of preparation, Takeuchi judged him to be ready and allowed him to play with the orchestra in an actual performance. Elated with his accomplishment, he called home to relate the good news to his family. As he described the thrill he experienced in all that he had done, he had to pause to allow his mother to excitedly share the news with other members of the family, and he was rewarded to hear their clapping and squeals of delight echoing in the background. The teacher in charge of the orchestra told Kenji that Minoru was indeed a born genius who would go far in the world of music.

Now his old friend was facing some very serious surgery. Dr. Yamaguchi did feel confident, however, that Minoru would make it through the operation and recover well enough to continue pursuing his career, due in part to his practice of yearly checkups and to the prodding of his wife demanding that he put all else aside and concentrate his energies totally to defeating this threat to his life.

Dr. Kenji Yamaguchi was well situated to face the task confronting him. His native talent coupled with his driving force for perfection in the many facets of his profession drove him to the prestigious position he now held as the chief surgeon of the No. 1 Section of surgery in the Hospital of Waseda University. His demanding reputation preceded him in his relations with the nursing staff, and his cold stare when things did not go as planned was truly frightening, especially among the young nurses who considered his anger to be "kowai" (frightening). In truth, he relied heavily on his subordinates and his head nurse to be well prepared and to keep everything running smoothly during an operation. Any kind of confrontation with the members of his staff made him feel uneasy and he tried to preserve harmony at all costs. He had developed the habit of speaking indirectly in a Japanese way. For instance, he did not like to say negative things in a straight forward manner. For instance, "That nurse. what's her name? She is an interesting person," meant that he did not approve of her and she was soon transferred out of the department. Kenji was a master of oblique conversation and the head nurse was his chief interpreter. At times he would say, "You know THAT," and she usually understood what "THAT" meant. When she truly did not understand, she would say, "THAT? What are you referring to?" The doctor would get miffed at not being understood. At that point she would guess at what he meant and she was usually correct. The head nurse who was usually not in the least afraid of him often said to him, "Doctor, I get annoyed when you insist on using the word "THAT" in such a way. How am I supposed to know what 'THAT' means?" Dr. Yamaguchi would just laugh it all off and say, "You do very well as my interpreter. I'm not worried. You understand everything." And they both laughed as they closed up the office for the day.

In all his relationships with the office staff Doctor Yamaguchi projected the image of a typical Japanese leader. Authoritative, yes. closed off to others, no. In fact, his subordinates on the hospital staff called him "Bucho" (Chief). In their daily work in the hospital they often had frequent and even frank discussions. When Dr. Yamaguchi said "That's a unique interpretation," everyone knew that it meant that Yamaguchi and the speaker did not agree. "I'll check that out with my superiors," really meant "Forget it and stop pushing." Although Dr. Yamaguchi himself smoked only one cigarette during a conference (he was hardly a smoker), the package itself was a signal. When the discussion seemed to be over and there was a danger of going off on a tangent, Dr. Yamaguchi would pick up his cigarette package and put it into his top pocket. Everyone would get the signal and stand up; the conference was over.

Dr. Yamaguchi had learned the use of authority from the older doctors when he was young and new to the staff. He followed in that same tradition in dealing with his subordinates: be authoritative yet open, strong yet understanding with the young interns and nurses, aloof yet friendly to those close to him on the staff. This is the Japanese way, he thought. We understand it in our guts. For this openness to Japanese tradition, Dr. Yamaguchi was very much respected and loved. He was a master at leadership. Harmony, that's it. It all gets down to that, he thought.

Kenji Yamaguchi was born in a small fishing village on the northern island of Hokkaido. His ancestors had all been fishermen and the sea was in the family's blood. His father went out on a fishing boat sometimes for a month at a time in the summer while his mother worked on the docks sorting fish, putting them into boxes, pouring ice over them, and stacking the boxes on big trucks which rushed the fish to the big cities in less than a day. It was very tiring, and at times, very dangerous work, especially for those setting out into the cold northern Pacific waters with seas that could turn violent and challenging when storms came down with terrible force on the small fishing boats. Kenji was a favorite of his grandfather who had worked on the boats for forty years and was now retired. Grandfather Yamaguchi would very often take little Kenji on walks down to the ocean, talking all the while about life on the ocean as he described the harrowing life of a fisherman plying his trade out on the open water. In winter, his mother bundled Kenji up in a big jacket, a muffler, mittens and a Russian type woolen hat. Kenji looked more Russian than Japanese. When the ice on the ocean inlets was frozen, sound like pistol shots could be heard when the ice cracked. In the spring, large sections of ice would drift by silently, bumping into one another as they lazily meandered out into the open water of the ocean. In the summer, only the hardiest would swim in the cold water. There was really no rainy season that far north and the chilly days of autumn came quickly in early September. When the wind came off the ocean in great gusts, Kenji was frightened that he would be blown away. He used to huddle behind his grandfather to block the wind. "Don't become a fisherman, Kenji," Grandfather would say, "It's a tough, lonely and dangerous life. I don't miss it one bit. Let's find another job for Kenji."

Kenji's father had a reputation for being silent, a man of few words. He rarely spoke or showed his emotions. Yet he was a hard worker, a good provider for his family, and in his own way, a sentimental man who wanted only the best for his children. He liked to smoke a long bamboo pipe with a bowl as small as thimble at the end. Only a small bit of tobacco could be put into the bowl. So after a few puffs, his father would empty the ash into a tray and refill the little bowl. This simple pleasure was his favorite pastime. When Kenji was a baby he would often fall fast asleep on his father's lap. In later years, when his Dad was long dead, Kenji would recall those difficult times and the tough old fisherman with great esteem.

Kenji's mother was the heart of the family. Besides working on the docks, she was a typical, loving Japanese mother who took the children's education extremely seriously. When Kenji was in nursery school, his young teacher, herself hardly out of her teens, told Mrs. Yamaguchi that her little boy Kenji was "riko" (very smart). "This little boy will really go somewhere, I guarantee you that," she said with a foresight beyond her age. Mrs. Yamaguchi wanted to send Kenji to cram schools where the studies would be long and very difficult, but the young boy adamantly refused because he had an obsession with playing baseball. All his energy was devoted to his time on the baseball diamond. Normally such a situation would doom a young lad to lost opportunities in the classroom. But Kenji was no ordinary young boy. He was gifted with an excellent mind accompanied by a fierce determination to excel at school. Out on the baseball diamond he drew attention for both his hitting and fielding abilities. In primary school, he would play every chance he could with the older boys in pickup games. Later, in the more organized teams in Junior and Senior high schools, he played two positions: right fielder and relief pitcher. During his final year in high school he led his team, a small public school, to the Prefectural finals and a chance to go to the big high school tournament in Osaka. They did not advance too far in that tournament, but the fact that they even made it that far was a source of great pride in the little fishing village. When their game was televised, the announcer even mentioned that the fourth batter was also quite a scholar who would be taking the exam for Tokyo University in the following Spring. No one could believe that a boy who did not go to a famous private high school, who did not attend cram schools, who spent his entire spare time playing baseball, could even think of taking the examination for this prestigious school.

Kenji's secret as a scholar was his phenomenal memory and a very organized method of study. He had heard that boys in private school read current American magazines to prepare for the Tokyo University exam. So Kenji asked his mother if he could subscribe to TIME magazine. In addition, Kenji bought twenty six copy books, one for each letter of the English alphabet. When he looked up a word in the big dictionary, he would file it under the proper letter: anxiety went under the letter "A", while opulent went under "O", etc. At first he could not understand the American style of writing, but with perseverance he could guess at what most of the articles meant. In class, he memorized all the exceptions to the ordinary rules of English grammar. He also discovered that exceptions to the rules of grammar were to be found on every exam in the country. With that in mind, he studied old exams from prestigious Universities and found that many of the difficult questions were often repeated.

Mrs. Akasaka, his English teacher often said that Kenji was "a walking English dictionary." When she led the class in a translation of some English text, she would ask, "Right Kenji?" who would give her a thumbs up sign of approval. Painfully shy, Kenji would on occasion wait until after class to suggest to the teacher another translation of the phrases she mentioned in class. Kenji confided to her that even though he was confident that he could pass the Science and Math exams, he was definitely worried about his ability to pass the English exam. His teacher, who had never had a student who was so organized and so intent, just patted him on the shoulder saying, "You'll do just fine, Kenji, just fine."

When Kenji left on the long train ride to Tokyo for the exam, his mother prepared a big box lunch for him: "o-nigiri" (rice balls), sausage, fried fish, cucumbers, potato salad and pickles. Along with the box lunch, she also gave him a big flask of tea. His family walked along the station platform as the train pulled out, and his long trip to Tokyo began on a note of homesickness. His last view was of Grandfather standing at the farthest end of the platform waving his hat in goodbye.

After the exam was over, Kenji felt that he had passed. He called home and told his parents the good news that he felt he had done well. His mother, however, cautioned him. "We should wait until the results are finally posted." Kenji Yamaguchi, a boy from a small fishing village, did indeed pass the rigorous exam and was granted acceptance into the academic world of the University of Tokyo School of Medicine. After the results of the national exam were published, it seemed like only a few minutes before almost the entire village was at the door wishing to congratulate the family. Mother kept wiping away the tears of joy from her eyes, while Dad continued puffing away on his bamboo pipe, taking it all in, while deep within his heart swelled with pride at all his son had achieved. A few days later, after Kenji had returned home to a tumultuous village reception, he and his Grandfather took their customary walk along the shoreline. "You made us proud, Kenji, you made us proud," the old man said over and over again.

When classes got underway and life at the University began to take shape, Kenji's rural background and his accent from Hokkaido let it be known that he wasn't from the 'big city in-crowd' he initially wasn't fully accepted by some of those who felt his background wasn't suitable enough for them. But what they could not deny and had to accept, however grudgingly, were his achievements in the classroom and labs. He consistently out did them by his work ethic and the results it produced.

Now he stood somewhat at the pinnacle of his career and facing a daunting challenge: returning his close friend Minoru Takeuchi to good health. The evening after the examination of Mr. Takeuchi, Kenji was talking to his wife, Hanako, in the quiet of his study. He often openly and lovingly called her "Boss," all along through the many years of their relationship, he both admired and respected the many talents she showed in so many different ways. So he had willingly surrendered to her abilities and gave her full power in running the affairs of the household. "Maestro Takeuchi will indeed have to have an operation, and it will be a difficult one at that," the doctor mused, his mind mulling over which way to turn in his attempt to save Minoru's life and health. "Kay is so worried," said Hanako. "I know you will take good care of him. Your reputation is well founded. You were even trusted to operate on the Empress two years ago, and you pulled her through successfully." "Yes, my dear," Kenji said after some thought, "that's true, but. every operation is a separate challenge. If you've seen one tumor, you know it could grow into a hundred different kinds of cancer. Each one is different. Each one challenges you. Minoru's an old and good friend; I pray that all will go well," Hanako said encouraging him."

Kenji and Hanako had five girls who were the love of their lives. When the girls were young and the evening shadows had gathered it was time for bed. From upstairs would come the sounds of fighting and arguing, the usual chorus of young children taking one more chance to get in the last word before settling down for the night and Kenji would march to the bottom of the stairs and shout, "Quiet up there." For a brief space of a few moments there would be quiet and then the giggling would start. "Stop giggling and go to bed," he would say and they would all laugh. All the girls went to private schools and Hanako had to make five box lunches every day. She would lay out everything the night before, rise the next morning before six and make the lunches. The girls would descend in a last minute rush from upstairs to have breakfast before leaving for school. Of course, along with all the rush came the arguing, teasing and fighting before they rushed out the door to catch the school bus. Finally when all were gone and a quiet peace had filtered throughout the house, Hanako would pause to collect her thoughts and pour herself a nice cup of green tea as she relaxed and watched the morning news. Later she would sometimes say, half in jest, to her friends as they talked on the phone, "It's a war every morning."

Hanako, being a good wife and mother to her family, was always concerned with the health of both her husband and her children. The question was always how to achieve what she wanted in ways that were pleasant yet forceful, a bit humorous yet very serious. Sometimes, as in this instance when she was planning a much needed winter holiday for the benefit of the whole family, she would kind of trap Kenji into doing something that he really needed to do but which he otherwise would have kept putting it off, letting a precious opportunity for the family just slip by unfulfilled.

One evening as she and Kenji sat in the parlor watching television, the girls all gone to bed in their rooms upstairs, she turned off the TV and said to a surprised Kenji, "When you were away at the hospital one day, the girls and I had a family meeting and it was unanimous that when the girls are on the winter break from school, we should all go up to Hokkaido for a week of skiing to relax together for a few days. Kenji looked at his daily schedule, thought for a moment and said, "I'll think about it and give you an answer later." When the girls had all come home from school, Hanako announced, "Papa said he might like to take us all on a skiing trip to Hokkaido during your winter break, and we would all stay in the same hotel we so much enjoyed last year. Wouldn't that be great?" Of course, Kenji was no match for the sea of smiling faces and excited squeals of delight when he returned late from the hospital that evening. The following day, as they gathered for lunch, Kenji would "complain" to his fellow doctors of how his family was "ganging up" on him. "I'm outvoted on everything, six to one. Even Miki, who is only in kindergarten votes against me'. Everyone would laugh and joke about his predicament. "Hanako, my wife, she is always three steps ahead of me. I just can't win," was his feigned complaint in response.

One year, during their winter holiday break, when they were staying at a hotel with a hot springs spa, they were enjoying themselves very much while having dinner sitting on the "tatami" (mat) floor, Kenji got into his cups and waxed eloquently, "I'll never let any of you girls become brides. Never." Hanako and the girls laughed out loud. Then they took turns imitating him in fake deep voices, "I'll never let you go. Never." They became so raucous that the other parties in the restaurant were staring at them. In fact, as the years went by, Kenji would weep openly when each daughter became a bride.

Getting back to the subject of our story, Dr. Yamaguchi, in a very lengthy and tense operation removed the tumor from the right lung of Maestro Takeuchi. Much to everyone's relief, no traces of cancer were found in the surrounding area of the operation and the procedure was judged to be a complete success. Nevertheless, the ever cautious Dr. Yamaguchi recommended further treatments as a follow up.

When Kenji made his daily visit around the wards and private rooms, he was always followed by several interns and medical students intent on watching the master at his work. Dropping in to visit Maestro Takeuchi, now recovering and receiving post-operative care, Dr. Yamaguchi asked his patient, "How are they treating you, Minoru?" "Oh, they're just fine. Everyone is wonderful," Minoru answered. "I hear that all the nurses are asking for your autograph," Kenji continued with some concern. "I told the head nurse to speak to them about that." "Oh, that's okay. My right arm is just fine," said Minoru cheerfully.

When the time came for Mr. Takeuchi to be released from the hospital, Dr. Yamaguchi , the head nurse, and some young nurses were at the door to say goodbye. There were also some television cameras and reporters there as well. "Did you get good care while you were here at the hospital, Maestro?" asked a woman TV announcer. "Oh yes, Dr. Yamaguchi took very good care of me," Takeuchi answered. The announcer then turned to Dr. Yamaguchi. "Was the Maestro a good patient, Doctor?" she asked. "Very good," he replied. "And it was a pleasure to see my old friend once again," Dr. Yamaguchi answered as the interview ended.

Our story comes to an end in Hokkaido where it all began a number of years ago. Dr. Kenji Yamaguchi, chief surgeon at Waseda University's Medical School is standing at the water's edge looking out to sea, as his mind drifts back with memories of all that had gone by in his life since he left these very shores as a bright eyed youngster carrying a box lunch and a container of tea his mother had prepared for him to take along on the long train ride to Tokyo. It was a lovely summer day, and a gust of wind blew through his premature gray hair. Kenji recalled with nostalgia his many walks with his beloved Grandfather on this very beach. He saw the old fishing boat, "The Sea Gull" that his father had sailed on lying on its side, all warped and broken on the sand. A few minutes later he walked over to the docks where his mother had sorted fish. No one recognized him. "How's business?" he asked a woman who was sweeping up. "Fair, fair" she answered without looking up. Kenji had left a long line of fishermen to become a doctor in the big city in one of the best hospitals in the world. He thought of how fortunate and happy he was to have met Hanako who was so encouraging and so full of fun. And the girls!. They were always fighting, arguing and giggling with one another, but they were his girls, his family and he dearly loved them. Taking one last look around the harbor, he turned and headed home to Hanako, his hands in his pockets, the collar of his jacket pulled up against the wind, the trace of a smile on his face, and with a heart full of gratitude. Yes, life had indeed been good to him.

Miki

----- The Accidental Architect -----

Grandmother Hanako's grasp of the English idiom, even to the fine points of slang, was truly amazing, given the fact that she had never lived in an English speaking country. From childhood she had persevered in listening to American programs on the radio, and for many years had taken the tests offered by the sponsors. True, even though she had majored in English in the university and worked in an American bank after graduation, she always contended that listening to the radio was her main road into the land of American English, of which she now had a near perfect mastery. She even liked to converse in casual everyday English with her husband, Dr. Yamaguchi, who likewise spoke the language fluently said, "This guy is a real absent-minded professor," she said in English hoping that the people seated nearby in the benches would not understand.

He was referring to the groom, Taro, who was standing in the back of the Catholic church, waiting to walk up the aisle with her youngest daughter, Miki. Looking to the back of the church, she could see her daughter, Miki, adjusting Taro's tie which had become askew, and brushing his suit coat free of the dandruff scales which had gathered on his shoulders. Shaking his head, Dr. Yamaguchi responded , "You chose him, m'dear," with a deep grin.

Miki, her youngest and the father's most beloved daughter, was about to take the plunge into married life. She was thirty years old and as headstrong as Hanako herself. Taro was a full professor at Keio University. He had a doctorate in German from a German university. He was forty years old, had never married before, and was as out of it as any typically absent minded professor. But he was available and Hanako had worked hard to get him matched up with Miki. Actually, Miki took an instant liking for Taro. Taro himself was infatuated from the beginning with this vivacious architect. He had never really been in love before. As they say, he fell head over heels in his love for Miki. In this ship, however, it was clear to all who knew the couple who would be captain. She'll mold him like putty, Hanako thought. Japanese men don't want a wife, they want a 'Mama.' So for a mother who came from the old school of 'arranged' marriages, this one looked to be just about perfect, thought Hanako as she wiped away a few tears from her eyes.

As her wedding day approached, Miki had been adamant about two things: first, that her father would not give her away in the traditional custom, and second, she would not wear a veil to cover her face. "We are not children, Mama," she protested when Hanako tried to control the ceremony. Hanako had been terribly worried ever since Miki had turned twenty five that she would end up with a spinster on her hands.

Arm in arm, Miki and Taro began their walk down the aisle of the church. The ceremony was now about to begin. Papa's shoulders were shaking now and tears were in his eyes as he tried to restrain his composure. He was about to lose his beloved Mi-chan. As the couple passed by the parents' bench, Mama gave Miki a low V sign and Miki winked and nodded in response. With her last daughter getting married, Hanako felt that this important aspect of her own life as a mother was complete.

The first children born to Miki and Taro were identical twin boys, who were a delight to everyone in the family. In their youthful exuberance, they were a challenge at times to their parents, but the joy of the childhood innocence they possessed captivated the hearts of all. Three years later, the time had arrived for the twins to enter kindergarten. Grandmother Hanako had already decided on the place where the children would go. It was a Catholic kindergarten run by a lovely nun from Nagasaki named Sr. Kataoka. There were two other nuns on the staff who were teachers. Hanako zealously tried to influence her daughter and son in law to enroll the children in this Catholic kindergarten rather than a privately run, somewhat prestigious kindergarten located nearby. "There is a nun there," she told Miki and Taro, "who will give the twins a good balance of love and discipline. Just what the kids need." Taro, the boys' father, was leaning in the opposite direction. He pointed out that the kindergarten Grandmother was suggesting was in need of repairs and had no central heating. Miki herself was leaning toward an institution that taught the children math, English and Chinese characters. The Catholic kindergarten's attraction was a nurturing of the heart. Catholic prayers were taught, and a rather spiritual atmosphere would be experienced with a kind and loving care being directed in a very personal way by the manner in which the teachers related to the children in their charge. However, they did not prepare the young children as totally as the private kindergarten did. For many mothers this was an obvious minus. "They'll be studying their whole lives," Grandmother remonstrated, "let them enjoy their childhood. That's what wrong with today's system. It's all study, study, study. That nun from Nagasaki is right in allowing them to enjoy their childhood."

Miki was not convinced and with several mothers who were her friends, visited other kindergartens in the neighborhood. Miki had taken a leave of absence from the architectural firm where she had worked for eight years. Miki and Taro decided to have the twins, Shinsuke and Akira, meet with the teachers of the Catholic kinder-garten and another institution that taught the children to study. There was fierce competition to get into these kindergartens. The parents' thinking was that if their child was not accepted at one place, the possibility was such that he or she could enter another competing kindergarten. Such was the way of thinking and planning among the young Japanese mothers before their child ever set foot in any one of the schools.

The tipping point for the coveted entrance admission, as everyone realized, was the interview with the head teachers before the children were selected. Grandmother Hanako came to Miki's house every day with a bag of M and M's as she helped prepare the twins for the first big test of their young lives. "What is your name, little boy?" Grandmother asked. "Shinsuke Ito, and I'm three years old." That was the correct answer and as a reward Grandmother would give him an M and M. "What is your name, little boy?" She asked and the other twin would reply, "My name is Akira Ito and I'm three years old." He also would get an M and M. Miki became upset at Mama when she went through this game-like preparation exercise with the twins. It was understood between Grandmother and the boys that a wrong answer would mean no M and M reward. "Look at what you're doing, Mama. They will never pass the test. Stop giving them M and M's." Everyone was asking the twins their names and ages. When Taro came home from work, he would chime in as well. "What is your name, little boy?" And they would dutifully respond, "My name is Shinsuke Ito and I am three years old." "My name is Akira Ito and I am three years old." They even answered correctly to Grandfather when he asked them. After hearing this go on for it seemed weeks on end, Miki was convinced they were indeed ready.

On the day of the interview, when the twins were secured in their seats in the back of the van, Miki sat in the driver's seat and Grandmother Hanako sat in the front passenger seat. "Now Mama, don't make them nervous. You make ME nervous, Mama," Miki said in a high pitched voice. Without being asked, the twins began to shout at the top of their lungs, "My name is Shinsuke Ito and I am three years old." and "My name is Akira Ito and I am three years old." Once when they stopped at a traffic light, the twins were silent but Grandmother Hanako brought them to life again when she asked, "What is your name, little boy?" "Mama, puulease stop that," Miki interrupted in a commanding voice, "You're all getting on my nerves." But that did not stop the twins. "My name is Shinsuke Ito and I am three years old." "My name is Akira Ito and I am three years old." Finally, much to Miki's relief, they arrived at the kindergarten, and Miki noticed that the parking lot was already quite a bit filled with cars.

Inside, the hall was packed with small children and nervous young and anxious parents, complete with all the chitter chatter, crying and all the attendant noise that goes with such a gathering. After registering, the Ito twins were scheduled for a personal meeting with the principal of the kindergarten and the chief teacher in one hour's time. Six teachers from the school were sitting on the floor, playing with the children while at the same time observing them and taking stock of their readiness for kindergarten.

All the children were tired and uneasy with all the new surroundings and so many strangers everywhere, so it didn't take long before some squabbling broke out. Shinsuke pushed a little girl and followed this up by calling her "baka" (stupid). The little girl's mother glared at Shinsuke in red hot anger. "Oh, I am very sorry," Miki said in apology as she shook Shinsuke. "Apologize to the little girl," Miki ordered. "I'm sorry," Shinsuke said, but the little girl continued to sniffle and the mother continued to glare at the boy. Akira next piped up, "Mama, I have to go to the bathroom." Miki was fearful that he would not make it in time and raced with him to the bathroom in the back of the hall. She had prepared two sets of underwear in case something like this happened. When they returned to their seats, only a few moments went by before Shinsuke said, "Mama, I have to go the bathroom," Again Miki rushed with the boy to the bathroom. When they came out and returned once again to their place, another little boy was standing there, and having noticed that Shinsuke and Akira were identical, he said to his mother, "those two boys look alike." The mother answered, "Yes, they are twins." "What are twins?" the little boy asked. "That means they were born at the same time and look alike," the mother replied with great patience. The little boy broke away from his mother and ran over to where Akira and Shinsuke were seated. "You twins?" he asked. Shinsuke shoved him and said "baka" (stupid). Before this new encounter could continue any further, a young teacher approached them and said, "Master Shinsuke and Master Akira will be next in line. Come this way." It was the ultimate moment of truth for the two little boys.

"What is your name, little boy?" the nun asked Shinsuke. There was a long pause and Miki nudged him with her elbow. "What's your name, little boy?" the nun asked again. "I dunno," Shinsuke replied. Miki's chin dropped. Turning then to Akira, the Nun asked, "What's your name, little boy?" "I dunno," Akira answered. "How old are you?" the nun asked. "I dunno," they both answered. Again Miki nudged them with her elbow. Then Shinsuke got up and hid behind Miki. Seeing that, Akira also got up and hid behind his mother. "Bachan, baka," (The old lady is stupid), Shinsuke said, and then Akira repeated his brother's phrase, "Bachan, baka," much to Miki's embarrassment.

When the twins were seated again in their proper chairs, the nun said, "Let's talk. Are you happy about coming to our kindergarten?" Shinsuke heaved a deep sigh (the twins were great actors) and said, "Well, I dunno, Papa says this place is all broken down and has no heat." Akira sighed too and said, "Yeah, and Mama likes the place down the street where they teach you to read." "Well, how about you?" the nun quizzed. This time Akira sighed and said, "It all depends on Grandma. She decides everything." "She does, does she?" said the nun, and then added, "Oh, I know Grandma. She gave us a great big box of castella, a pound cake delicacy from Nagasaki. She is so nice." Miki, who was by now completely disappointed over the twins' performance, was now furious at Mama for interfering. Shinsuke huffed again,

"I think Grandma will cry if we don't come here." "Well, we wouldn't want Grandma to cry, would we?" the nun replied. "Yeah, maybe," said Akira, "we go to church with her sometimes and it is real boring. There's this little fat guy who is all bald, and he talks and talks. Grandma likes him, though, and gives him cookies." Miki was just about at the end of her rope and was looking for a small place where she could hide. "Well, that is all for now," said the nun, and turning to Miki she said, "They are so cute." "Yes," replied Miki, "and so bad. Such chatter boxes." Miki was persuaded that the twins did not make it through to acceptance. Tears were in her eyes on the way home. "Mama, how could you go behind my back like that and give that cake to the nun?" They will NEVER let the kids in now." Hearing that the twins had done poorly in the test, Grandmother Hanako was extremely quiet. Of course, nothing could suppress the twins. "My name is Shinsuke Ito and I am three years old." "My name is Akira Ito and I am three years old." Too late, too late, thought Miki, as the tears rolled down her cheeks. It was a long ride home.

The following day, Grandfather, Grandmother, Taro, Miki and the twins were seated around the kitchen table waiting for word from the kindergarten. Miki, calmed down by now, could not maintain her anger at the twins because, after all, they were just babies. Looking back at all that happened, the whole experience was extremely funny and would remain the source of great family humor for many years to come.

It was indeed comical. They all laughed when Miki repeated her description of the whole encounter that had occurred, first in the waiting room and then with Sister Kataoka. She laughed at Mama and the cake episode as well. "And you, Mama, giving castera to the teachers! How could you?" "I was only trying to help, you know," Grandma answered. "Nagasaki people love castera. It's a Spanish pound cake that the missionaries brought over years ago." "Yeah, but it looks like a bribe," retorted Taro with some indignation. Dr. Yamaguchi spoke up in a mild but real defense of Hanako when he said, "Well, you know Grandma. She can't stop trying to help. She was born like that."

In the midst of their laughter, the sudden ring of the telephone startled them, especially when they realized this may be the call from the school. They all listened intently as Miki rushed to the phone and answered, "Hello. Yes, this is the Ito residence….Yes, Sister, thank you for the call." Miki continued in a VERY nervous voice. "Yes, I understand. Thank you for calling." Miki put down the receiver and then ran over and hugged the twins. "You did it. You did it," she said excitedly and then hugged Taro, Grandma and Grandpa. "We did it. We did it," Grandma said, and then checked herself. "I mean, THEY did it. They did it." Happiness is passing the test into kindergarten.

Before the orientation talk for the new students of the kindergarten, an Irish Catholic priest, Fr. Michael Harrington, gave a talk to the parents on being thankful for all the gifts they have received from God. Miki and Taro were both in attendance. Miki whispered to Taro, "The must be the little fat guy who is all bald and who talks at length that the twins were referring to." In fact, Fr. Harrington was about five foot six inches tall and weighed over two hundred pounds. True to their description, he had hardly a hair on his head. As is the case with many foreigners, Fr. Harrington spoke fluent but heavily accented Japanese. In fact, his talk turned out to be very good. Both Miki and Taro were moved by the priest's presentation with frequent mention made of Japanese culture. Miki recalled now with affection the way the twins had described Fr. Harrington: "A little fat guy, all bald, who talks a lot." He taught English to the children and was very popular with them. He always started out his introductory talk to the new children by saying of himself, "The children all call me 'Fats'," which always got him a good laugh from his young audience.

As part of the orientation talk, Sister Kataoka mentioned to the parents that the Board of Directors was entering into a building program to improve the school and its facilities. According to the master plan, the present structure would be torn down and replaced with a more modern building which would include both heating and air conditioning. She said that very soon the Board planned to put the design of the building out for competition to four or five architects. The Board of Directors would then choose one design from among those submitted as the winning design for the new kindergarten building. Immediately, this talk of a new building and its design being submitted to architectural competition struck a responsive chord in Miki's imagination and interest because she herself was a professional architect and would be overjoyed to have the opportunity to enter the competition and submit a design. She felt very strongly that she was up to the challenge and could submit a design the Board of Directors might like. When she returned home, she right away phoned her architectural company where she worked and told them about this coming opportunity to design and build the new kindergarten. The president of the company said that as a firm they were not interested in this type of construction, but that Miki herself was free to present a design if approved by the Board. Miki immediately talked over the opportunity with Taro, Grandmother and Grandfather. Taro, perhaps trying to avoid disappointment or even failure for Miki, took a very negative position and tried to dissuade her from making any attempt to secure such a challenging commission. Grandfather was encouraging, but felt that the Board of Directors might have objections to a member of a family with children in the kinder-garden being so fundamentally involved in the construction of a new school. "It may be too delicate a situation. I am sure myself that you could do it, but the question is, would they accept a parent of a child in the school undertaking such a plan." Grandma Hanako, on the other hand, was delighted and fully supportive. "Go for it, Miki, go for it. You can give it a woman's and a mother's perspective." Miki herself was somewhat apprehensive, not so much at the challenge of the project itself but at the timing. The twins had just been accepted for entrance to the school; they hadn't even so much as attended class there yet. She felt it might be too presumptuous at this early date for her to meet Sister Kataoka and ask her for permission to present her own concept for the new building.

One day, for other reasons, Miki received a phone call and was asked to come to the school. It was about two weeks into the school year when the call came, and Miki became very apprehensive right away. This was all new to her and she did so want everything to go smoothly, especially after that rocky beginning on the day of the interviews for registration. Sister said that she and the twins' homeroom teachers would like to have a word with her as the mother of the twins. Miki immediately thought the worst and feared that somehow her two boys had wound up on the wrong side of the law and were in trouble at school.

After a rather apprehensive drive over to the school, a very jittery Miki Ito was met by Sister Kataoka, the principal and the two homeroom teachers, Keiko Sensei (Miss Keiko) and Atsuko Sensei (Miss Atsuko). Miki recognized right away that these were the first names of the two teachers because that was the way they were addressed in the classroom situations with the students. The four women then retired to the principal's office where they were seated at a table with Miki on one side of the table and the principal and teachers facing her. It was not a comfortable situation, but the tension was relaxed somewhat when Miki observed that the two young teachers, barely in their twenties, were looking down with their faces, but Sister was wearing a very gentle smile on her face and seemed relaxed rather than angry or upset. "The twins are so cute and so popular. Everyone loves them," Sister said. "Yes, replied Miki, "and I am sure have been up to something. What did they do?" Miss Atsuko began by saying that Shinsuke had discovered a way of opening up the teachers' supply cabinet and examining all its contents. He singled out the super glue which had been put up on the top shelf for security's sake. Fascinated by what it could do, he then spread the glue on the teacher's classroom chair. When she sat down, she became stuck to the chair which, of course was embarrassing enough, but then she had to hobble with the aid of another teacher to the teachers' study room to get help. Fortunately she had another skirt out in her car which was brought to her so she could continue her classes for the rest of the day. "I scolded him severely and he began to cry," Miss Atsuko said. Miki immediately stood up, bowed profoundly and said, "I am so sorry. I am so sorry. I will pay for your clothing. I will talk to him at home and explain to him that this kind of activity is totally unacceptable." Tears came to Miki's eyes as she turned toward Sister and said to her pleadingly, "You are not going to put him out of the kindergarten, are you?" "Of course not," came Sister's reply, "If we sent children home who were naughty, we would not have a kindergarten." After a moment of quiet, Miss Keiko spoke up. Now it was her turn. "Mrs. Ito, I too have had a problem that we need to discuss," she began. "Akira somehow got up on the roof the other day and could not get down. We don't know how he got up there. But we ourselves just could not get him down. It was just too dangerous. We had to call the fire department which sent over a special emergency squad to get him down. The fireman and I both scolded him. It was very dangerous. He could have been killed." Again Miki stood up, bowed profoundly and apologized, "I am so sorry for their conduct. We will reprimand them both severely at home. I am so embarrassed." When they came out of the office and went into the teachers' room, the twins were sitting there with their heads down. Miss Atsuko and Miss Keiko both hugged the children. They all began to cry. On the way home in the car, Miki was completely silent. "Mama is angry. Mama is angry," the twins finally whispered to one another, sensing correctly that were going to get punished once they got home.

Taro was very embarrassed because he himself was a teacher who naturally wished only the best for his children as they took their first steps on the ladder of education. Like so many adults, however, he had his own experiences with the often rude behavior of the students in his University, and would at times find himself saying, "These kids today have no restraint. They text each other even during class!. It's the families!." But this was different. This was trouble right here in River City. Taro and Miki took turns in lecturing the children and decided that as punishment for their bad behavior they would not be allowed to return to the kindergarten class for three days, and also that it was only appropriate for them on their return to each make a public apology to their classmates. The twins loved going to kindergarten and their homeroom teachers so much that for them, this was considered a great punishment. "We'll be good. We'll be good. Honest," they both said almost with one voice. Miki uttered one more and final admonition, "If you are not, they will put you out of the kindergarten. Do you understand that?" She was furious. "When in doubt," Grandma Hanako counseled Miki, "bow profoundly, apologize and give Sister a big box of castera" Miki had been thinking of a way to properly mend fences with the faculty at the kindergarten and listened eagerly to her mother's advice. "You can never go wrong with an apology and a box of castera" the elderly lady said. Hanako's words came from her heart and from the many experiences she had resolved in her lifetime. And so it would be. Miki, encouraged by her mother's wise advice, went to the nearby cake store which was well known in the neighborhood for making the special pound cake called castera which was very popular in the southern Island of Kyushu, especially in the Nagasaki area. As soon as she came back from the store she called the kindergarten and arranged for a meeting with the principal, Sister Kataoka. "Just maybe," she thought, "I might use this opportunity to suggest offering my idea for the new kindergarten."

Sister Kataoka invited Miki into her office so they could talk privately. She was very appreciative when Miki presented her with the box of castera, and bowed slightly in recognition for Miki's thoughtfulness. As Miki took her seat, Sister took a moment to prepare and serve some tea, which eased the tension in the room. "My husband and I are so embarrassed by the conduct of the twins," Miki began, giving a deep bow. "He is a teacher by profession and was expecting much better of the twins. He was very angry with them," she continued. "The two home room teachers are so kind. The twins love them." "Please do not worry, Mrs. Ito," Sister replied. "They are so cute and are very popular with their classmates." "Oh, I was so mortified when I heard of their escapades from the teachers," Miki said in reply.

Sister Kataoka went on to say that she had entered the convent at an early age. "My dad was killed in the Burma campaign and my mother died in the bomb. My brother and I were raised in an orphanage. I joined the same Order of Nuns when I finished college." As Sister was relating these facts about her early life, Miki couldn't help realizing that only close friends are given insight to one's private life. This was something that Miki was quite unprepared for, yet something that touched her very much, and she felt a great touch of affection for this nun who had evidently known considerable suffering in her life and was now sharing some of those emotions with her.

There was a long pause as they both considered momentarily how their two lives, so altogether different in their respective beginnings, had now converged in the one same effort of getting these two little energetic boys off on the right track in life. Miki sensed that this might be the moment to change the subject by tentatively presenting her proposal about submitting a design for the new school, and so she said, "At the orientation ceremony, Sister, you mentioned that you and the Board of Directors were going to put the design of the new kindergarten out to four or five architects, asking them to submit their respective plans for your consideration." "Yes, that is so," Sister replied. Seeing the opportunity open up before her, Miki took a breath and made her proposal. "Sister, the reason I mentioned this is that I am an architect myself with some degree of experience in the field. I have a whole host of ideas and suggestions that would fit in well with your needs. Do you think the Board of Directors would allow me to submit a design for the new kindergarten?" Miki asked with great concern. Sister put her head down and thoughtfully considered Miki's offer before answering with some questions and observations of her own. "If you are not selected, how would that be? Would you be angry? Do you feel there might be any objections against you by some who would accuse you of having a 'conflict of interest' by obtaining a contract like this while your own children are students here in the school? Some Board members might well object to your getting the contract on that basis. Tell you what, I will put your request before the Board at our next meeting and see what happens. I'll get back to you and give you an answer." With that, their brief meeting in Sister's office came to a close, and for Miki the long period of waiting for an answer began. As she drove home, she felt that her chances for success were indeed slim. Time would tell.

Later that same week, Miki dropped in to spend a few moments with her mother and met Mrs. Charlotte Carpenter, an American interior designer, who was visiting with Grandma Hanako. Miki had heard of Charlotte's late husband who had been a highly respected architect in America. In the course of their conversation Miki mentioned to Charlotte about her dream to build a new kindergarten for the school. Charlotte gave her what turned out to be a splendid piece of advice. "Did you ever think of building all in wood? You could import wood from Canada at low cost which could be then incorporated into your design and give you a building that would be very appealing to the Japanese. The Canadian Embassy would be glad to give you contacts with architects and builders in their country who would give you all the information you need on imports and design. My husband and I often used imported Canadian wood in our work, and with the proper skill and attention to detail, the results were always very attractive and appealing.

It wasn't long after that when Sister Kataoka called to say that Miki had been selected by the Board after much discussion to be one of several architects who would be invited to submit a basic design for the new kindergarten. After further evaluation by the full Board at their next formal meeting, a winning design would be chosen from among the several offered for consideration. Miki recognized immediately the name and firms of the other architects against whom she would be competing. They were well known, some of prestigious reputation. This would indeed be a fierce competition. She would have to come up with some technical and artistic designs to win this competition.

Miki called the Canadian embassy the next day as Charlotte Carpenter had suggested, and received a very favorable reply. Their country had been blessed with many natural resources, of which good strong hardwood trees excellent for building were among its very best assets. The Canadian embassy was advertising and promoting the sale of this lumber and even had a list of importers whom Miki could contact. The Japanese assistant at the embassy who was in charge of imports from Canada highly recommended a Mr. Michael Brown who had imported large quantities of Canadian wood which he used in the construction of many buildings throughout Japan. Although he himself was not an architect, he had many good ideas which he offered to Miki as a result of his having worked with many architects in the rebuilding of Japan after the war.

Michael Brown was the son of a Protestant minister and was born in Japan. He attended Japanese public schools and was therefore, quite fluent in Japanese. There was not even the trace of an accent in his superb Japanese. Michael was delighted to hear from Miki and listened with great attention to her proposal. The use of Canadian lumber in its construction, he thought, would make it very solid throughout and would give it a unique appearance, certain to attract the attention of young parents seeking to place their child in a kindergarten of some distinction.

They met later in his downtown office where they began to outline in great detail all the features they wished to incorporate into the new facility. Miki's basic design called for the kindergarten to have a high ceiling throughout, wide corridors, and plenty of natural light from the outside. In addition, it would have a teachers' room that would overlook the whole site for safety and control purposes, a large hall for assembly purposes. Special features would include a kitchen for the mothers, modern bathrooms, and ramps instead of stairs. The entire facility would be housed on one floor with a large wrap-around outdoor deck as seen in many American homes. Michael also told Miki of modern advances in technology for in-floor heating and air cooling sufficient to handle the climate changes on a year round basis. These latter two suggestions by Michael appealed greatly to Miki and she insisted they be incorporated into the final design.

In the matter of actual construction of the building, Michael also had some very practical suggestion, some of which would be very worthwhile and also cost-cutting measures that would please any Board of Directors. For instance, Michael told Miki that there was a company in Canada which cut wood by precision computers far more precise in measurement than anything previous. They would ship the wood already precisely cut to Japan in large protected containers which could then be assembled on location exactly according to pre-cut measurements. Canadian engineers would be necessary to put in the foundations with Japanese carpenters assembling the building itself. Michael estimated from previous work he had done that such a procedure in their case would save them about one third of the cost. From a thorough examination of the property lines, and after a close examination of the square footage available, they were able to determine that it would be able to construct the new building on a slightly different location than the present structure, thereby enabling much of the old school to remain in use during construction, and opening up the use of two fields where the children could play. One additional benefit, never before utilized proved to be of significant value once the property was laid out in its new configuration. Fortunately, right after the war when the nation was just getting back on its feet, the nuns purchased a large piece of property which was then selling for a low cost. A lot of that land, still owned by the Sisters but never developed, could now be paved over and become a fairly large parking lot for the teachers and for those families bringing their little one to the kindergarten. This would be a big attraction since many kindergartens did not have enough property for such a luxury. Together they had a model made of the new building located in an in-scale drawing of the whole complex. One could take the roof off the model and see the floor plan from above. The whole master plan gave the impression of a building set back from the road with plenty of parking spaces and a large field for the children to play in. Miki couldn't be more pleased, and confidently submitted her plan to the full Board of Directors for their evaluation and judgment.

SUCCESS!!! WE WON!!! WE DID IT!!! JUBILATION ALL AROUND!!! Miki and Michael, Dr. Yamaguchi Sensei and Hanako, even the twins were all excited and thrilled when Sister's phone call came to announce the approval of Miki's design for the construction of the new kindergarten. Sister herself went on to praise the plan for its being both functional and artistic at the same time.

Now they had to produce! While Grandma Hanako watched the children after school and at other hours, Miki and Michael worked ten hour days on the plans. Recalling other encounters he had experienced with government agencies, Michael informed Miki that sometimes city and prefecture officials were very demanding before giving permission for building permits. The fire department especially, would be very demanding, and rightly so since the lives of children were at stake. Michael, in his previous work, knew the people on the city level, but he had not had many dealings with the prefecture office where the educational department was found. Miki decided that she would take that challenge on herself. Fortunately, the lady in charge turned out to be a woman around Miki's own age with small children at home. Coming from a similar background, she was open to understanding Miki's plans since she herself had similar concerns regarding her own children. The two ladies got along well which made everything go smoothly. The corrections demanded by the prefecture were reasonable and able to be accommodated without too much of a problem. It wasn't long before the full approval was issued and construction was allowed to begin.

Four Canadian engineers appeared shortly thereafter to begin examining the property in great detail and laying the foundations for the new building. It took about a month's time. A local construction company was hired to assemble the building itself. First, however, a considerable amount of time was spent with officials and foremen of the company to be certain that they were fully aware of the need for the absolutely precise alignment of the various pre-cut sections of the building soon to arrive from Canada. While Michael focused his attention on the external and physical parts of the construction while Miki focused her attention on the finer details of the interior and the needs of the teachers. The insights and recommendations coming from the teachers proved to be invaluable and were welcomed by both Miki and Michael. They wanted spotlights for the stage in the hall, and an outdoor speaker system for the days when the children played outside and for the day when the annual field-day was held. They were especially concerned about the type of bathrooms they wanted for the children. Slowly the building arose and drew sidewalk spectators from all around the neighborhood. The windows, doors and heating system arrived on time from Canada. The foreman of the construction company listened patiently to all their concerns and desires and tried to implement them whenever possible. He explained with great patience what could or could not be done under the contract. This gentleman was a man of great experience and one of the best in the company. And he knew how to deal with people effectively and politely. He was very deferential towards Sister Kataoka and tried to accommodate her wishes whenever possible. In fact, he was taken quite by surprise regarding her knowledge of construction details.

In less than a year, the building was nearing completion with the dedication ceremony only a month away. The Japanese are very conscious of ceremonies, and this new kindergarten was no exception. Sister Kataoka and her staff at the school worked long hours preparing the sequence of events that would take place at the dedication. The Catholic Bishop of the diocese was invited by all means, and he would bless the new building and say a few words. Gifts and awards would then be given to Miki Ito, the architect, the importer and principal advisor, Michael Brown and to the president of the construction company. Each in turn would give a short speech upon receiving their awards. Speeches would also be delivered by the Minister of the Prefecture, speaking for its Education Department and by the President of the Private School League. The President of the Board of Directors spoke on behalf of all the Board who were there with him on the stage. The Provincial of the Catholic Sisters then spoke for the Community of Sisters, and last of all, Sister Kataoka would deliver her message of appreciation and praise for all the parents and staff for their considerable efforts of support.

Of course, this was a day of special importance for Miki who had designed the plans for the new structure and who had engineered its construction from the ground up. She was feeling great that day, proud of what she had accomplished, and sure now beyond all self doubt about her abilities as an architect. Her speech reflected that new found self confidence, and so she told the audience in a light hearted manner of how badly the twins had acted on that first day and interview with Sister. She thought a the time that the twins had utterly failed, but that Sister in her kindness had allowed them to enter even though they had called her "Baka," (Stupid.) "If the twins had not been allowed to enter, I would not be here today," Miki said with gratitude in her heart. She then went on to thank Sister also for giving her a chance to present a model for the design of the new kindergarten.

Sister Kataoka, when it came her time to speak, praised the design of the new building in glowing terms. "It's far and away beyond my dreams," she said. She went on to say that the twins, far from being intentionally fresh, were genuinely fine little

167

boys to whom she had taken a great liking. "They are a bit mischievous, to be sure…," she said, bringing a laugh from the section where the teachers were sitting.

"I won't go on to tell you about their boyish escapades," she continued, "let's just say that this is the era of the Ito twins." With that, the teachers all clapped and the audience laughed. "Their mother," Sister continued when the laughter and clapping died down, "is so very artistic. Truly, without her vision, we just would not have this beautiful new building. Just look at it, beautiful in its design, all in Canadian wood, and dedicated to God's glory. Thank you, Mrs. Ito; thank you Michael, and thanks to all those who worked in building this magnificent structure. Well done!!, Well done indeed!!" When Sister descended from the stage, she went directly over to Miki and embraced her. They both cried in each other's arms. With that, Shinsuke rushed over to his teacher and excitedly said, "Mommy always cries when she's happy."

Later that same year, Miki received an award from the Canadian Embassy for her artistic design of the new kindergarten. The building was featured in both Canadian and American architectural magazines. It goes without saying that her smashing success in this her initial venture in the field, opened many a door to further invitations to offer designs in architectural competitions. Miki was now a bona fide competitor in her chosen field.

At the first graduation ceremony in the new building, the twins were in the first commencement class. "Master Shinsuke Ito," the teacher called. "Here," Shinsuke answered and proceeded to approach the Principal and receive his diploma. "Master Akira Ito." "Here," Akira responded and he too walked up to the Principal to receive his diploma as well. Gently releasing a sigh of relief, Miki thought to herself as she recalled the near total misadventure of their registration day, they have indeed come a long way. Looking across the aisle, she caught Hanako's eye and flashed a big smile. Hanako smiled back in return, slipped her daughter their common 'V for victory' sign and thought to herself, "I came here this morning to witness the twins take a big step forward and graduate. That they did, and I am so proud of them. But their mother graduated as well, from being a young, uncertain, untried, untested architect into a shining example of professionalism at its best. and I am so very, very proud.

Ai Kataoka

------ The Nun -----

I am writing this from my hospital bed in the hospice section of St. Francis Hospital in Nagasaki. I was put under obedience to do so by my Provincial who wants to gather material for the history of our Congregation. I am reluctant to put my personal feelings on paper since I have always been a very private person. I find it painful to recall my past life and some of the sufferings I endured. My name is Sister Luke in Religion. My family name is Kataoka, an old Nagasaki Christian name, which goes back, I'm sure, to Francis Xavier and the time of the persecutions.

There are hundreds in Nagasaki to this day who bear that ancient name. My first name is "Ai" which means Love in Japanese. My baptismal name, one I rarely ever use, is Theresa, named after the Carmelite Nun, the Little Flower, to whom my mother evidently had great devotion. I have one brother, Nobuo. My sister, Nozomi, perished in the bomb along with my mother. "Nobuo" means Faith in Japanese, and "Nozomi" means Hope. One can easily imagine my mother's deep faith as she named her children: Faith, Hope and Love. My father was killed in action in South East Asia when I was one year old. The atomic bomb occurred shortly after my father's death while in action.

I was still an infant when the bomb fell on Nagasaki. My brother, Nobuo, who was ten at the time, was attending school along with my elder sister, Nozomi. Nobuo survived, but Nozomi did not. Her body was never identified either. Nobuo recalls my baptism in Urakami church when he was a little boy. Of course, no records remain as the rectory where the documents were kept was burned to the ground.

According to Nobuo, they found me hidden under my mother's body two days after the explosion. Evidently, my mother noticed the flash and shielded me with her own body. The house collapsed on top of us. A search squad looking for survivors heard a baby crying under the debris. I was completely safe under my mother who was dead.

When people hear that I grew up in an orphanage, they feel sorry for me as one who never had a mother's love. What can I say? I was saved by my mother who had sacrificed her life for me. I have felt her love throughout my whole life and have always felt that she is very close to me.

I learned about my mother chiefly from Nobuo. He said she was kind and gentle, but she got very angry if they missed catechism after school. My mother, you see,

169

was a catechist at Urakami church. Her first name was Midori and she was called "Teacher Midori" by the children. She had them memorize the whole book as was the custom at the time. Someone once showed me a picture of my mother standing with some First Communion children. I think she was very beautiful and a woman of faith. She went to Mass every morning, washed altar linens and did other acts of service in the parish community.

My earliest memories are of the orphanage. I remember many young Nuns who wore a white veil. I learned later that they were Novices, and part of their training was working in the orphanage. They cooked our meals, gave us baths, took us on walks, and when we got older, observed our studies. People always ask if the Nuns were harsh or unreasonably severe, but that is not part of my memory. I remember we had to make our own beds, clean the floor, peel potatoes, wash dishes and rake leaves, but I have no memories of harsh treatment. The Novices were forbidden to eat anything outside of meals, and we came to trust them when they said, "We eat what you eat." The young Nuns would often hug us when we cried. Life was strict with no nonsense, but it was not harsh. I am indebted to those Nuns, and showed my affection for them by joining their Congregation.

My brother, Nobuo, hated the orphanage with a passion. I remember perfectly the day he turned sixteen and could leave the orphanage. He tried to take me with him. He put all my belongings in two big "furoshikis" (squares of cloth used for wrapping), took my hand and said, "Come on, Ai-chan, we are leaving this place." He was leading me to the door when the Nun in charge stopped him and said that he could not take me with him because he was not capable of caring for me in a proper way. When he tried to push the Nun aside, she said that she would call the police who would restrain him. She was right, of course. Nobuo hugged me for a long time, and with big tears in his eyes he promised to visit me every Sunday, which he did. When he married young, he went to the city office, did the needed documentation to become my legal guardian, and without a word of thanks to the Nuns, took me out of the orphanage and into his home. His wife, Emiko, became my second mother. Emiko was a practicing Catholic. They had their own children later on, my nephews and nieces, but I considered them to be my brothers and sisters. Once when one of the boys said that Ai-chan was not his real sister, Nobuo said, "We'll have no talk like that around this house. Ai-chan is your sister and don't you forget it!" It was never mentioned again. Instead, they called me "Neechan," (older sister.) I must have been 11 or so when I left the orphanage. My new mother, Emiko, enrolled me in a nearby primary school. At the time, before there was official privacy, all one's private life was written into one's family registration in city hall. So my homeroom teacher, Mrs. Matsuo, without saying so, knew of my background. My intuition was that she felt very sorry for me. I loved that teacher, Mrs. Matsuo, who had studied catechism under my mother in the old Urakami church. I was very close to her even until the time of her early death from atomic bomb sickness. She had been a young teacher just out of college when she was caught in the big explosion that turned everybody's life around. She survived, but many of her beloved students did not. She was under the debris for three days before she was rescued. She said she almost died of thirst. She drank a whole thermos of tea in one gulp. She died a few years ago in the atomic bomb hospital. I attended her funeral Mass and was invited to their home by her husband. I told him and their children how kind she was as a teacher and that we all loved her. Her husband handed me a little cup and poured sake into it. All her children did the same. We offered a silent toast to her memory.

When I entered Junior High School, I joined the volleyball team. We had to practice every day, even Sunday. Nobuo, who did not practice the Faith himself, insisted that I go to early Mass on Sunday mornings. Emiko often drove me to church and packed a box lunch for me. So I went to the 6:00 a.m. Mass and then went on to school for practice. I never missed practice even once, and was elected captain of the team in my third year at school. We had a strong team that year and went all the way to the Prefecture finals where we lost in a close game. We cried all the way home on the bus, hugging each other and taking responsibility for the loss. "It was my fault," each of us said repeatedly on that long ride home.

We treasured our friendships. Even to this day we continue our commitment to each other. We lived by the old rugby law, "all for one and one for all." Japanese schools at the time were treasuries of friendship. We still meet every couple of years in a Chinese restaurant and tease each other as we used to do when we were young. Someone called me "Sister Ai-chan" after I became a Nun and that name has stuck with me ever since. To my old friends, whenever or wherever we happen to meet, I am still called "Sister Ai-chan." Sadly, in today's schools one does not find the same sense of bonding. Instead, only too frequently one finds cases of bullying and even violence. As a result, many children fear, object and refuse to go to school. This was almost unheard of in our day even though there were some bad actors in the big cities. Friendship was the chief reason we went to school and were so happy to do so.

I had only one run-in with my brother, Nobuo, and this took place when I was in my third year junior high school. While we were eating dinner one evening, I casually mentioned that I was going to take the test for the public high school with all my friends. Nobuo dropped his chopsticks on the table and glared at me. "No, you are going to go to Junshin Catholic High School for girls. Mama would want that. Do you understand?" he said with a severity that stunned me. Now I am glad I went there. I loved Junshin in so many ways. Among other things I played volleyball under a great coach, a Junshin Nun, who had been a star player in her time. In my Senior year we went to the area semi-finals but lost. As difficult to accept as it was at

171

the time, we nonetheless enjoyed a good run in the play-off tournament. We had not been seeded, but after we knocked off two seeded teams, the local papers were watching and gave us a good write up. We thought the championship trophy might be ours to take home, but we stumbled in the final game and lost, a bitter pill for us to accept. Junshin had a Junior College attached to it and I applied to the Educational Department to get a certificate to become a teacher. At that time, I had not fully decided to become a Nun even though the thought was always in the back of my mind. I lived in a dormitory during my college years and used to say prayers and attend Mass with the Junshin Sisters. They pressured me pretty strongly to join their Community, but I told them that I was not ready to decide. I knew if I DID become a Nun, it would be with the group who had taken care of me when I was a child.

When I left college, I became a part time teacher in public Junior High Schools. The experienced teachers told me to be very strict on my first day and to get the attention of the students. They advised me to not show any weakness or else the children would take over and there would be chaos for a whole year. You can never get order back once you lose it, they said. So I started glaring into the mirror. "Nobody will mess with me," my face said. So on the first day of class, I walked into the room, slammed a book down on the desk and glared, I mean glared (just as I had practiced in the mirror.) "I want order," I said, "and no fooling around or I'll knock your head off." It worked. It worked. They all gave me a deep bow and sat down quietly. I never had any trouble the whole year, even with the boys who towered over me. The principal supervised my teaching one day and said later in the teachers' room, "Miss Kataoka's glare scares even me. I started bowing to her too." I taught Geography for two years at two different schools. Geography is dull, really dull, but I loved my pupils and never had any trouble with discipline.

I was 23 when I decided to join the convent. I was warmly welcomed by a Nun who had been my guardian in the orphanage. She remembered me. "Aren't you Ai-chan?" she asked and then hugged me. I felt at home. Sister said that I had been a quiet child, but that Nobuo was always trying to escape. "I'm sorry," she said "that Nobuo had such bad memories of the time. We were under strict orders not to be harsh with the children, but I guess we did not have enough warm love to reach Nobuo's heart which was torn by his tragedy." She went on to tell me how Nobuo hated the Americans. "After the war, Catholic GI's would come to the orphanage with blankets, towels, soap, clothing and food. Once when they came to give out ice cream, they handed Nobuo a big double-decker. Well, he took the cone and dumped the ice cream on the GI's shoe. "Why don't you take your ice cream and go home?" he said. When we translated for the soldier that Nobuo had lost his family in the bomb, the young GI reached out and tried to shake hands with Nobuo. "I'm sorry, kid, so sorry," he said, but Nobuo shouted, "Why don't you go home and leave us alone?" He then ran out of the room. Later, one of the Sisters took Nobuo aside and said that he must learn to forgive just as Jesus had forgiven on the cross. Nobuo shook his head and said, "That was Jesus and I'm me. I'll never forgive." So you see that Nobuo's problem was his deep seated anger. I must say that I understand Nobuo completely because I lost my family too. I have found it hard to forgive, and I am a professed Religious. Sister turned from me and she began to weep. Her body shook with emotion. Then, turning back to me, she said, "Think of all the people killed in other countries under our military. We are not without guilt by any means.

I wore a white veil as a Novice and had class every day with my Novice Mistress. There were ten of us in the class. We had Mass and prayers every day and confession once a week. We got up at 5:30 A.M. and had prayers and meditation before Mass. All the meals were taken in silence. We took turns reading from the Bible and Catholic spiritual books. You could get a scolding if you did not prepare the reading and stumbled through it. We had recreation outside where we could walk in the woods or play volleyball. We also had a short recreation period after dinner in the evenings. There was a lot of stress under this oppressive schedule. "Do your best and leave the rest to God. Stress is not healthy," Sister said. The tension eased and the atmosphere became more relaxed. Sister had so much heart and so much love. I think she was a living saint. "Let's find God together," she would say, "that's what the Religious life is all about."

After I professed my vows, I was sent by our Order to teach kindergarten in Tokyo. I served there for a few happy years until I myself, to my astonishment and concern, was appointed Novice Mistress.

I repeated exactly what I had learned as a Novice. I even used the notes of the previous Novice Mistresses. I lectured the young Novices on being calm and to not allow stress to interfere with their formation. I repeated to them what had been told to me, "Do your best and leave the rest to God." I reiterated to them the words my own Novice Mistress said to me, "Let's find God together."

I found that there were many pious women under my direction. I tried to point the way to them to find a solid prayer life. I told them how Jesus had emphasized above all the ideals of patience and perseverance in prayer. St. Paul wrote about yielding to the Spirit . Asian people in general, including we Japanese, have an innate sense of prayer. I'm sure it comes from our Buddhist background. I urged the Novices to sit on cushions or specially made kneelers to keep their spine straight and their breathing even. Japanese women flourish in this style of prayer, and I did my best to encourage it. My Provincial must have approved my methods for she kept me in that work for several years. I wrote a book on Japanese style prayer that was warmly received both in and outside the Church. The book was about traditional Catholic prayer said with a Japanese heart. It received a favorable review from a Japanese Bishop and sold many copies. Also it was translated into English, German and Korean. I wanted more than anything that my Novices find complete happiness in walking with the Lord as indeed I had found. That can only come about by a solid prayer life and complete generosity in the community. Prayer and generosity, they are the two keys to happiness in the religious life. We must have been doing something right because we continue to get vocations from every walk of life. I hear the Novices still feel stress as they begin their new lives with us. The period of formation in the Religious life is a happy, but difficult one at the same time in one's life.

I was sent back to Tokyo, this time to be principal of the kindergarten where I formerly taught when I was a young Nun. Along with the assignment, I incurred the responsibility to build a new facility because our old kindergarten did not measure up to the new laws the Japanese government had established. The building itself was in very bad shape and there was no equipment in the building for heating or air conditioning. Clearly I had a major task confronting me. We hired a young lady architect who put up a very fine building for us and kept it within our budget. She was still young at the time, and the innovative architecture she devised greatly advanced her career. She now builds throughout Asia and is known worldwide. It was a big undertaking, but we did it with the help of God. It is a tribute to modern Japanese architecture in both its design and Canadian wood structure.

Along the way I developed a bad cough that just wouldn't go away. My doctor had me take a series of tests in his attempt to find its cause. When he finally determined the cause of my problem, he met with me and revealed the bad news to me. It was difficult to accept at first, but my being a Nun with a strong faith in God enabled me to accept what was happening to me. The doctor's analysis which he shared with me was that I had developed a bad case of leukemia with a very poor prognosis. Many survivors of the bomb have come down with this special kind of cancer. I must say that I have never felt any degree of pain, thank God, but I am getting weaker and weaker with each passing day. Not too long ago I asked to enter the hospice in Nagasaki. The Nun who runs the hospital is an old friend of mine.

I know my time is getting short, and the end of my life is fast approaching. We Japanese like the word "reunion." It is our custom that at New Years and "O-Bon," (the time of the dead,) any Japanese who can do so, returns to his "furusato" (native town,) to be reunited with his family and visit the graves of his ancestors. "Reunion" is a word I love. It's so thoroughly Japanese. Naturally, as a Catholic and also as a Religious, I look forward to be joined fully with God's love and Divine Mercy. All my heart's desire is for that fulfillment I do not fear death. My human heart tells me to hang on to what I know and not to jump into the ocean of the unknown. In the end, like a trapeze artist, it will be for me, a "jump" into God's everlasting love. I pray every day for the grace to be able to make that "leap of faith."

I look forward also toward a "reunion" with my family, with my mother, father and sister Nozomi. That "reunion" will be a special joy for me. We will be together again, never to be separated from one another.

Nobuo and Emiko come almost every day to visit, and they bring fruit, cookies and yogurt. I tell Nobuo frankly that I am praying for him that he will receive the grace of forgiveness. I told him that he will never be free until he forgives, and that he will always be a slave to resentment. This morning, he squeezed my arm as he was leaving and said, "Not for God, not for Jesus, not for anyone will I forgive. But for my Ai-chan, my beloved sister, I will let it go. I will let it go. Maybe I'll find God again." This evening Emiko told me that Nobuo had gone to confession and received Holy Communion after all these years. They were turning out the lights here in the hospital at the end of visiting hours when Nobuo suddenly appeared at my door and came over to my bedside. He took my hand and whispered to me, "For you, Ai-chan, I have let it go." It was the answer to my prayers.

Signed,

Ai Kataoka
Sister Luke

Tadashi

----- The Sushi Master -----

"Shall I call you a cab, Mrs. Yamamoto?" Tadashi asked his customer who was sitting, slumped over, on the counter from her customary stool at the counter of his sushi shop. "It's 2:30 AM and I've got to close up. You know I have to go to the pier early tomorrow morning to buy fish." With a wet cloth, he wiped the brown wooden slab that served as his counter. Without lifting her head, Mrs. Yamamoto lifted her glass and slurred out the word, "another." "You've had enough already," Tadashi said, but filled her glass anyway with Suntory beer. "I hated that old bum," she said. "He made some illegal deals, but he just didn't care. He had a heart of stone." "'Everybody does it,' was his motto. Do you know why I stayed with him?" she continued to rattle on as she answered her own question. "It was for the money, yeah the money. I was gonna get myself a deal from that old guy. And it worked! I stuck it out with him till the end, but it paid off when his will was read. I came away with a very nice inheritance. I still hate the bum though…Another." Then she changed the subject. "Maybe I'll take off from here and move over to Vancouver. What do you think about that? For $300,000 over there, you can buy a three bedroom house with two bathrooms and a space for a garden. Here in Japan, you can't even get a decent condominium for that price." She held her glass and said, "Another".

As much as he felt sorry for Mrs. Yamamoto, drinking away her life one day after another and constantly harboring those negative thoughts about her late husband, there was at the same time an attraction to her that he felt in his heart. He himself was a widower, having lost his wife, Mako, just a year ago and was still feeling the pangs of loneliness that are so common to all surviving spouses. Mrs. Yamamoto was, thought Tadashi, still an attractive woman in her early 50's. She played golf almost every day and flew to Hawaii frequently with her rich girl friends to play there as well. Just this year, they all flew to Hawaii in February and returned to Japan in time to see the cherry blossoms in late March. Maybe, he thought, I might ask to take her to dinner some evening. After all, both of us are now alone in life, now that our spouses are deceased, and we could appreciate some companionship. I'll have to think about that.

Tadashi was up early the next morning, mounted his old bicycle and headed off to the pier where the ships had docked after a night of fishing out in the deep off Korea. He began his breakfast with some raw fish seasoned with a healthy helping of horse radish and some soy sauce which was prepared and sold right on the pier by the

177

fishermen's wives. A cup of near scalding hot green tea topped off the meal and gave him some warmth as well.

After he returned to his shop with his supply of fish for this evening's customers, he ate the second part of his breakfast consisting of some "miso" (fermented bean paste) soup and a portion of white rice. He finished off this second part of his morning meal with another cup of hot green tea, after which he got to work icing down the fish he had just bought to have it ready for his "guests," as he called them, when his customers would arrive that evening. Then it was time for a long nap before getting ready to open up his shop around 5:00 p.m. Once again his thoughts returned to Mrs. Yamamoto and her constant tirades against her husband, his shady business practices and how they both affected her life is such an unending way. That's no way to live, he thought, letting the past eat away at you like that and offering you no tomorrows, no hope for a new day. She should somehow say 'good bye' to those memories and try to start a new life.

Thoughts like this brought to light remembrances of his own marriage which almost broke apart over one incident that caused great pain to both him and his wife. Mako was her name, and many years had passed since they first met. At the time, Tadashi was working as an apprentice in another sushi establishment. He was working behind the counter learning the art of cutting and preparing the fish and spreading the rice just so with the fish in order to create a real delicacy. Mako was a regular customer for sushi and so got to know Tadashi over a period of time. On those occasions when the owner would correct Tadashi for mistakes he made in preparing or serving the sushi, Mako would tease him or make him laugh. They gradually got to know and like one another until their relationship developed into genuine love. Before long they were married, settled down and had one child, a daughter. All was well between them until Mako learned of a brief fling Tadashi had with another woman, a customer from the sushi shop who lured him into a relationship that was headed nowhere but for trouble. Mako, of course, was furious when she found out about everything and threatened to leave him. At long length they reconciled only to have Mako fall victim to cancer which took her life after a long and difficult struggle.

Now Tadashi was left alone with his thoughts, about love, about marriage, about what he was going to do with the rest of his life. "Let's face it," he said to himself one day, "life in the sushi world is tough. It's an art and I've mastered it, but it's the same thing, the same customers, day in and day out." Marriage, love and a home life were all appealing, but he had been badly shaken by the turmoil caused in his marriage to Mako by his infidelity. She had always wanted more affection, more open assurances of his love for her. But he was not one who could openly display his affection and true feelings; doing so had not been part of his early life as a child and he found it difficult to do so now as an adult. He just did not know how to show love and affection with ease and sincerity. "Love is a strange thing," he thought. "It is easy to receive love, but difficult to offer it to another." But it is part of life, and the desire to share his life with another was still strong within him. Could it be that now that he was older and more mature, that he might seek love and happiness once more, with a woman who needed someone to show her true love and affection, even if not perfectly? A woman like Mrs. Yamamoto....

After a midday nap it was time to rise, spruce up and then get to the shop to prepare for its 5:00 p.m. opening. Business has been brisk, especially in the last couple of years as word got around about Tadashi's skill at his trade. The title of "Master" was a coveted honor sought after by all sushi shop owners. There was no school or other formal preparation that qualified one to be called "Master." In the world of sushi shop owners, however, to be ranked by one's peers and by one's customers as "Master" was a distinction with a difference. It was a title that assured one of much respect in his trade, and financially made a significant difference in one's profits, even at times survival in the highly competitive world of business.

Tadashi was an expert with the long sharp knife used for cutting fish. He honed it every day prior to opening for business and kept it as sharp as a straight razor. It had taken him some five years to master the technique of cutting fish quickly, deftly and with a speed that attracted the attention of all his customers watching him prepare their orders. He could cut a red snapper with lightning speed. To finish the order, he would then take a handful of rice and squeeze it just so, adding it to the fish and completing the order, presenting it to the customer in a short ten minutes. They liked that. As they say in the business world, location is essential for one to succeed in business. Tadashi was fortunate in that regard for his shop was located in a location that assured him of a wide variety of customers. His shop was in the downtown area, somewhat near the docks, fairly close to a thriving business center and not too distant from a university. That allowed for a diverse mix of customers and provided for a rich interplay of chatter and conversation. While this never ending supply of sushi loving customers was good for business, keeping up with the pace on a daily basis was wearing on Tadashi and he began thinking seriously of retiring. Mrs. Yamamoto, his regular customer with whom he was developing a close relationship, had hinted strongly of her desire to escape from her past unhappiness and to start anew in Canada, a place she had found to be very attractive on her many vacations there. The thought of starting life anew, of sharing his life with someone he loved and cared for was very inviting. He'd have to think some more about this. Meanwhile it was 4:00 p.m. and while Tadashi was making his final preparations for this evening's customers, he turned on the TV and watched the sumo tournament as he worked. Two young ladies walked in and took a table near the door. They worked for the same company and were close friends. They were dressed very fashionably and their speech reflected a well bred and cultured background. They ordered raw fish and began drinking beer, pouring some into each other's glass as they chatted away. They obviously had just finished work and just wanted to relax, talk about the latest office and social news before heading home. After a while they ordered some sushi and some sake. When they had finished, Tadashi gave them a bottle of beer. "My father will scold me if I come home tipsy," said one of the girls. "Well, it's time you got your own apartment anyway, and got yourself some freedom," her friend replied.

Around 7:00 p.m. three professors from the local University came in. Two of the teachers were young and showed an undue amount of respect for "the chief," the director of their department. They lit his cigarettes, poured sake into his cup when needed, and seemed to be alert to every nuance their mentor was making as he continued talking. "We are most of all interested in providing a quality education and in attracting students of superior quality. Our graduates must be prepared to compete in a business environment of some first class companies. That is our mission. Internal school politics is not on our agenda," he said in a voice Tadashi could overhear from behind the counter and knew that it was a pretty picture of academics, but it really wasn't shot full of holes. Tadashi knew this director. He came in fairly regularly, always with new teachers in tow, supposedly giving them an idealized vision of life at the university. But Tadashi knew that it was politics, cliques and academic rivalry that really energized the chief. Talk at that table was all about academic politics. The chief complimented his protégés on their sense of responsibility and loyalty. It was obvious to Tadashi that these young teachers, like others before them, were drinking it all in and would certainly be advancing up the ladder under the tutelage of this man. As long as they would remain in this man's department, choosing the right clique would be their road to success. Shaking his head Tadashi finished wiping down the counter and moved on to wait upon other customers.

After 10:00 p.m. the stools at the counter and the two tables in the back were filled with people. At one of the two tables, the newscaster from the local TV station was seated with her retinue, a make-up artist, a secretary (both young women) and a male agent who was busily engaged on his cell phone. The announcer herself was charming. She was a graduate of a Protestant University in Kyoto. People from the area knew her quite well. She was a local girl who had done well and had achieved a degree of fame. Tadashi was an old friend of her father. In keeping with her status as a person of some prominence in the TV industry, she was watching her diet and was eating just a small portion of raw fish with white rice. Not only was she the anchor of the local news, but her channel had recently assigned her to do documentaries and personal interviews. Clearly she was a first class talent whose star was quickly rising.

As the evening wore on, just after 11:00 p.m., a detective, just off duty, came in, a man who Tadashi knew well as a frequent customer. You could tell he was tired; it had evidently been a tough night with some difficult calls. He told Tadashi that he had pursued some rowdy motorcycle gang members. There was quite a scuffle as he and his partner subdued three of them and arrested them for disorderly conduct and resisting arrest. "Clowns," he said, "Damn idiot clowns," as he wearily sipped some cold beer. "Then shortly after that," he went on, "we found a body in the river. Poor guy! He was suffering from depression, they told us later. Then the really tough part came, finding his family and telling them the bad news. Oh man, that's really rough. There's denial at first, then shock, screaming and crying, and a lot of confusion when relatives and neighbors come in to find out what happened." Tadashi listened intently and couldn't help but feel sorry for his friend, the detective. Suffering, death and the human condition were mysteries whose solution he could not comprehend.

As for his friend the detective, it was a tough, mean world out there, where he saw unhappiness every night. And the price he paid was great. Like so many others in many big city police departments, he paid a steep personal price. His marriage suffered, and then he wound up with a decree of divorce. Now he lived alone, devoted to his duty on the police force, but pessimistic in his view on life, at odds with his superior in the department and subsisting on sushi, sake and playing pin ball machines.

Mrs. Yamamoto came in after midnight. She liked to watch TV dramas at home during the prime time hours. After that came the 11:00 p.m. news and weather information on the local news channel. Then it used to be that she would take the brief walk over to Tadashi's sushi shop to drink and complain. Of late, however, a not so subtle change began to appear in her nightly routine. She spent more time, for one thing at the sushi shop, not just drinking and complaining about her former life, but just helping out when things were very busy and Tadashi needed an extra hand. They talked a lot too, especially in the late evening hours as she and "the Master" prepared his shop for the customers who would be arriving. It was his busiest time. Occasionally also, she would take her bicycle out early in the morning and ride along with him to the docks where he would buy the fresh fish that he would prepare and serve to his customers later that evening. Those early morning rides would also give them the opportunity to stop and have some breakfast together. It was apparent that through all these times together that this man, in spite of his lack of polish, was manifesting a real concern for her, trying to lead her away from the negativity of her earlier life to something better, something genuine that offered an inner peace. She found a growing affection developing within her for Tadashi, an affection that in time matured into love.

Tadashi too felt his own emotions for her growing deeper as the days went on. He was not a man of intense or even smooth interaction with women. After Mako's death, he had lived the solitary life of a bachelor, driven by the many needs to succeed in a one man operation at his shop amid the many demands put upon him by his competitors. It was indeed a tough, competitive world out there. The strain of its demands were telling on Tadashi. Perhaps it was his own drive to succeed and maintain his high standards that drew his attention to Mrs. Yamamoto who "had it all" in her comfortable life style, but seemed to be throwing it all away by her excess in drinking and her empty tirades against her deceased husband, however bad he may have been. Tadashi hated to stand by and see a person throw her life away. Such a concern led him to denying her "just one more" when he knew she had reached her limit, and to tell her also to "knock it off" when her outbursts against her former husband's conduct erupted. Gradually his concern for her touched a responsive chord within her and she responded by correcting herself and drawing closer to this one person who was showing respect and concern for her even in her worst moments.

That's all it took, really. Respect for oneself and others, concern for someone in trouble, and opening up in mutual conversation were all the basic ingredients that led up to their decision to seek a new life together. Their love blossomed and was sealed in a brief Shinto ceremony at a nearby Shrine with only a few close friends in attendance. Mrs. Yamamoto brought up the idea of moving over to Canada and starting a whole new life in a new and different environment. She even secured a buyer for Tadashi's sushi shop from one of her husband's cronies who knew a good business deal when he saw it. Tadashi was thrilled. He had managed his shop successfully, sold it off honorably and had a new life awaiting him. Yes, there were a lot of details to take care of as he stepped away from his old life and looked, albeit with some hesitancy, to a truly new life, but he had his new wife by his side and together they would make a go of it. Yes, they would.

At Narita, Tokyo's main international airport, they sought out Japan Air Lines and began the process of going through security and through customs. Their travel agent, sharing in their excitement, had secured two seats for them on the airline's newest plane, the Boeing Dreamliner 787, because she said that was the perfect plane to whisk them away to their new life.

About an hour passed, and then at a signal the plane backed away from the gate and lumbered slowly through the roadways leading toward Runway 125W. Once they reached the runway and positioned themselves for takeoff, the pilot revved up the two powerful jet engines until he heard the command, "Japan Flight 1412, cleared for takeoff." With a surge of power the huge jet surged down the runway and swept upwards to the sky. Inside the jet a new life was beginning for a newly married couple who took their individual weaknesses, said, "No, I can do better," and joined their hearts together to make that future possible.

182

Fumiko Tajima

----- Lady With a Badge -----

Fumiko Tajima, a plain clothes detective, was standing at her post in Ueno Station in Tokyo. Her commission for that early month of the summer was to be on the lookout for young people, runaways, truants, druggies, the whole gamut of a new leaderless gang of misfits who were filtering into the capital groping and scratching for some kind of action that would fill the void in their otherwise empty lives. There was a reception committee there too to greet them and to try to lure or snare these wayward youngsters into lives of crime or bondage. The Japanese "yakuza" (gangsters) are a formidable bunch, ruthless, devoid of compassion yet oozing with promises of excitement, easy money, and lives of uninterrupted pleasure. It was a dangerous mix, fraught with disaster for young dreamers. Standing between these two groups, the hunters and their prey, stood people like Fumiko Tajima, specially trained and highly motivated police doing everything they could to keep the two groups apart.

Uneo Station was natural place for these two groups to meet. It was both a transportation hub and also the traditional terminus for long distant trains from northern Japan, the upper regions of Honshu (Japan's main island), or the northernmost island of Hokkaido. Fumiko drifted over towards the platform where people were waiting for the arrival of an incoming train, scanning the crowd at the same time to pick out any unsavory characters who were up to no good. Two men sided up next to her, one a heavily built middle aged man, was wearing a pink tie with an expensive pin, the other a very young man in his early twenties sported dark sun glasses. Speaking in a low voice with a hint of violence in its tone, the older man said, "Buzz off, "Neechan," (elder sister), this is our territory." After a quick glance in their direction, Detective Tajima looked straight ahead, and in an equally low and determined voice replied, ""Where did you get that pink tie? It looks like something you picked up in a second hand shop." "Very funny," answered the hood. " You're supposed to be inconspicuous, but any dumb jerk could pick you out in a crowd of two people. Why don't you just wear a white suit and blow a whistle?" Annoyed at this crude attempt to distract her from her duty, Fumiko turned and said, "Look, Buster, you take your little friend here and move along or I'll signal my back up guys to pick you up and bring you downtown for an afternoon of questioning. Wouldn't that be a lot of fun!! Now, move on!!"

With those two out of the way, Officer Tajima returned to her task of scanning the incoming passengers from the train to see if she could spot the young man she was looking for. There he was, looking much like the grainy FAX picture she had been carrying around for the past three days. Since he was only a youngster, and having come in from a small town up country from Tokyo, he had that slightly bewildered look that betrayed his vulnerability. Figuring that he would be hungry after the long train ride, Fumiko let him walk by her and then followed him to the public lockers where he deposited his bag, and then to the end of the station where he entered a noodle shop for something to eat. She allowed him to take some nourishment and then she entered the shop and took a seat at a nearby table. When she saw her back up enter the shop and take a table near the door, Fumiko made her move, walked over to the boy and putting her hand on his shoulder said, "Son, we've been searching for you. Your parents are frantic about you." Before she could say another word, the young lad bolted away from her and rushed to the door, only to have his flight curtailed by the two police officers waiting for him.

Back at the police station when they began questioning him, the young man was very uncooperative, much to no one's surprise. At first the male police officers questioned him, and he held his ground refusing to speak. It was "a man thing to do," and while it didn't accomplish anything, it gave Officer Tajima time to reach his parents by phone and assure them that the boy was safe with them and that she would personally bring him home the following day.

When Fumiko began her questioning by saying that she herself was a woman with feelings and understanding like his own mother must be having about his safety and his future, his defenses began to crumble. Defiance gave way to some tears once he realized what an impact his impulsive act must have had on his parents, especially upon his mother. Yet his defiance reasserted itself, "Look, I don't care how they feel. All I hear is 'Marks' and 'Studies' again and again! No matter how hard I try, I can't please them. They keep saying that I'm lazy and don't try hard enough." After a while, Fumiko had had enough. Putting her face directly in front of him, she spoke slowly and firmly, "Enough of that stuff. Now you listen to me. I've done my homework and checked up on your family and background while the other officers were in here listening to you whining and wailing about the demands your parents are making upon you. You have two very fine, wonderful parents who care about you and your future and want only the best for you. Most of the kids I pick up don't have both parents at home to talk to. Some are in jail, some are addicted to drugs, some are violent and some don't work and are not even on welfare." To have all these ugly facts come at him in a non-stop staccato fashion cut through all his bravado, and there were tears. A lot of them. Fumiko gave him time to compose himself and then continued, now in a more gentle but firm manner. "Now here's what we're going to do. We're going to get you something to eat right now and then let you spend the night here in the Shelter. Then first thing in the morning you and I will catch the first available train north to your home.

As the train for northern Honshu sped north from Tokyo and the kilometers clicked away one after the other, the young man and Fumiko had the opportunity to talk. Conversation was halting at first for the young lad was very apprehensive about the greeting he was going to receive when they would reach his house. "My Dad especially will never forgive me. I embarrassed him. Like you he is a cop and can be very severe." Fumiko broke in, "Yes, he is a cop, but before he ever put on a badge he was your father. I understand where you are coming from, but I assure you that his love for you is very sincere. He and your mother have been worried sick about you, …were you all right, …did anything bad happen to you, …why did you run away? All these questions, and many more besides, have been tormenting them ever since they became aware that you had run away."

Once his fears had been allayed, the young lad opened up some more and revealed that he actually admired his Dad for his moral integrity and courage in facing down some threats hurled at him by some drug-crazed thugs he was arresting. Maybe he could do something like that, or even go beyond police work into law and become a lawyer. Fumiko assured him that it was indeed possible, but there was a great deal of schooling, self discipline and hard work involved. He would really like to be a lawyer, he said. "In America they have thousands of lawyers," he said, "but in Japan they limit the numbers. So it is very competitive." "Yes," Fumiko answered, "in the United States they like to 'go to court' so to speak, they like to litigate. We Japanese tend to compromise on an issue before going to court. But things are changing, and now more Japanese are engaged in litigation. Being a lawyer and helping people, especially poor people, out of difficult legal problems is really great work, but it takes a lot of study and hard work in the classroom to be a lawyer." And with a wink in her eye, a smile on her face and a jab in his ribs, Fumiko reminded her young runaway friend that he couldn't run away from all that he would have to accomplish if he really wanted to achieve his goals.

The distraught parents were waiting at the small country station as the train pulled in. After they stepped off the train, Officer Tajima and the boy approached his parents. Fumiko sensed the propriety of the occasion and showed her badge and offered her name card to the boy's father. The father, himself a policeman, looked carefully at the badge and the personal card before giving a profound bow to Officer Tajima. The boy's mother meanwhile gathered her son into her arms and with tears flowing welcomed him home. A moment later, the official introductions having been made by the father to Fumiko, he too put his arms around the boy who by now was awash in tears of joy at the joyous welcome he was receiving. Later, sipping tea at the humble home of this family, Fumiko took the opportunity to speak in a positive tone to the parents about their son. His flight away from home, in typical teenage fashion, was done very impulsively and with little long term planning, she said. But on the other hand, once he had been apprehended and settled down, he cooperated very much with the authorities. Later, the boy himself stressed to his parents that Officer Tajima took the time to speak at length with him and pointed out in real life terms that if he wanted to realize his dreams, serious study and discipline would have to be part of this life. With Fumiko's encouragement, he said, he accepted this challenge and had resolved to meet it head on.

After tea, the boy's father nodded to Fumiko to come outside. They slowly walked a scenic route beside the river that coursed its way through town. "I'm a cop, too, you know," the father said. "I'm used to lecturing people, but I guess I still have to learn something about the need to show affection and love. I taught my children a good deal about rules and making an effort, but I'm learning that there is a deeper quality about education that is only transmitted by the heart. It is love, and I must admit that I am not very good at expressing it to others. That's a confession from one cop to another." Fumiko was wise enough to say nothing at this moment. Listening quietly, she knew, was very important in the art of conversation.

The time was approaching for Fumiko to catch the late afternoon train back to Tokyo. After the appropriate goodbyes, the father drove Fumiko to the railroad station. He accompanied Fumiko to her platform and waited with her for the train to depart. As the train edged slowly away Fumiko stood in the aisle and looked back at the solitary figure looking in her direction. They saluted each other one last time. Fumiko noticed a white tissue in the father's left hand. He was trying to control his emotions. Fumiko sat down and pulled out her own tissues to dab her eyes. One thing about cops, she thought, they understand each other.

On the train back to Tokyo, Fumiko tried to concentrate on a police manual she carried with her, but she was full of distractions. Her memory flew back to the time when she had attended the police academy and her early years as a rookie. She recalled how proud and in such high spirits she was that first morning as she left home and headed for her first shift as a Police Officer. The fact that she had been assigned to the Ueno District precinct gave her added confidence because that precinct encompassed the busy Ueno Railroad Station, a hub for much rail traffic entering and leaving Tokyo. Here she was sure that she would be challenged by assignments involving a wide variety of police work. Fumiko was prepared for that; she had been at the high end of her class all through the Police Academy which, of course, was the reason she had been assigned to the Ueno District precinct to begin with.

It was one thing to be prepared to meet whatever challenges that came from the misfits and low-life hoods she would encounter on the streets. It was quite another to deal effectively with the initial cold shoulder treatment she experienced from Sargent Hara and some of the other male officers with whom she had to work. The initial aloofness and wariness on the part of the other patrol officers toward female officers gradually melted away as the women proved their mettle out on the street working alongside their male partners in the daily challenges of street work. The situation involving Sargent Jun Hara, the senior patrol officer of the Ueno District precinct was a bit different. He was an older man, of sterling reputation and held in high regard by all the officers in the precinct. He just couldn't connect with Fumiko as a police officer on a par with the others under his command. Whenever he was in charge, he was forever giving her what Fumiko considered "housekeeping assignments" around the station, desk duty, making sure all records were accurate and up to date, interviewing complaints in family cases, and questioning all female prisoners. The other female police officer on the same shift as Fumiko at the station didn't really object to such duty. She was slightly older than Fumiko and was content to just fit in, do her work and go home. She was not 'driven' as was Fumiko to go out and grapple with the daily challenges of police work in the real world.

While the everyday give and take, the practical jokes, etc. between Fumiko and her fellow officers was easy and relaxed, the situation with regard to Sargent Hara and Fumiko was different, more formal and more reserved. He was content with this situation, but she was not. She craved more 'action,' getting into more street work, mixing it up with the crowd, even taking on the "yakuza" (hoodlums) on occasion. Sargent Hara was a nice enough guy, and there was nothing personal in the way he was treating her. So she, in desperation, crafted a plan which might work, which would 'break the ice' between them, and at the same time let him know that she was competent out there on the street. It was bold and it was putting her reputation within the department right on the cutting edge. If it failed, she would surely be transferred out of the Ueno Precinct station. But if she pulled it off successfully, she would certainly win acceptance by her fellow officers, and hopefully with Sgt. Hara as well.

One busy day, in the midst of the crowded Ueno Railroad Station, Sargent Hara was making his rounds, checking out, not the crowd but his own men, to make sure they were on station and doing their assigned work. Slowly an elderly lady wearing a typical Japanese kimono with a wide black "obi" (kimono sash) cautiously approached him giving evidence of someone needing assistance. The elderly woman was bent over and walking with the aid of a cane. "Officer," the woman asked, "can you tell me where the taxi stand is?" "Taxi stand?" retorted Officer Hara, "it's right behind you. You can see the taxis from here." "Whaaaat?" asked the old lady. Sargent Hara gestured at the taxis lined up at the curb and said, "Right there. Can't you see them?" "Whaaaat?" the old lady asked again. The sergeant began to shout directly into the old woman's ear. "THE TAXIS!! THEY ARE RIGHT THERE BEHIND YOU!! CAN'T YOU SEE THEM?" "Whaaaaat?" asked the old lady once again. Exasperated, Sergeant Hara took the old lady by the arm and led her over to the spot where people were waiting for taxis. "STAND HERE!!" he all but shouted to her. "Thank you, Officer, you are so kind," were her parting words as he walked back to his station. The sergeant had lost his cool and was quite irritated. After the late afternoon crowd had thinned out and he had a moment to himself, he sat in his cubicle in the railroad station, made himself some tea, and gradually calmed down. It had been a very busy midday shift, and that old lady with her incessant questions still echoed in his mind. It was at that point, as he was closing up his office and preparing to leave for home, that he noticed his expensive gold ballpoint pen, the one his wife and family had given him when he was promoted to sergeant was missing. Rapidly and with mounting apprehension he went through all his pockets and then all the drawers on his desk, but for the life of him, he could not find it. Where could it be? Where could he have left it? Who would have taken it? Could it be that little old deaf lady? No, it couldn't be, no little old street tramp could beat me!! But if she did, the next time I see her she will regret having fooled Sargent Hara!! No, it must be somewhere here in the station house. He looked all over, but in the end went home empty handed.

The next morning at the precinct formation for duty assignments, Sargent Hara approached the Captain and asked him to make an announcement about the lost pen. After all, it was gold plated, engraved with the inscription, "To Sarge, Congratulations, From the Family" and meant a lot to him. The announcement was made, but before the line-up could be dismissed, a hand went up in the back. "Yes, Tajima, what is it?" the Captain asked. "Sir, I have Sgt. Hara's pen here in this little bag. You see, yesterday was my day off so I was not expected to be here at the station. I decided to do this impersonation to prove to Sgt. Hara and all my fellow officers here that I could really do serious police work, even undercover work, if I were just given the chance. Ever since I came here I have been assigned to do only what I call 'protected work,' and I appreciate your concern for me. But I want to do 'real' police work, out with the public where I can really help people. So I planned this "little demonstration" as I call it. I meant no harm to Sgt. Hara, or to you, Captain, and I apologize to everyone here if I hurt your feelings." After a moment of stunned silence, the whole room erupted with laughter, even applause, and comments from just about every one of the uniformed police officers. Sgt. Hara rushed to the back of the room to retrieve his personalized pen, and it was easy to see that he was about to verbally chastise Fumiko, but the Captain, however, took immediate charge of the situation and showed his qualities of leadership which defused what otherwise might have been a disruptive and long lasting feud. "Wait a minute, Sgt., calm down, now, calm down!! Our young officer here pulled off a really good joke in this little make-believe stunt she concocted. Now let's let her show us whether she is as good out in public as she thinks she is. Assign her some patrols that will really test her mettle. Let's let her prove to everyone here that she can come through as a partner on a patrol, or by herself in some real life situations. All right, that's enough. We all got a big laugh out of this. Now let's get back to work. All Patrols, dismissed." Even Sgt. Hara had to go along with what the Captain said, and even though his meetings with Fumiko were cool and formal for a while, in the end, after she had proved her worth in several difficult and even delicate cases, he began grudgingly at first, but later in time, to have a warm admiration for this brave officer who put everything on the line among her peers to prove again and again that she had "the right stuff."

Fumiko Tajima's rise in the Tokyo Police Dept. continued to progress "in the fast lane," partly because of the high quality of her police work, but also because of her being one of the first female officers whose career was being closely watched by the Commissioner and his associates who saw in Fumiko role model potential for the new female recruits constantly being added to the police force. In time she had received various commendations for excellent police work, which of course, made her very proud of her accomplishments. The one promotion that she had desired most of all was to become a detective. When two male detectives retired, her dream came true.

Detective Tajima was not long into her new position when she received notice to report to the Commissioner's office. During the interview with the Commissioner, Fumiko was told that she had been selected to fly to the U.S.A. to attend the famous FBI school in Quantico, Virginia, where she would learn advanced techniques in investigation, surveillance, crime scene procedures, fingerprinting and DNA evidence and management. This was an awesome opportunity to excel even further in police work. As she prepared for her trip to America, she recalled a film she had seen of the actress Jodie Foster who had portrayed a student in that very FBI school. Before boarding the plane, however, Fumiko had to attend and excel in an intensive English language program in Tokyo, to be followed by another refresher course when she arrived in Washington, D.C.

Her class at the FBI academy was made up of police officers from the United States and some foreign countries. That particular year, Fumiko was the only officer from Japan. In general, those who attended the academy were mature, seasoned veterans from differing police departments which allowed the students to pick up additional insights into police work from hearing different techniques discussed in class. The students had a good sense of humor together with a tinge of cynicism which Fumiko took to be a universal mark of people working in the imperfect conditions connected with law enforcement. The academy tried to instill a spirit of camaraderie and loyalty, virtues that were needed in everyday life on the street. Some of the American officers, especially those from large metropolitan areas, told of being shot at and wounded as they described some harrowing situations they had been in.

Fumiko's group leader was a tall good looking man from the New York Police Department. Very much an extrovert with a heavy Bronx accent, he quite easily fell into his role as spokesperson for his group. "Hi," he said, "my name is Hugh Dugan," as he introduced himself to his charges, "I'm thirty two years old, as Irish as 'Paddy's pig' and still living at home with my mother." Many of the others laughed at this bit of humor, (acknowledging that many Irish men tended to remain at home and marry later in life). Coming as she did from the Orient, and being totally unaware of the strong Irish American culture of the NYPD, (as it is frequently identified), Fumiko missed the whole point of Dugan's somewhat clumsy attempt to put everyone at ease. But he did manage to break the ice and soon everyone was relaxed and engaged in some form of conversation. There were thirty student agents in the class, divided into three groups of ten, twenty four men and six women.

Inevitably the practice of self-defense came up as part of the program. Fumiko had learned judo and karate from experts in Tokyo when she was attending the police academy to qualify for the police department. After that, she had practiced regularly at the gymnasium especially provided for the police. "Can you do any judo or karate?" Sargent Dugan asked Fumiko on the way to the gymnasium. "A little," she answered, in keeping with her Oriental disposition of having a quiet and inscrutable demeanor. "I try to keep in shape." Later, when she was paired with Sgt. Dugan, she demonstrated very clearly her previous training and innate ability. He had been misled by her earlier off handed reply regarding her ability and relied too much on his size and weight advantage as he tried to quickly throw her. With quick and sure movement she turned her shoulder on him, pulled him off balance and flipped him over. He landed on his back with a thud. Surprise registered on his face. Quickly he got up and came at her again, more determined than before. Fumiko deftly stepped aside, tripped him and sent him sprawling. A third attempt went pretty much the same way with the big Irish cop from the NYPD on his back. "OK, little lady, you know your stuff," he muttered with some admiration as he got up off the mat.

After these customary "get-acquaintance" routines ran their course and the new trainees got to know more of their real selves, the training settled into its regular routine by offering new material and techniques. There was indeed a lot to absorb in the short ten week period of the course, crammed with a very tight schedule that left little time free for socializing. Nonetheless, Fumiko noticed that Hugh Dugan was paying increasing attention to her beyond what he was paying toward the other five women in the group. This was indeed flattering and she responded appropriately in her own somewhat shy Japanese way. At the conclusion of the course just before the American celebration of Labor Day, Hugh invited Fumiko to spend the long holiday weekend and the next several days before she was to return to Japan on a whirlwind tour of New City. In addition to the customary tourist sites, he gave her a "behind-the-scene" tour of the inner workings of the NYPD headquarters, which because of their common interest, was especially fascinating and deeply appreciated by Fumiko who by this time was responding with warm affection for Hugh. By the time she left New York to return to Japan it was clear that a bond of deep affection had developed between Hugh and Fumiko. He promised to keep in touch, a promise he kept by means of the many e-mails, Facebook messages and phone calls he made in the ensuing months. Their relationship became more serious during the following year when he suggested that they meet for a week in Hawaii. He would be bringing his mother for what would be a 'trip of a lifetime' for her and Fumiko would come with a long time girl friend of hers who had become a police officer like Fumiko thereby strengthening the bond between them.

The trip to Hawaii turned out to be everything they expected it to be, and then some, since it was during that time together that Hugh proposed to Fumiko and she accepted to become his wife. Later that same year they married at a Catholic ceremony in New York and later at a Shinto ceremony in Tokyo. After their marriage, they moved back to the United States. In keeping with a common practice among Japanese married women, after her marriage Fumiko retired from the police department to devote her time fully to their home. Hugh continued to work as a member of the NYPD, having risen to the full time rank of detective, and was assigned to the homicide squad working out of a busy midtown precinct. In time, three children were born to the couple, Hugh Jr, Aiko and Kenneth.

One Japanese custom which caused some confusion among the children happened when Fumiko spoke of Hugh by the familiar term used by Japanese women in conversation. The word in question was "anata" (you) which is a term of respect and endearment when used by a Japanese wife speaking to her husband. When the children were small they used to kid their mother about the way she pronounced their father's first name. "Daddy's name is not 'you,' Mommy, it's 'Hyuuu' as if there were a "y" in it." "No, no, no," Fumiko would answer, "I want to say it like you do but it just sounds like I am saying 'you.' We Japanese have difficulty with some English words and expressions. She went on to say, "There is also special words that a husband uses to speak of his wife in a humble way. If he is in a group of people and he wants speak of his wife, he would use the word,"kanai" or "nyobou." Learning about little differences such as these, the children later came to appreciate the delicate nature of the Japanese language and other oriental languages as well. Those languages were centuries older than American English and had histories of development.

One incident which took place on the subway, forever secured the admiration and love for Fumiko in the minds and hearts of Hugh Sr. and the children. It came in the middle of an afternoon shopping trip for Fumiko and her two very young children, Aiko and Kenny. They came out of Bloomingdale's and got on the Jerome Ave IRT subway line for the trip home to the Bronx. As a now practiced New Yorker,

Fumiko, with the two small children in tow, boarded the express train rather than the slower local. As the train sped north, Fumiko became concerned at two rather shiftless young men eyeing them in a menacing manner. When the train stopped at 125th St. for its customary three minute lay-over, she nudged the children and stood up intending to step out of the train, move to another car and re-enter the same train. Before she and the children could move, the two thugs made their move, one saying mockingly to the other, "Look, the Chinese lady is going to leave us. What'cha got in your bag there, lady?" Fumiko said in reply, "Back off, pal, or you'll be sorry." When he ignored her and tried to grab her purse, Fumiko quickly reacted with a hard karate blow to the stomach followed in quick succession by a two handed shove to his shoulders after having slipped her left leg behind his right leg thereby tripping him and sending him sprawling. As he fell to the floor his head hit the hard plastic seat with a resounding thud which momentarily stunned him. His partner lunged at Fumiko, but she thrust up her right forearm catching him hard in the throat, right on the Adam's apple. That hurt! Before either thug could react the transit cop on duty on the platform, alerted by a passenger, entered the car through the open doorway along with his police dog, Zeke. One look at Zeke with his teeth bared and emitting a low growl to indicate that he meant business, the two thugs knew that this little game was over, right now, for good. With that, a second cop, riding on one of the rear cars of the train entered the car and finished the scenario for good. As the two hoods were about to be led away, Fumiko looked the first one right in the eye and said in a low but very firm voice, …"I TOLD YOU TO 'BACK OFF.' …WHY DIDN'T YOU LISTEN? …STUPID!!"

When they arrived back home, Aiko and Kenny were wild with excitement as they told their Daddy and older brother of Mommy's exploit on the subway. Hugh sent out for pizza and the whole family celebrated!! Later, as she prepared the children for bed, Fumiko said to them, "Now you know why I go out each Wednesday morning to the gym while you are at school to keep practicing the judo and karate lessons I learned in Japan many years ago."

Life continued on for them as a family, and all for the good. Hugh was made Captain in the NYPD and later that same year was named "Father of the Year" in their local parish church. At the dinner in the church hall, Kenny was explaining to a lady sitting next to him about his mother's sometimes difficult pronunciation of American English. "She calls Daddy 'you' because she can't say 'Hyuuu.'" Fumiko laughed and said in return, "That's my Japanese background. It's hard to explain. In Japan, wives call their husbands "anata" (you).

During the summer after Hughie's graduation from grade school, and before he entered Cardinal Spellman High School in the Fall, Fumiko took him with her on a trip back to Japan, partly as a reward for his having achieved rather outstanding success thus far in school, and partly as a way to broaden his understanding of the world he was about to enter into in his high school and teen age years.

One day, while they were visiting different places in the Tokyo area, Fumiko brought young Hugh over to the Ueno Railroad Station so he could see, and she could re-visit, a place rich in memories for her. On the way into the railroad station she showed him the police precinct station nearby out of which she used to work. Then inside the busy station she brought him over to the area of the taxi stands and recounted for him the story, which he had heard often before, of how she had donned the kimono with the wide black belt and fooled Sargent Hara by deftly taking his gold engraved ball point pen, only to present it to him the next day in the precinct station in order to demonstrate to him and to all her police comrades that she was indeed worthy to perform serious police work. They both had a good laugh once again at how well she pulled off her deception, Sergeant Hara's frustrated response, and how her gamble paid off by laying the groundwork for her being chosen to go to the FBI training center in Virginia where she had the good fortune of meeting her future husband.

Finally she brought Hughie over to the little noodle shop in a corner of the station for a visit and a short snack, sitting at the very table where she had detained and brought in for questioning the young boy from northern Honshu, one of her very first successful challenges on the police force.

After leaving the noodle shop, the two of them walked slowly through the crowds in the station and took the subway back to their hotel. A few days later, it was time to leave for the airport and return to New York. Each of them left Japan with many thoughts and memories, Hughie with a greater admiration and love for his mother, and Fumiko with renewed memories of the past and cherished hopes for her family and all that the future would hold for them.

Grandpop

----- The Cabbie -----

My Grandpop is retired now from driving his cab from one end of the city of Fukuoka to the other, from its best districts to the humblest of homes in areas far away from the center of society. Old age can be very boring and tiresome for someone who was so active and who interacted with all sorts of people for so many years. So, I often asked myself, how does an older person like my Grandpa pass the time now that age and his infirmities have so much altered his life? He tells stories of the many things he can recall from meeting so many people in his days of driving his cab. My mother believes that whereas many of the stories are factual, many have been dramatized to make Grandpop come out a hero, or at least someone important in the story. As with so many older people, so it is with Grandpop, he repeats the same story over and over again. So I know all his stories by heart, even the ones with different versions. Funny thing, though, as Mom often points out, Grandpop's stories are great fun, full of humor and humanity. I decided to put some of his stories down on paper for others to read. I don't think Grandpop will be with us much longer after the stroke which left him largely incapacitated. I hope my children, and indeed their children, will read these stories and learn what a great character Grandpop had been. I hope he will be fondly remembered. That is the chief purpose of my writing these remembrances of him.

Grandpop, in his younger days, right after his marriage, was a bus driver in the country town of Miyazaki, one of the most beautiful areas in Kyushu, if not of the whole of Japan. However, since he did not take home enough of a salary to support his wife and child, they decided to move to the big city of Fukuoka where Grandpop took the test for a bus driver, passed it and began to work at his new job. He did make more money than he did in Miyazaki, but Grandpop still felt that he could do better if the right job came along. He fixed his eyes on any other promising job that came into view.

One day a friend happened to mention that a relative of his was planning to retire from his job as a privately run cabbie and was asking around for anyone who might be interested in taking over his route and position. Grandpop jumped at the opportunity and applied for the job. He was successful in obtaining the license and considered himself fortunate in becoming his own boss in a position where he could work his own hours and at his own pace.

In his new position Grandpop would go out early in the morning to capitalize on the morning rush hour for people trying to get to work on time or trying to make early morning appointments. Business would taper off later in the morning, and after a mildly busy time around noon Grandpop would come home for a light lunch and an afternoon nap. Mama says that the family would have an early supper immediately after which her father would again take to the streets to accommodate people in their rush to get home after work for their own evening meal. It was always worth his time to remain cruising for fares until around midnight, especially on rainy nights, for those leaving the theaters or sports events. And this schedule went on all through my life as a child and on into my teenage years. On the other hand, Grandpop was consistent, a good father, reliable for all his regular fares, and always on the alert to pick up new customers. We were not rich as a family, but through his honest and reliable work Grandpop made enough money to support his wife and raise three children. Toshihiko, his eldest son, is my father. Grandmom died so Grandpop came to live with us.

In his relationship with the other cabbies, my Grandpop learned to walk a thin line of prudence and circumspection. In Japan, many men customarily spend time at the end of their day having a drink or two with their immediate superiors as well as with their fellow workers. It's an old Japanese custom considered to be part of the job. Over sake, many a man would receive praise or admonishment from the boss and much encouragement from friends on his level. One had to be always careful and aware lest true judgment be compromised by too much sake.

Grandpop was always assured of a regular supply of customers if he parked his cab near the bars or the Japanese restaurants towards the end of the evening. Very often he would get a tipsy customer who wanted a safe ride home. Cab drivers quickly learned that people who drink too much like to unload their troubles on any eager listener like my Grandpop who quickly became quite adept at providing just the right line in reply to whatever the story might be. "You don't say...Wow, that's something! Yeah. You're dead right on that."…. They were all were expressions Grandpop had honed into an art over the years. He mastered the art of saying the correct response to satisfy whatever story was coming from the fare in the back seat of his cab. Of course, the art of listening and responding appropriately was not completely disinterested. Saying the right thing at the right moment often merited a fat tip. "Being a good listener is the secret of getting tips," Grandpop would say proudly as he philosophized about this art. "You see, in general , the Japanese do not like the western concept of tipping. But for some reason, the Japanese like to tip cabbies. 'Keep the change,' people would say even if they did not believe in tipping as a way of life. Japanese are funny that way. They hate tipping as a practice, but are quite generous to the cabbies they like."

What follows are but a few of the many stories Grandpop used to tell about some of the more dramatic happenings that came his way as he drove his cab around the streets of Fukuoka those many days and nights. We are sure that many of them are truly factual, told in great detail by Grandpop and very believable, whereas others have been "edited and amended" by my Grandpop as he retold the stories over and over again to captivate and entertain his many customers and family members as well.

There can be dangerous episodes in a cabbies' life as one knows. Picking up an unknown person who wants to go to a destination that turns out to be very threatening is an obvious example. At the same time, bringing a stranger to just about any destination can quickly turn into a disaster, depending whatever that person has in mind. One such incident in Grandpop's life on the job illustrates just what can happen to an innocent cabbie. One night, a man wearing a baseball cap with a white health mask covering the lower part of his face, entered the cab and quickly put the blade of a knife he was carrying to Grandpop's neck. "Drive me to Kurume" (a city near Fukuoka) the man said. Grandpop quickly realized the danger he was in and tried to remain calm. Without saying a word he drove the cab directly to the man's destination. Before the man leapt from the cab, he cut Grandpop's throat very badly. There was blood all over the cab. Holding a towel to his neck, Grandpop drove directly to the ER at the nearest hospital. Fortunately the doctors there were able to close his wound and save his life. It took the surgeon's ten stitches to do so, and Grandpop had a long ugly scar on his neck for the rest of his life. Grandpop told the detective who interviewed him that he was convinced that the thief was a native of Fukuoka. His accent and the dialect betrayed him.

Eventually the man was apprehended on another charge, and under questioning admitted that he had robbed Grandpop (although he adamantly denied that he had cut Grandpop). In his confession to the police the man explained that he was high on drugs and could not remember any details of the incident. He was later convicted in court and spent some time in prison. My mother says that every time she sees that scar on Grandpop's throat it reminds her of what he must have gone through that evening and of how dangerous a cabbie's job can become at any given moment.

Now for a story that mother believes certainly has been embellished and made more dramatic by Grandpop because it's so human and heartwarming and cries out to be heard. As Grandpop tells the story, one day as he was cruising through a residential area, a visibly excited and nervous man flagged him down and said that his wife was in labor and must be rushed to any nearby hospital. When the woman got into the back seat of the cab, she said, "Oh my God, it's coming." Grandpop rushed through the streets, all the while calling the police on his wireless. "Woman in labor. Alert the hospital," he said. When he pulled into the Emergency Entrance to the hospital, a doctor and two nurses came rushing out to the cab. The baby's head was showing. They put the mother onto a hospital gurney and immediately rushed her inside the hospital. The baby was born in the corridor outside the delivery room. While all this was going on, two aides came out with buckets of water, towels and brushes to wipe down and clean Grandpop's cab. Then the husband appeared and offered Grandpop a reward for his kindness. "I wouldn't think of it," Grandpop said and drove off, his part in the drama now complete.

But that's not the end of this dramatic story. As Grandpop relates it, the father of the baby was a writer for the local newspaper who later wrote an article on his daughter's birth mentioning how gracious Grandpop had been. Grandpop, of course, kept the article on the dashboard of his cab and would often show it to his customers. "The father said I was a hero, but nah, I was just the guy on hand. I did what I had to do." Naturally, Grandpop did not hesitate to embellish and make even more dramatic the story of that afternoon ride to the hospital. "The baby was born just where you are sitting. It was born right before my eyes. Just where you're sitting." Mom laughs every time she hears the story repeated another time. She knows the story is basically true, but cringes every time she hears Grandpop tell it, just one more time.

Now we come to the subject of "ghosts " (o-bake), not the kind of ghosts people in America tell fearful stories to impressionable youngsters about around Halloween time, nor the kind that inhabit so called haunted houses or other similar places guaranteed to spook a person or send shivers of fear up and down one's spine.

No, these "ghosts" are those whom taxi drivers learn to spot and be leery of, who in their own way, can provoke fear or at least anxiety in the mind of cabbies whenever they are encountered on any working shift. From older cabbies, Grandpop learned the meaning of the word "ghost." These "ghosts" are customers who ask to be taken to a distant place, sometimes miles and hours away. The "ghost" usually does not talk and there is none of the usual banter or conversation between the cabbie and his passenger. A "ghost" who talks, Grandpop was told, is not a "ghost" in the true sense of the term. A real "ghost" does not talk; he just sits in the back and waits to arrive at his destination. Grandpop was told that there are no female "ghosts."

While sitting around in the cabbies' stand, waiting for calls to come in, new men are given some basic advice from older and experienced cabbies. "Before leaving any such long trip, always make an agreement to receive double payment for the trip back. Never let a customer get out of your cab without first paying after you have arrived at the destination. He will try to leave. So you have to keep the lock on the back door so that he does not escape," the older drivers instructed the newcomers.

Well, Grandpop kept all this advice in the back of his mind and committed it to memory. Indeed in his time he did have many "ghosts," but they were all polite people who really needed to get to their distant destination. They paid their fare and often expressed their appreciation to the cabbie before departing. Grandpop began to think that the old troopers were exaggerating the situation about "ghosts" who try to escape without paying.

But one night, a "ghost" asked him to take him to Saga, a city quite a distance from Fukuoka. "For my return trip, pay double?" Grandpop asked, and the "ghost" nodded in agreement. Not a word was said during the entire trip to Saga. When they arrived, however, the "ghost" somehow lifted the lock on the back door and as he jumped out said, "I have to make a phone call from that convenience store." Grandpop sensed correctly that the "ghost" would probably exit from the back door of the store, so he pulled around and parked directly behind the store. Sure enough, the door opened and the "ghost" came out of the store, took one look at Grandpop waiting for him, and took off running down the street into the crowd. Grandpop raced after him shouting aloud "Thief!!, Thief!! Help!" The crowd formed around the man allowing Grandpop to catch up and to grab the man and hold him in a stronghold. Seeing the crowd and hearing the commotion, a police officer who was patrolling nearby hustled over, separated the two men and ushered them off to a nearby police station. In the questioning that followed, Grandpop explained what had happened. The man, however, said he had every intention of paying and that Grandpop had over reacted. The man pulled out his wallet and tried to give Grandpop some money. The young police officer, stopped that game right there and asked the man for some identification. When the police officer put the information into his computer, however, he discovered that the man was a convicted felon who had recently been released on parole. This led to the man being indicted for breaking his parole thereby sending him back to prison. The young police officer, as Grandpop related the story, then took some bills from the man's wallet and paid Grandpop the full fare that had been agreed upon which enabled him to drive back to Fukuoka a happy man. This was one of Grandpop's favorite "ghost" stories. "Live and learn. Live and learn," he would say every time he told this tale. The story entered into the folklore of the cabbies where they would say, "You just can't be too careful," as they told the story to one another back at the taxi station between calls.

And what does Mom think about this story and its reliability? She thinks it has most of the hallmarks of being reliable. The only weak spots occur when Grandpop described the police officer in the city of Saga who arrested the man. Sometimes he is described as being "just out of the police academy," whereas at other times Grandpop describes him as "a veteran officer who had earned his stripes over the years." She thinks that Grandpop may have been playing up to his audience in varying his remarks. Everything else, however, in the story remains the same and appears to mesh with the facts of what happened that night.

One of Grandpop's favorite stories involved an American. It seems that one day he was flagged down by a big African American man who was impeccably dressed. On his right hand he sported a big expensive ring. "The dome, please," the man said and Grandpop guessed correctly that he was a baseball player. "You… You… play good," Grandpop said. The big athlete flashed a smile and replied, "Thanks, Gramps, I appreciate that." For a while as they wove their way through the afternoon traffic the player was silent, and then he burst out, "Tonight… wife… and son… come from America . See me play. I'm very happy." Grandpop understood the words 'wife' and 'son.' Grandpop put up three fingers and said, "you, you, three home runs…" "I'll try, Gramps. I'll try to hit four, one for you, Gramps."

That night Grandpop listened to the radio to pick up the broadcast of the game. The number four hitter, an American from Philadelphia, did indeed hit three home runs to the utter surprise of Grandpop. When the player was interviewed after the game, he told the announcer how a cabbie had predicted he would hit three home runs, for his wife and little boy. He said he had promised the cabbie that he would hit four home runs, one for the cabbie too. "Hey, Gramps, if you are listening. Sorry about that." he said.

The next day a reporter picked up the human interest story and interviewed Grandpop. In the article, a picture of Grandpop was shown standing next to his cab. "Thanks, Gramps," was the caption. Grandpop delighted in this story and had the clipping to back up his story. Even Mom did not suspect that story as being false in any way. "I've heard it a thousand times with no change in it from start to finish. Did you ever hear the story of the time I picked up an American baseball player and took him to the dome."

Grandpop always got indignant when he told stories of professional thieves who had duped him or one of his fellow hard working cabbies. "…Fleeced, …betrayed, …lied to, …" Grandpop would say and his face would turn red in anger. Incidents like this didn't happen too often, but when they did occur, the hurt they caused ran deep and the pain was real.

The life of a cabbie is difficult, long hours, uncertain pay, dangerous trips made at the direction of unknown customers, etc. However, generally speaking the public is made up of good and generous people who are supportive of a businessman-cabbie just trying to make a living and put food on the table for his family. But there are exceptions to that general rule; there are, out there, people who will try to deceive and take advantage of a cabbie of good will. This hurts, financially and as a human being who has been taken advantage of. What follows is but one example of such a happening which occurred to Grandpop and left him infuriated and frustrated.

One day Grandpop received a call to pick up a fare at a certain address in a rather respectable neighborhood. When he arrived at the site, there was his fare, an apparently middle aged man holding a piece of paper in his hand, nothing else. The look on his face was that of a person suffering from some degree of dementia with a somewhat confused look on his face, with eyes that seemed unfocused and with steps that were unsteady. He said nothing but just offered the piece of paper to Grandpop. On the paper the message said, "This is my father. He has Alzheimer's disease. Please leave him off at this address, ring the bell and I will pay you."

The destination was a bit distant, and all the while they traveled the man said nothing, just stared straight ahead. His eyes brightened a bit as they rolled to a stop. He got out, smiled and bowed a bit as he turned and walked slowly into the house. Grandpop busied himself writing up the details of the ride in his log book, and then walked up to the front door, rang the doorbell and waited for someone to come to the door. Nothing happened; no response. He opened the door and shouted, "Anyone home?" Again, no answer. Grandpop then entered the house and opened the door to the living room. There was no furniture in it, nothing. He walked through that room and out into the kitchen area. Nothing was there either, no appliances, no furniture, nothing. One thing stood out; the back door was halfway open. Looking outside, Grandpop could see that it opened into a fairly busy city street. His so-called "fare" was gone. He had simply run through the house, rushed out the back doorway, and fled down the street. Grandpop "had been taken." He was livid with rage. His attempt to offer service and kindness to a sick person and his family had been thrown back into his face. There was little he could do, but return to his own neighborhood and try to continue his daily search for customers. Reporting the matter to the police would have been futile; it would have been judged only a misdemeanor, and there was little hope of catching the man. The only recourse open to Grandpop was to warn the other cabbies back at the taxi stand to be wary of any such calls they might receive. My mother told me later on that when Grandpop came home that evening he was visibly upset, not so much at losing the money from that call, but that someone could be so low as to masquerade as an elderly sick man to fleece a hard working cabbie who was going out of his way to do a charitable deed.

Mom says that there is no doubt that some of Grandpop's stories are shameless fabrications. She says that the way one can judge some information to be false was to observe any change in important details. "Some are like a Kurozawa movie with all different points of view," Mom would observe. Grandpop was as clever as a novelist and came up with stories that had the plot of a Hitchcock movie. One such story was told in three different ways, each with its own point of view.

Version Number One: "I carried the boss of a crime syndicate to his girlfriend's apartment. He found another man there with her and shot them both. He received life in prison, but was out in sixteen years."

Version Number Two: "I picked up this woman who wanted to be taken to the crime boss' apartment. When she entered the apartment, she found the boss with another woman. During the violent argument that followed she reached into her purse, pulled out the very gun the boss had given her for her protection, and shot them both. At the trial, she received a sentence of thirty years and is still in prison."

Version Number Three: "I took this crime boss to his girlfriend's apartment, but members of a rival syndicate followed my cab. After I left the scene, they burst into the apartment and shot the boss and his girl friend with tommy guns.." This is a very weak story because weapons are not permitted in Japan, and tommy guns are unheard of.

Mom contends that Grandpop was a fan of the movie directors Kurozawa and Hitchcock, and that this is seen in some of the stories he told. When we tried to pin him down about the details of these stories, he would say, "NO, NO, NO. That is not the way it was." Then without hesitating he would proceed to tell another version of the same story. Some people have told me that they heard of such a story in which a crime boss killed his girlfriend, but the locality and the details of the story were entirely different from Grandpop's version in his story.

Finally, here is one last story from Grandpop. According to Grandpop, he once picked up a man carrying a black leather briefcase. When the man exited the cab, he forgot the briefcase and Grandpop drove on without realizing the briefcase was still resting on the back seat. When the next customer entered the cab, a lady was honest enough to call his attention to the briefcase. After thanking her for her honesty, Grandpop drove her to destination, and then he opened the case to reveal its contents. It was filled with money. Realizing the value of what was in the briefcase, Grandpop locked the case in the trunk of the cab for security and returned to the place where the man had gotten out of his cab. When he turned onto the street as he remembered it and stopped for a moment to look around at the neighborhood, his cab was confronted by several tough looking thugs who quickly hemmed it in and surrounded it. Grandpop opened the window a crack and asked what was going on. "If you want to stay healthy, just give us that briefcase and drive on," the leader of the mob commanded. Grandpop, an honest hardworking man, and not fully realizing the dangerous situation that confronted him, naively said that he wouldn't release the briefcase until he had a signed receipt for it. The gang leader exploded in anger, smashed the driver's window of the cab with his pistol and yanked Grandpop physically out of the cab. He jammed the pistol directly under

Grandpop's chin, told two of the thugs to get my Grandpop up into the building, and told two or three of the other thugs to tear the cab apart until they got that briefcase and brought it upstairs to him.

When Grandpop was brought into an apartment, there was his passenger, bound up and tied to a chair. He had obviously been roughed up from a beating and could say little to Grandpop. Before long, the thugs from downstairs came in with the briefcase and said they had ripped apart the cab before finding the briefcase in the trunk. At that point, an argument erupted among the gang members about what to do with their two captives.

Suddenly and without any warning, the apartment door was flung open and police with guns drawn rushed in and apprehended the gang without firing a shot. It turned out that some neighbors in the lower floor apartments looked through their windows and heard the ruckus going on out in the street as Grandpop was being dragged away. They quickly reported it to the police and immediately several cars were dispatched to the location. The responding officers were given a description of what was happening from the tenants who were awaiting their arrival and they rushed quietly upstairs and burst into the apartment. Their quick arrival put an end to what might well have been the murders of both Grandpop and his passenger.

Of course, a story like this, filled with all the details and excitement Grandpop could put into it, made great entertainment as he recounted it over and over again. But how true was it? Grandpop would never say, but the twinkle in his eye as he told and retold the story of how he was almost killed protecting his passenger's money and saw his assailants dragged away by the police to spend years in prison, certainly made for good entertainment on a rainy afternoon at home for us kids.

Stories? Well, Grandpop had a million of them! Without a doubt, some were true and were a testimony to the often harrowing experiences that all cabbies everywhere undergo as they go about their work each day offering service and assistance to complete strangers. Some, on the other hand, were spun out of the fertile imagination of my Grandpop, told not to deceive but to entertain children like myself when I was a little tyke, eager to imagine the many exploits my Grandpop, my childhood hero, had encountered in his fascinating position as a taxi driver serving the public, whoever they may be, wherever they wanted to go.

I just came out of Grandpop's room. It was very sad to see him in such a weakened condition. He was whispering so low, I could hardly make out what he was trying to say. So I drew closer to him, even turning my head just a bit to put my ear close to his mouth. "Did I ever tell you the story of the time..."

Need I say more? Could I say more? He was a great man, my Grandpop! Together we made many a trip side by side, sometimes in the front seat of his cab, many other times in the fertile spaces of my imagination, as I listened to him tell one story after another. He was my very own personal cab driver, and any time now when I get into a cab and the cabbie says to me, "Where to, Mister?" my eyes tear up with memories of my Grandpop, the greatest cabbie of them all.

Eiji and Keiko

----- Love Conquers All -----

Kumamoto is a city about two hours away by bus from the large commercial center and academic city of Fukuoka on the southern island of Kyushu. Kumamoto is famous for its climate (hot and mucky in the summer, damp and cold in the winter), a feudal castle, organized crime syndicates and Mt. Aso, a sleeping volcano. Even small children make a pun out of the word "Ahso." For instance, if someone says, "We're going to Mt. Ahso," the usual reply is, "aSOH, (Is that right?)." Kumamoto's blistering heat in the summer is often compared to the ancient city Kyoto which is equally uncomfortable. Our story begins and ends in this castle city where the two lovers grew up.

Eiji Tagawa's parents were divorced. His mother worked as a cleaning lady in the city office. His uncle owned a barber shop near the castle and the hope of all was that Eiji would someday work in that shop and later, inherit it. Eiji, however, wasn't great in his studies. "All he does is play video games," his mother would complain to her friends. He never got into trouble with the law and was rather quiet and disinterested in class. Everyone thought that the barber shop would be a good place for him.

Keiko Oka, on the other hand, was the daughter of a rich farmer. Her family grew mostly vegetables and fruit on their farmland. Mr. Oka had two helpers who worked the fields with him. He used a small tractor which he bought through the farmers' union. Mrs. Oka had high hopes for her children. Elder brother, (the proper pecking order and title in a Japanese family), would, however, turn out to be a bachelor, much to his mother's disappointment. Younger sister wanted to become a hair dresser, but her mother hoped instead that she would go to college and then make a good marriage with someone who had money and prestige. Like many Japanese mothers, Mrs. Oka was very calculating when the marriages of her children were involved. She expected that Keiko would go on to college and marry a businessman or a teacher. Keiko was a cute little girl who wore a charming smile. Her father had a special love for her, but tried not to show any favoritism in his dealings with his children.

Keiko and Eiji did not know each other in primary school, but met when both entered the same middle school. Keiko immediately joined the basketball team. Eiji and Keiko got to know each other because they worked together giving out food to the students when their turn came around to serve lunch. Keiko was known as "Kei-chan" ('chan' is a diminutive attached to the abbreviated name of young girls). Eiji would often wink at Kei-chan and she would giggle. When Eiji heard that Kei-chan was on the girls' basketball team, he joined the boys team so he could meet her. When a ball would roll over to the girls' side, Eiji would go to retrieve it and would wink at Keichan. The girls basketball coach was furious when she saw that and reported the incident to their homeroom teacher. Mr. Teruo Yamazaki, who was a strict mathematics teacher, was in charge of Keiko and Eiji's homeroom. He called them in one at a time. He had them kneel in "seiza" style (legs tucked beneath the body). He scolded both of them for showing affection to each other. "I was just joking," Eiji said, "and teasing Keichan. We hardly know each other." "Well," the teacher said in stern language: "Everyone knows you ride your bikes home together and you carry Miss Oka's books. To me, that's flirtation. I don't want you winking or going home together. What would her parents say?" "Yeah, but," Eiji said but couldn't get the whole sentence out. "Don't yeah but me. I don't want you to see each other. I'm going to call Oka's father." After the lecture, Eiji sheepishly left the teachers' room and Keiko was called in and knelt down before the teacher. "I hear that you two are flirting. Everybody is talking about it. Some of the teachers are angry. You should be ashamed. I'm going to call your father. I don't want you two to see each other. Got that?" Keiko, who had a strong backbone, looked into Mr. Yamazaki's face and answered, "How can I stop seeing him? He sits right next to me. I think this is ridiculous." The teacher got very red and said, "I'll tell your father that you're insolent too. No student has ever talked back to me like that." He dismissed her with an angry gesture. Outside the school, as they were getting on their bikes, they agreed to not ride home together. When Kei-chan arrived home, her father was working on some flowers in the family garden. "Hi Papa," she said. "Did my home room teacher call?" "Yeah, he seemed very disturbed over your flirting with some boy and he said that you talked back to him," her father answered with a perplexed face. "There's this boy in my class who is a great teaser. He winked at me during basketball practice and sometimes we ride our bikes home together. Flirtation? That's ridiculous," Kei-chan said and started to sniffle. "You mean that kid, Eiji?" he asked, "he seems like a nice kid. How did they get flirtation out of that? Tell you what, Kei-chan, I'll call back that Yamazaki guy and tell him that I scolded you and that you wouldn't do it again. How's that?" Kei-chan continued to sniffle and said, "this is ridiculous." Eiji stopped winking at Kei-chan, and Eiji would ride very fast on his bike to go home and then he would return to meet Kei-chan on her way home. As they passed each other on their bikes, Eiji would shout, "Hiiiiiiiiiii," as he approached and Kei-chan would answer, "See yaaaaaaa."

In third year junior high school, it came time for the students and their families to make a choice regarding to which high school they would send their child. It is a very important step which families take very seriously. Eiji's mother wanted him to go to the public high school where the tuition was almost free. He flunked the entrance exam, however, and had to enter a lower level private high school. In Japan, the public schools in general are for gifted students. Students who do not pass the stiff entrance exam have to go to private schools. In other countries, the public schools are for all the students.

From early childhood, Keiko had wanted to be a kindergarten teacher like the loving ones who taught her when she was a child. Her parents were aware of her aspirations and chose to have her take piano lessons when she was four years old. To secure a position in a high class kindergarten, the ability to play the piano was a must. Her mother had decided that Keiko should go to Fukuoka and board at a high school which had a Junior College connected to it. Many kindergartens preferred Junior College graduates because they would have a longer time to progress in teaching. Keiko herself was agreeable to this idea and after graduation from middle school, she moved to Fukuoka to enter Nakamura high school. She did very well in the entrance exam, and because of its outstanding sports program she liked and enjoyed her high school years. Eiji wrote to her at least once every week. He would begin his letters with the word "Hi" and finish with "see ya." He told her that he had transferred to night school and was working in his uncle's barber shop. He also told her that whenever he fell asleep in class, one teacher would always throw a piece of chalk at him. He also mentioned that he had to finish high school before he could enter barber's school. He reminded her in his teasing way about the time she ran over a long snake which was lying on the street. Eiji would write in block letters, "That snake you ran over now lives right below your dormitory window. One of these nights he is going to slither up the wall and take revenge on that girl, crush her and then swallow her whole." Keiko would then check the windows to see that they were all safely locked. She would then quickly jump into bed and pull the covers up over her head. "Oh, Eiji, you're such a tease," she would write back.

After graduation from high school, Keiko entered the Junior College that was attached to the high school with no trouble. She found that there was a good spirit in the school and that the girls looked after one another. The teachers were exemplary and prepared the students well for their teaching professions. In their second year at the school, the teacher in charge of employment opportunities counseled them frequently. This highly professional teacher, Mrs. Yuki Noguchi, prided herself at finding jobs for very close to one hundred percent of her students. She was also highly respected by the principals of the local kindergartens. Her first responsibility was to find kindergartens where the students could carry out two weeks of practice teaching. She counseled her charges on comportment, use of polite language, (but not too polite), knowing one's place as a "kohai" (junior) and respecting one's "sempai" (senior), trying always to have a smile on one's face, and finally, to listen and follow closely all instructions.

The kindergarten to which Keiko was sent was named Ropponmatsu Kindergarten. It was a private facility, and the principal was very much open to suggestions from the teachers. There was Japanese harmony which was reflected in the relationships between the teachers, the teachers and the children and the teachers and the parents. The principal and the head teacher met with the parents (mothers mostly) and had long discussions with them when there was a problem or a misunderstanding. "Beware of 'monster mothers,'" the principal, Mrs. Chikako Nakashima, would say with a grim face that evolved into a chuckle. Some mothers were very aggressive and sought to control the kindergarten itself. The principal and her head teacher were quite good at neutralizing these women. They both were very political when it came to choosing the new president of the Mothers' Club every year.

When Keiko went to the kindergarten chosen for her to begin her teaching career, the head teacher, Miss Sumiko Fujisawa, became her mentor. Sumiko had been a teacher for eight years and was the chief confidant of the principal. She first gave Keiko many chores such as wiping windows, cleaning the floors and toilets, raking leaves, and serving tea to the "sempai." The first week Keiko observed the head teacher's method and style. She could hold the children in the palm of her hand. She disliked scolding a child in public. She would take the naughty little one aside, kneel down and go eye-ball to eye-ball with the child. She was very firm and sometimes stern. Then she would hug the child for a long time. She prepared her classes the night before and rarely went home until long after eight o'clock in the evening. Keiko praised the children to their mothers on those occasions when she met with the parents of the children. In her attempt to present the children in a very positive light, Keiko would almost always describe the mother's little one by saying the same phrase, "ninki mono da wa" which means "he/she is very popular." Jump rope was one of the principal's favorite exercises. At that early age, the girls were usually more agile than the boys who tended to be rather clumsy. A child received a different color ribbon as he or she perfected the art of jumping rope. A winter festival on jumping rope was held in the winter, and the parents marveled at the excellent techniques of the children. This type of exercise helped to make the kindergarten better known in the area. Jumping rope was a perfect exercise for the little ones in the winter months as it stimulated the blood and kept them from just standing around shivering in the damp and cold weather. Sumiko, Keiko's mentor and guide as a teacher, was a great model for the children as well, for she could jump rope longer and with greater ease than any boxer preparing for a match.

When Keiko's turn came to lead a class of small children, she was extremely nervous. First, she had the children sing a song they all knew, and then she proceeded to teach finger painting. The children were all quite cute at the end of this exercise with their hands all covered in various colors. Then Keiko got them to march out to the washing station to clean their hands which she then inspected as she handed out towels and had them get presentable once again. After their return to the classroom, Keiko made sure to praise them abundantly for their good work in painting. When time came for recreation, the children all flocked to "Keiko sensei" (teacher Keiko) and she hugged them all one by one. When the two week training course was finished, Keiko had a long conference with the principal and Sumiko. They said that she talked too fast and didn't emote enough. "You have to be an actor," the principal emphasized. However, they praised her for her attention to detail, her evident love for the children and her backbone. When Keiko returned to her college, the teacher in charge of employment gave her high praise. "I'll bet they'll pick you to be a teacher there next year. Just wait and see," she said with encouragement. A few months later, Keiko was called into the counselor's office and told that the Ropponmatsu principal asked if Keiko could come in for an interview. Shortly thereafter, Keiko was selected by that principal for the coveted opening. She called her parents right away, and tears of joy flowed both in Fukuoka and Kumamoto. The following April, her parents attended the entrance ceremony. Keiko, their beloved daughter, was introduced to the parents of the prestigious Ropponmatsu Kindergarten School as assistant teacher under Sumiko Fujisawa.

Her first year of teaching was extremely taxing. She lost fifteen pounds in the first six months. The "sempai teachers" nicknamed her "Olive" after the character in the Popeye cartoon. Sumiko told her to buy a crockpot and to prepare her dinner before leaving home in the morning. This way, her mentor advised her, Keiko would not have to worry about fixing dinner after she had returned home on her bicycle. After a long day, she could eat, enter the hot bath and then fall into bed for a night's rest. At school, in addition to her work in the classroom she had to fulfill all the chores of a "kohai" and serve tea to the "sempai." Under Sumiko's supervision, she was permitted to give frequent classes to the children. The principal also observed her, and in the afternoon they critiqued her, sometimes rather sternly. By the end of her first year, the principal asked Keiko if she would prefer to continue as an assistant or become a homeroom teacher on her own. When she approached Sumiko for her advice, her mentor answered in a very forthright manner saying. "You're definitely ready, and I will not have you return merely as an assistant, and the other teachers are of the same opinion. I have already talked to them. This should come as a compliment to you. Like ourselves when we were just starting out, you will learn by making some mistakes; we all did too. But remember, we'll all be right behind you supporting you.

The following year, Keiko was the homeroom teacher for the five year olds. She learned the important word, "renraku" (communication). Keiko had so many things to remember that inevitably she would forget some things that would prove to be very important. Some examples include occasions when she would forget to call the parents when a child got sick at some point during the day. Another occurrence happened when she failed to tell the principal that a child had fallen off a swing. There was the time when she failed to tell the other teachers that her class intended to use the field. Still another was the time when she forgot to tell the piano teacher that the children were going home early. Yet another time she forgot to tell the children to bring plastic spoons to school to eat jello during a class break. And so it went. She was often reprimanded by the principal for repeated failures to make "renraku." On one occasion the parents of a young girl were very upset when the child returned home and said that she had fallen off a swing and cut her leg. Forgetfulness, for Keiko, turned out to be a big failing after she became a homeroom teacher. Sumiko admonished her to keep notes, and cross each off the list after she had corrected the problem. "Mama, I have much trouble making "renraku," she would cry on the phone to her mother. Little by little, however, Keiko progressed in her ambition to become a good teacher.

The years passed, and Sumiko married a fire fighter. He was a quiet young man who kept in shape for his job by jogging and lifting weights. Keiko spoke at the wedding, and asked the groom to take care of Sumiko. He saluted Keiko and with his body language inferred he would take care of Sumiko. Keiko, in turn, became a mentor for the new teachers coming into the facility, and used the example of Sumiko in her own attempts to encourage both students and first year teachers. During these years when Keiko was teaching, Eiji finished high school and barber's school. He was working as an assistant in his uncle's shop. His uncle was very demanding and thought nothing of berating Eiji even in the presence of customers. Eiji, as an assistant, had many different chores to fulfill around the shop. There were always the hair clippings to be swept up, and in Japan where every customer has his hair washed and shampooed, Eiji was the one to set up the special sinks that were placed jut behind each chair as he prepared to give this special treatment to the customer. What followed, of course, was the washing and drying of the towels that had just been used. He also would cut some customers hair when the shop was busy, and it was expected that he would keep the shop orderly and attractive inside as well as cleaning the premises on the outside. All this made for a busy day which got on Eiji's nerves after a while. Being a youth, young and energetic, he would often complain about all these many details that he had to fulfill each day when he spoke to his mother after returning home tired and frustrated. "Taking orders and doing all these seemingly small chores every day," she counseled him, "is part of growing up and are part of life in the adult world. Just learn to do them well and be proud of every little thing you do. That's how you become successful in life, doing everything well and being proud of what you have accomplished." Eiji listened to his mother, realized that she was correct in what she said. Gradually his relationship with his uncle improved and they became good friends. His uncle, Satoshi Oka, liked the young man, and often they would sit around after the shop had closed for the day to drink some sake together. One such day, his uncle surprised Eiji by saying that he was considering retiring and would allow Eiji to buy the shop and pay the cost through a long term, no interest loan over a period of years.

Eiji would often take the bus to Fukuoka and visit with Keiko, and on days when both of them were free and were able to enjoy one another's company in a carefree and romantic setting the couple would walk around the big pond near Keiko's apartment, chatting about their individual lives with some hints about an uncertain future they both might share. Their walk around the pond always wound up at the ice cream parlor for a long chat before it was time for Eiji to board the bus for his return trip home. When Keiko returned home for the New Years' Celebration, and as well for the Festival of the Dead in August, she would meet with Eiji and they would drive up to Mt. Aso in his uncle's car. There they often would kiss and embrace. "I love you, Kei-chan," he would say shyly. Their childhood friendship had indeed endured and had blossomed into love. Of course, when two people are in love, it's impossible to hide it from others who are close to them. Both Eiji's mother and Keiko's parents picked up the rumors and forbade them to see one another. Keiko's mother was very upset that Keiko would choose to marry Eiji and become a barber's wife, way below her status. "You can't marry that rich girl. She's out of your class," Eiji's mother would repeat angrily. Both Eiji and Keiko, in spite of all this, kept denying that they intended to marry. "We're just friends from childhood," they would say over and over again.

The principal also heard the rumors and called Keiko into her office. "You're not thinking of marriage, are you?" she asked very bluntly. "Eiji is a nice kid, but look, you'll never be happy with him. How would you like to be an assistant in a barber shop? My goodness, it would never work. You should meet a lot of boys so that you can get a better idea." "We're just friends," Keiko answered. Sumiko called her one evening and asked her to go out to a sushi shop. Keiko knew that her "sempai" would discourage her from seeing Eiji. Of course, she did just that. Sumiko was very forceful in her advice, "Fixed marriages are old fashioned, that's true, but all statistics show overwhelmingly that they last. Keiko, ask your parents to find a suitable boy for you." "We're just childhood friends. He's such a tease. He makes me laugh all the time. He used to wink at me in school. We were forbidden to ride home together. The teachers thought we were lovers, or something. We were only fifteen" Sumiko was deeply concerned that Keiko might marry Eiji.

The following August, when Keiko was home for the Festival of the Dead, Eiji invited her to go up to Mt. Aso again. Keiko fixed a box lunch and a flask of tea. When they arrived at their favorite spot on the mountain, they sat down together on the grass. Eiji was unusually serious and quiet. There were no jokes or teasing. "What's up, Eiji?" Keiko asked. Eiji put his head down, rubbed his forehead in agitation and blurted out, "Well, Kei-chan, I've been thinking about this for a long time. I need an assistant in my barber shop. I ahhhhhh, you know, you know." "For heaven's sake, Eiji, you know what? Why are you so nervous? What do you want to say?" Keiko pressed him. "Well, you know …I was going to ask …you know …I

211

have a ring in my pocket and I want to propose to you. Will you marry a barber who can't promise you anything?" Keiko looked down and didn't answer. Eiji knelt down on the grass and pulled out a small box. There was a ring in it. He tried to show it to Keiko, but it fell into the high grass. Keiko giggled and they both looked for the ring. Keiko found it first. "Oh Eiji, you're so romantic. It's just like you to drop our wedding ring." She put it on her finger and said, "How beautiful it is, Eiji, it must have cost you a fortune. I kept wondering when you were going to ask me. "I've always loved you, Eiji, and I will marry you. It'll be tough getting permission, and they will put all kinds of obstacles in our way. If it is our fate to marry, nothing will stand in our way."

When it was revealed that they were indeed going to marry, all hell broke loose. Keiko's mother cried and cried. Her father was absolutely opposed to the marriage. Eiji's mother was equally against this step. "It'll never work. It'll never work," she said over and over again. The principal and Sumiko took Keiko out to a sushi shop and tried to talk Keiko out of what they felt was a great mistake she was about to make. They repeated what everyone else was saying, "It'll never work, not even six months. Oh, Keiko, you are being so foolish."

Eiji was the first to crack. "Let's give up, Keiko, they'll never permit us to marry," he said. Keiko also was torn apart. The idea of offending her parents in such a serious matter that she began to think that Eiji was right. Eiji and Keiko climbed Mt. Aso once again and sat down at the spot where he had proposed to her. "Let's call it quits, Kei-chan, there's just too much opposition and hard feelings in our two families," Eiji said. With tears flowing down her cheeks, Keiko offered this counter proposition to Eiji, "Let's agree to wait a full year, and if we still feel the same way, we'll then get married."

A year later, they each told their families that they were going to go through with the wedding. This time, however, everyone finally, but with great reluctance, realized that the young couple was adamant in their desire to marry. A small Shinto wedding ceremony was held with a low key reception (no speeches except for a toast offered by Sumiko). The couple went to Nagasaki for a brief honeymoon. Keiko resigned from her position in the kindergarten in Fukuoka and began her new responsibility as assistant to Eijii in his barber shop. She did all the chores expected of her and truly added something special to Eiji and his barbershop. Her bright smile and perky personality brightened up the shop, and her feminine elegance added a distinctive atmosphere which all the customers enjoyed. She chatted along with all the men as she shaved their necks and washed and shampooed their hair. As one could imagine, Keiko was very popular with the customers who would chatter with her far more than with Eiji. On Mondays, their day off, they kept to their custom of climbing Mt. Aso and just spending the day together relaxing and enjoying the peace they were now experiencing after all the tension of earlier times. It was on one of these trips to Mt. Aso, two years after their marriage, that Keiko revealed to Eiji that she had become pregnant and that he would soon be a father. Eiji was, of course, jubilant at the news and both families were absolutely delighted. "It's a girl," the nurse said. Eiji, who had been pacing up and down outside the delivery room, downright fainted upon hearing the news. He was a father!! His head swirled in disbelief and in awe as he started for a chair to sit on, missed it and collapsed onto the floor. His head hit an empty umbrella container which clattered away noisily. Just then, a doctor came out of the delivery room, saw what was going on and asked Eiji if he was all right. Eiji, his head now cleared, asked the doctor, "Did you say my wife had a baby girl?" Seeing Eiji's delight upon receiving the news, the nurses all applauded at his good fortune. When he entered the hospital room, Keiko was quietly nursing the baby. Eiji came over to the bed and the nurse gently took the baby from Keiko and placed her in Eiji's arms. "She's beautiful, just beautiful," he said softly, repeating it over again as he walked about the room holding her and forever locking this moment in his memory. Looking over at Keiko, he said, "I thought of a name for her that you might like. In the Chinese language, the character for our Japanese language, "kei" means "megumi" (a grace from God). How about the Japanese sound "Megumi" for her name? It would really sound nice and would signify something really beautiful." Keiko nodded her head in agreement. "Megumi-chan, Megumi-chan, that's just perfect." After Eiji left, Keiko held the baby in her arms and whispered, "And you, little girl, what will you be when you grow up? You've got to choose, you know, and follow your heart.

Happiness is choosing love. Be happy, my Princess, be happy."

CPSIA information can be obtained at www.ICGtesting.com
Printed in the USA
BVOW10s1500100714

358701BV00003B/16/P

9 780877 231141